BEING
GERRY MULLIGAN

BEING
GERRY MULLIGAN

MY LIFE IN **MUSIC**

GERRY MULLIGAN
WITH KEN POSTON

Backbeat
Books

Essex, Connecticut

Backbeat Books

An imprint of Globe Pequot, the trade division of
The Rowman & Littlefield Publishing Group, Inc.
4501 Forbes Blvd., Ste. 200
Lanham, MD 20706
www.rowman.com

Distributed by NATIONAL BOOK NETWORK

British Library Cataloguing in Publication Information available

Library of Congress Cataloging-in-Publication Data

Names: Mulligan, Gerry, author. | Poston, Ken, author.
Title: Being Gerry Mulligan : my life in music / Gerry Mulligan with Ken
    Poston.
Description: Essex, Connecticut : Backbeat, 2022. | Includes index. |
    Summary: "Being Gerry Mulligan: My Life in Music is Gerry Mulligan in
    his own words. This autobiography tells the story of the iconic American
    jazz saxophonist, clarinettist, composer, and arranger"— Provided by
    publisher.
Identifiers: LCCN 2022013941 (print) | LCCN 2022013942 (ebook) | ISBN
    9781493064823 (cloth) | ISBN 9781493064830 (epub)
Subjects: LCSH: Mulligan, Gerry. | Jazz musicians—United
    States—Biography. | Saxophonists—United States—Biography. |
    Composers—United States—Biography. | LCGFT: Autobiographies.
Classification: LCC ML419.M79 A3 2022 (print) | LCC ML419.M79 (ebook) |
    DDC 788.7/165092 [B]—dc23/eng/20220323
LC record available at https://lccn.loc.gov/2022013941
LC ebook record available at https://lccn.loc.gov/2022013942

♾™ The paper used in this publication meets the minimum requirements of American
National Standard for Information Sciences—Permanence of Paper for Printed Library
Materials, ANSI/NISO Z39.48-1992

CONTENTS

INTRODUCTION

IN 1995 I suggested to Gerry that he could start recording his oral auto-biography. He liked the idea, but as an incentive to take on the project he would need an expert to work with him as an audience, who wouldn't interfere with his chain of thought, but at the same time would refresh his memory if he lost the thread. I thought he could work with Ken Poston, who knew Gerry very well. Ken is himself a jazz musician and historian with a strong knowledge of Gerry's music and career. He is also an experienced moderator of panel discussions.

We called Ken and offered to fly him out to Connecticut to work with Gerry and to record him. Luckily Ken was enthusiastic, and the two of them had a wonderful time together. If Gerry couldn't remember a certain time or concert, Ken was there to jog his memory without interrupting Gerry's train of thought. It was an ideal situation.

The following spring of 1995, Gerry returned to touring and performing with his quartet all over the world, and in October he played a benefit concert in Milano for the Sera Je Monastery University. He played with the Tibetan monks, which was the first time an outside musician had performed and improvised with them. In a press conference before the concert, he was asked how he had become friends with the Venerable Thamthog Rinpoche, director of the university and the center of Buddhist study in Milano. Gerry responded, "My wife, Franca, is a student of Rinpoche." The journalist asked Gerry if he was a Buddhist. Gerry paused for a moment and then said, "I think at the back of my mind I always was."

From the fourth to the eleventh of November, he performed aboard the SS *Norway* with his quartet as part of the annual Floating Jazz Festival. Gene Lees was present, and he wrote in his *Jazzletter*, "His music was out of this world."

Dave Brubeck said, "When you listen to Gerry Mulligan, you hear the past, the present, and the future."

That December, three weeks before his passing, he recorded a series of his songs and lyrics with engineer Phil Ramone at Carriage House Studios in Stamford, Connecticut.

Gerry never looked for money or fame. He was a self-taught musical genius and could be volatile; however, he had a great sense of humor and was a joy to be with.

I would like to give special thanks to my assistant since 1981, Cathie Phillips, for her valuable help with Gerry's oral autobiography.

Gerry, from an interview in Verona, Italy, 1990:

> There are some words that have been lost from modern usage that I like to bring to my music and have striven all my life to do, *beauty, grace, nobility*, these are the things that music can bring to us as human beings. I think it is well that we who make music keep that in our consciousness.

Franca Mulligan

PREFACE

I FIRST MET Gerry Mulligan in 1990 while working at KLON-FM in Long Beach, California, which was the jazz radio station that served the greater Los Angeles area. My job was to produce concerts and events, and I had put together a celebration of the Pacific Jazz record label that included Bud Shank, a reunion of the Chico Hamilton Quintet, and Gerry Mulligan's Quartet.

Having Gerry at that event was something that had been a long time coming for me personally. Gerry had been one of the first jazz musicians I discovered as a young music student growing up in Kansas City. The quartet recordings with Chet Baker were among a handful of records that were my first exposure to jazz, and those records were extremely influential and life changing. I had always dreamed of seeing Gerry in person but had never had the chance.

When I arrived at KLON, I immediately started to plan events to feature artists who were significant to the development of jazz in southern California. It turned out that audiences were as excited to see and hear the musicians who had defined the West Coast scene of the 1950s as I was. I felt that many of those artists hadn't received the credit they deserved, so I continued to expand upon the idea with a variety of live events and radio programs. Each event brought me into further contact with Gerry, and we developed a very nice working relationship.

In 1991 I produced a big Jazz West Coast event in London at Royal Albert Hall in which Gerry was the headliner. In 1992 we featured a West Coast presentation of Gerry's *Re-Birth of the Cool*. Finally, in

1994, I put together a four-day Jazz West Coast festival in Los Angeles that featured a who's who of the West Coast scene of the 1950s. In addition to concerts we showed historic films and presented panel discussions featuring the various artists reminiscing about their days on the West Coast. I ended up doing a one-on-one discussion with Gerry, which turned out to be a high point of the entire festival. He was such a masterful storyteller that he had the audience hanging on to every word. I would simply ask a question or bring up a specific subject and he would take it from there. The crowd response was so amazing that it's difficult to describe. I remember when it was over that Gerry was very happy with the results, and the whole experience seemed to be very meaningful to him.

About a week or two later I got a call from Gerry's wife, Franca, who said Gerry was wanting to write his autobiography and wondered if I would be interested in helping him with it. Franca and Gerry felt Gerry and I had developed a really good rapport and thought it would be very helpful if I could be there to ask questions and help get Gerry's story down on tape. Needless to say I was thrilled with the idea and beyond thrilled to have been asked to be part of it. I ended up going to Gerry and Franca's house in Connecticut three times in 1995 to conduct the interviews. The first two trips I stayed at the house for about a week each time. The third trip was part of a National Public Radio project, which enabled us to do a final, daylong session that helped fill in a few missing pieces.

During the initial sessions we usually did an hour or two each morning and more again in the afternoon. I created a loose timeline that we followed but left plenty of room for Gerry to take things whatever direction he wanted. At night I would listen to the tapes and formulate follow-up questions that we would deal with the next day or sometimes at the end of the week.

Gerry was extremely intelligent and articulate, and he was an engaging storyteller. It was fascinating for me to be able to spend that much time with him, and Franca made me feel right at home on each occasion.

Once we were finished with the initial sessions, the original plan was for Gerry to use the transcripts to assemble the book himself, and I was going to be available to help. Unfortunately, he never got the chance to begin work on it himself.

I am so pleased and honored that Franca and John Cerullo of Rowman & Littlefield asked me to finish the book. Spending the time with Gerry and Franca is one of the highlights of my life on both a professional and personal level. It was a joy to work directly with Gerry all those years ago and a joy now to be able to see the work through to conclusion.

I would also like to acknowledge Cathie Phillips for all of her work on the original transcripts and my longtime colleague Ken Borgers, who was a tremendous help with encouragement and advice.

There have been jazz giants who have excelled as writers and others who have excelled as instrumentalists. Gerry Mulligan was unique in that he set new standards in both areas. His compositions featured distinctive original melodies while his arranging style introduced a linear approach and an innovative use of counterpoint. As an instrumentalist, Gerry was arguably the most significant baritone saxophonist in the history of jazz, who single-handedly established the instrument as a solo voice. Both his writing and playing influenced entire stylistic movements.

In a brilliant career that spanned six decades, he created a body of work that established him as one of the true giants of jazz and twentieth-century music.

This is his story, told in his own words, the way he wanted it told.

Ken Poston
November 2021

1

ONE TO TEN IN OHIO

Starting at the beginning, I was born in Queens Village, Long Island, New York, and depending on which album notes or biographies you read about me, I was born in 1926, 1927, and 1928, simultaneously presumably! I've got hometowns in various places, mentioned in various publications, all over the East actually, including Philadelphia and Reading, Pennsylvania. The truth of the matter is, though, I was born in Queens Village, Long Island.

The way my family wound up there, was my father was from Wilmington, Delaware, and his family had worked on the railroads like a lot of the Irish that came to this country. The Irish built a lot of the railroads in the East, and my father's family had worked on both the Baltimore and Ohio (B&O) and the Chesapeake.

My father was born in Keyser, West Virginia, which was a railhead. In fact, his father, and probably his uncles as well, worked on the building of the B&O that goes through Keyser. Keyser, according to my brother, was a railhead for the construction of that branch of the system.

My mother's family were also railroad men. My grandfather on my mother's side was an engineer on the Pennsylvania, and bowing to pressure from my grandmother, he also got my great-grandfather a job on the Pennsylvania, for which my great-grandfather never forgave him. I don't think he spoke to him after that because he didn't want a job anywhere!

So my mother was from Philadelphia, my father was from Wilmington, and when they married they had three sons in Chester, Pennsylvania, which is just south of Philadelphia. Then my father took a job with a maritime company, Merritt, Chapman, and Scott. They had floating dry docks for rebuilding boats and ships, and they had the kind of dredging equipment for ports and harbors.

In fact, I remember very well that some of my favorite reading as a child in my father's library was a book called *Canadian Ports and Harbors* from 1924. Another book I liked a lot, I can't remember what it was called, but it was about municipal accessories, like traffic light systems and sewage systems. I thought they were great, better than a good novel!

Anyway, my father took a job and moved us to New York, and I was born in Queens Village, Long Island, in 1927, April the sixth. You know, there's been so much confusion about my actual birth date, and to compound the whole thing, the passport department, the last time my passport was issued, made a mistake on my birth date and moved me up to May! So now, according to the United States I was born May 6, 1927. I can't win! And if I were going to lie about my age, I could have at least knocked off ten years or something! This way it's hardly worthwhile.

One of my mother's favorite stories was about the day I was born. Being her fourth child, she felt she knew pretty well what was going on. Apparently, it was an easy pregnancy. She said to my father one morning when he was getting ready to go off to work, "I think today's the day." So he called the doctor, and the doctor came over and examined her and said, "Well, I don't think so. I think it's all right today for you to just go about your business," and he took off. Well, the doctor no more than got in his car and took off down the street, and I started to be born. So her favorite story is my father chasing down the street after the doctor and he can't reach him and there was a midwife in the neighborhood who was supposed to help. So he got her and I was born in the kitchen. Her great story was that the midwife told her that after I was born and dried off a little bit, they laid me down on the floor and I lifted up my head and looked around. She loved that. And I amended that story by adding to it that I took a look around and decided to try to get back in. I've tried to get back in all my life.

I guess I was less than a year old when my family moved to Marion, Ohio. My father took a job as a vice president and general manager, well something like that, something important sounding, at the Marion Power Shovel Company. Those are the memories that were first for me, in Marion. That was all the town that I knew. When we got out there, my mother had her hands full with a big house and four boys to take care of so she got someone to help her. She hired an African American woman named Lily Rowan. Her job was supposed to be kind of a nanny to me. I became her baby and she was very protective of me. When I got older I remembered some of these things, so apparently it happened early on.

Gerry's parents, Louise and George Mulligan, 1932.
COURTESY GERRY MULLIGAN COLLECTION,
LIBRARY OF CONGRESS, MUSIC DIVISION

Gerry as a baby.
COURTESY GERRY MULLIGAN
COLLECTION, LIBRARY OF
CONGRESS, MUSIC DIVISION

Gerry with his mother. COURTESY
GERRY MULLIGAN COLLECTION,
LIBRARY OF CONGRESS, MUSIC DIVISION

My father could be a pretty stern fellow, not given much to a sense of humor, and he had some very authoritarian kind of rules. Even as a small kid, if I was not eating something I should have been eating, and by God you're supposed to eat everything on your plate, I don't know if he smacked me or what, but Lily would come flying in from the kitchen and say, "Don't you hit my Bonzo." I was her baby.

And it's funny, because in that way my relationship with Lily is really the thing that was so different between my childhood and my brothers'. I suppose the youngest always gets the rap of being spoiled, you know. In this case, what seemed perfectly normal to me, my relationship with Lily, must have seemed to the rest of them like I was really spoiled, to have a protector and a woman who was so warmhearted and outgoing.

She adopted me and as I got older, I used to go over to her house and spend days there with her and her husband. Her husband was the head waiter at the hotel in town. It's maybe hard for people today to picture a city like Marion. It was a city of about thirty thousand, but it was a very

Gerry with his father, 1930 or 1931.
COURTESY GERRY MULLIGAN COLLECTION,
LIBRARY OF CONGRESS, MUSIC DIVISION

Gerry with tulips, 1934.
COURTESY GERRY MULLIGAN
COLLECTION, LIBRARY OF
CONGRESS, MUSIC DIVISION

Gerry with his brother Phil. COURTESY GERRY MULLIGAN COLLECTION, LIBRARY OF CONGRESS,
MUSIC DIVISION

Gerry and his brothers, Christmas 1930. COURTESY GERRY MULLIGAN COLLECTION, LIBRARY OF CONGRESS, MUSIC DIVISION

successful city industrially because it had this big power shovel plant and another plant that made diesel engines and all kinds of road equipment, kind of like the Caterpillar company. Publishing and all sorts of things went on there. So it was a very prosperous town. It had a big luxury hotel with a very nice restaurant and a big theater done in kind of the Moorish style, one of the grand palaces of the 1920s. When I was a kid, they still had a band playing in the pit before and after the movies.

There was a lot of music around in those days, in places that you wouldn't expect it. The movies didn't just displace live entertainment overnight. It was a long, slow, downward process that was of course hurried along by the Depression. But still, my earliest recollection of going to the big Palace Theater was the band in the pit, and that was where they had all the best movies. In the days before my memory, the days of the silents, the big expensive pictures went around to theaters like the Palace in Marion, and they went with a score and parts for a symphony orchestra, or in this case, a cut-down version of it. And this is what made the difference between just the ordinary run-of-the-mill, B and C houses running the cheaper films, and the big A vehicles from MGM or Paramount. It's a fascinating sidelight of the period and every place I can think of, where music was playing, is someplace that you wouldn't think about or expect to hear it.

I took piano lessons in the second grade, and I apparently wasn't a very good student according to the nun teaching the course. At my first recital I was supposed to memorize a piece and got halfway through and forgot and started over and went halfway through again and forgot and started over. They took me off stage, bodily, and the nun told my mother, "Save your money because he'll never learn to play this stuff the way it's written." And because that was what the nun said, that was the end of my piano lessons. It never occurred to my mother to go to another teacher, because after all, this woman was a nun and the nuns knew best.

But there really wasn't ever anything else I was interested in. Nothing that held my interest for very long, and in fact music was always there. I was always more conscious of music and more concerned about music than anything else. After my kind of fiasco of piano lessons, I kept on trying to play the piano, playing by ear and writing tunes down that I could play. So I was involved in a learning process.

I more or less taught myself to read music. I never learned to read fast and I never could read piano music. Those are techniques that I just never got to, and since I didn't have access to that kind of musical education, I kind of struggled along with what I could figure out myself.

As a child I spent a lot of time at Lily's house. She had a player piano and I used to love that. She had Fats Waller rolls and all sorts of things. So as soon as I was able, I'd be leaning against the piano bench with my nose at keyboard height pumping away playing this stuff. There were things that happened that I just thought were the normal way things were. I didn't know any different to spend that much time in the black part of town and learn things about that community. It was totally different from the rest of the town, but I didn't know it. It just seemed perfectly natural.

For instance, when the various black bands would come through, there were no hotels for them. So when a band came through town, the community would put them up. Often there would be musicians staying at Lily's house. She'd let them use a couple of her bedrooms while they were there, and this is how the black bands traveled around. They'd go into a town and the community absorbed them, which is something that made for a different kind of atmosphere for the players and their involvement with the people of their own community. It's kind of a heartening part of the whole picture.

But thinking back on it, what I really was, was a small-town kid that lived a pretty regular kind of American-boy childhood that consisted of Saturdays devoted to the cowboy movies and looking at the new models of cars when they came out. They put the new models in parking lots behind the showrooms, and they would put them under canvas so you couldn't see them. The kids had to go around and peek under to see what the new cars looked like.

I remember a high point for us was my uncle John from Pittsburgh. At that point they had two sons, later they had a third, but Uncle John and Aunt Marie were kind of the sporty relatives that used to show up with their Auburn. They were made by the same company that made the Duesenberg and the Cord. It was such a beautiful car, and they always used to joke because Uncle John was a kind of fast driver and he had a good car for it. And on Aunt Marie's side, the passenger side, she had the floorboards worn through from trying to put the brakes on!

It was a bustling little town with a couple of busy main streets. One of the things that is still a point of interest in Marion is the fact that four railroads come together there. It was a very busy rail center, like New York Grand Central. They had what they called the Nickel Plate Road, which ran down to St. Louis. The Pennsylvania had a line and I don't remember the other lines now, but they are all still functioning.

Marion was one of those towns that was hit by the move to the shopping mall on the outskirts of town. We were there a few years ago when we played a concert with the Columbus Symphony, and the poor downtown section is just like a wasteland. There are hardly any stores, all empty shops, and it's just such an incredible thing to see. A whole town kind of disintegrates into dust, and I guess nobody was thinking of trying to protect the communal centers as entities. It was good business to build a shopping mall, and that was all that was important. Whether the town died was not important. You know, save the operation, lose the patient.

My brother Phil and I were running buddies, and a town like Marion was nice because it was surrounded by parklands, both town parks and preservation areas. There were a lot of Indian mounds. We'd be playing as kids do in the wild, or what felt like it.

We lived a block away from where they had made a kind of memorial out of the home of Warren G. Harding. He was from Marion. He was the publisher of the local newspaper, and of course they had built a big monument to Harding on the outskirts of town. He was kind of a slightly hollow local hero, although he was well enough known and liked in Marion. They say he died under mysterious circumstances. The thing with Harding and the Teapot Dome Scandal happened a few years before I was born, but when you're a kid anything that happened before you were born seems like ancient history. The rumors were still rife when I was a kid there that maybe somebody in the family had helped him on his way to the hereafter, because they weren't able to face the scandal.

That was one of the earlier things I remember about the kind of journalism Edward R. Murrow did. I know Murrow (or someone else) did a program on him, but you'd hear recordings of this robust-sounding speaker who was Harding. He was every inch the matinee idol, you know: this handsome fellow with a kind of American gusto and gung-ho. After a couple of years in office with the corrupt cronies he had, he just sounded like a broken man, like he'd aged twenty or thirty years instead of two. I think he was the one who said that it's not your enemies you've got to look out for, it's your friends. I guess in his case it was true.

But it was a really nice town for a kid to grow up in. There were things going on that were, of course, interesting to a kid. You could go out and play like Tom Sawyer and Huckleberry Finn. Marion was a good-sized town with a population of about thirty thousand. I don't know what the population is now. It was barely recognizable to me when I went back and saw it. The house we lived in was an old brick farmhouse and one of the few houses that was still there on the street. Most of the houses had been torn down and replaced. I remember getting a letter (it must have been in the 1950s) from some advertising company that was making their headquarters in our old house, and they invited me out to the inauguration ceremony of this new company because they had taken the old house and incorporated it into their buildings. Now those buildings apparently had been torn down. So here's this big old square pile with the porches on it all gone. It really looked like something out of Charles Adams! And it was hard to imagine, because the yard that we used to play in with the apple tree and the cherry tree and the garage that my brothers and I almost burned down smoking corn silk was all gone. It was all a parking lot with asphalt. It's really sad to see a town that's like a disaster area. You know, people think everything is going to last forever. That's one of the earliest lessons I learned, that everything is temporary. Nothing lasts. The only thing we can count on is change and that whatever it is, is of short duration. Humanity has got a tremendous conceit about that. We're always building monuments to ourselves, and many times of course, the monument never gets built, so you're left with a hole in the ground.

2

OHIO TRAVELER

WHEN I WAS TEN YEARS OLD, we started an odyssey. My father at that point was general manager for a company that made Hercules road rollers and things like that. At this particular time, his company had an order of road rollers that they sold to Puerto Rico. They wanted him to go down there and teach them how to use the machines.

So he was down there for months and before he left, my grandfather on my mother's side died. So mother and we four boys closed up the house, left Marion, and moved down to New Jersey to be with Grandma.

When it came time to leave Marion at age ten, I really hated to go. I really liked it there. And of course it was all the kids from the school that I knew. It had been four years with the same kids, and I never experienced that again in my life. I always missed that. I think it probably had a lot to do with the feelings of being an outsider that I've always had, and which I've nursed, pretty much to this day.

It really wasn't hard for me to be an outsider in the music business because I had set the precedent for it. When I'd go to the country school, I was the city kid and shunned for that, and I'd go to the city school and I was the country kid and was shunned for that too. No matter where I went, I couldn't win!

My brothers and I were quite close together in age actually. My brother Phil was next to me. We were always hanging out together. He was a year and a half older than me. Then there was a two-year gap to the next brother, Don, and a one-year gap to my oldest brother, which reminds me of the way that things happen in families sometimes.

I remember telling a friend not long ago, "You know, I've realized that mine was a dysfunctional family." And she said, "All families are dysfunctional." But the thing that's hard to realize when you're a kid is that when a child is born to a family, they don't include a book of instructions. The first time out is pretty much a new adventure to the young parents, and so you have to realize they were doing the best they could and the mistakes they made were honest mistakes. You collect injustices as a child, but you finally come to an age when you realize that your parents were doing the best they could. They didn't necessarily mean to do it; they were trying to help you. I say if you want to help me, don't help!

My oldest brother, George Jr., was labeled with the unwelcome nickname of June, short for Junior. He was June all his life. He was kind of a sickly kid, apparently, and had some kind of an ailment as kids sometimes do. He was a colicky baby so was underweight and undersized because he couldn't keep his food down. By age four or so he recovered from that and was perfectly normal.

The next son, born a year after, was, as second sons often are, extremely competitive with the firstborn. June was kind of easygoing you know, even as a kid I remember he was easygoing, devil may care, a breezy image. And brother Don was very, very serious and, as I said, very competitive.

My mother and father felt George Jr. wasn't quite as physically strong as he should be at the start of school so they held him back. He wound up going through school with the two brothers together; the first son and the second son. When I was old enough to appreciate the situation, I felt really sorry for my oldest brother because that put him in a terrible position, and in some ways he was never able to get away from it. You spend all of your growing-up years constantly looking over your shoulder.

I used to admire my brother Don because he was so good with his hands and could make things. I never could understand why he was so mean to me. I never understood all that competitive thing with me being the youngest. You know it wasn't either my position or in my nature to dominate the scene. I was a pretty happy, easygoing kid, but I think another factor that helped shape my later personality problems was the fact that my brother Don took a great deal of pleasure in upsetting me. He pictured me as the spoilt kid who got everything for his own. And I had Lily, which I guess really must have riled the rest of them. I can understand that too, because I had my own source of warmth in life that they didn't have access to.

So Don used to take real demonic pleasure in making me mad. And when you're a kid, it's easy to do. I don't know if highly strung is the way to put it, but I was very full of vitality and was easy to steer in that direction. It was so easy to make me mad.

My mother always used to say, "Well, Gerry, you've just got to learn not to show your feelings." You know, "Sticks and stones will break your bones but names will never hurt you," and all that. Well, by the time I learned that lesson it was too late, and it was really destructive because I was thoroughly unprepared for the real world when I started working with the bands.

The first job I had was all right, but I started almost immediately drinking too much and hanging out too much. It's like when I left home, I just threw away the ideas of discipline that I had learned and managed to make a thorough mess of the ongoing business of living. As time progressed and I became more involved with people, I became more and more defensive. Other guys I've known have suffered from the same thing. They feel inadequate because of the things that they think they don't know, and they become defensive. To this day I have to be careful because if somebody snaps at me, it's my way to snap right back again.

It's been a long, long process to try to learn not to do that. Not to be sucked into saying dumb things, because it's just an automatic reflex response to somebody saying something mean to me. In those days I hadn't learned that lesson at all and the idea of hiding my feelings, in a way made it worse, because I'd bottle it up and then when it came out, it was an explosion. You know I lost so many opportunities because of just not being able to cope with change, the constant changing climate of emotional relationships with people.

We spent a year in New Jersey. After that my father went with a concern from Chicago, so we wound up living there through one school year. That had the advantage of being a very active city where music was concerned. It was something that was available to a kid my age because my brother Phil and I would be off to the theaters all the time to hear the bands. There were four or five theaters in Chicago that played name bands week after week, so I saw all the bands at that point. We lived up on the North side just below the Edgewater Beach Hotel and around the corner from the Trianon Ballroom. Those were both places where bands played, but the only thing available to me was the theaters because I couldn't go to the clubs. We spent one school year there with access to all of those theaters.

Then we went to Kalamazoo, Michigan. In Kalamazoo I ran into a brand-new situation because we lived in kind of a suburban area. Like something out of a TV sitcom. It was very nice with a modern public school, but the kid across the street, Jimmy Schumacher, played trumpet. He could play all the flashy stuff like the "Carnival of Venice" and the "Flight of the Bumblebee." He taught me a lot of things on the trumpet, but I was one envious kid; to be able to have that kind of training on an instrument. That really gave me the desire to play a horn. I had wanted to play trumpet before then, and that was the push that I needed.

Well, the next year we went downtown to Kalamazoo to the Catholic school in a very old, old building. The recess yard was bordered by a big brick wall, and behind the brick wall ran the main line of the central Michigan railroad tracks where the Michigan Central and the New York Central luxury trains would go by. Every day at recess in the morning, I'd go out back and there would be the Wolverine pulling out of the station and people sitting in the dining car with white tablecloths and silverware. I thought "Man, what am I doing here?" That was my idea of heaven, to be sitting in the restaurant cars instead of being out in the cold and messy schoolyard.

There was very little going on at that point, but then the next year the school moved into a new building and, along with getting a new building, they established some kind of music courses. They brought a man in to teach music. He was a trumpet player but he taught all the instruments. So I changed my mind at that point for some reason and decided to play clarinet.

We tried to start an orchestra with all of us beginners on these instruments. It was a fairly ungodly instrumentation; one clarinet, one violin, one drum, one piano player. God knows what all was there; seven or eight of us and still, I had the desire to try to write something for it. I was fascinated with the tune "Lover" and its chromatic progression. I felt it was beautiful, so I sat down and tried to write out an arrangement of it; *very* simple, with a lot of whole notes and quarter notes and I tried to get the moving parts and all that stuff from our instrumentation. So that was my first arrangement. Ultimately, I never heard it because the school was taught by nuns, and like a fool, I put on top of each one of the sheets the title "Lover." The nun took one look at the title and that was the end of that. We never even played the thing! So that was the abrupt end of my burgeoning writing career.

After Kalamazoo we moved on to Detroit where, among other things, my father put himself through night school in aeronautics to broaden his engineering horizons. My father was kind of funny about education because he had had a dream that all his sons would become engineers and we could be George B. Mulligan & Sons Engineers. At that point my two eldest brothers were in high school and getting ready for college. He would put them into college if they would go to an engineering school, but if they didn't want to go to engineering school, they could just fend for themselves. My oldest brother didn't want to go to engineering school and fought it, but ultimately he gave in and went anyway. My second-oldest brother wanted to go, so that was all right.

My father really didn't seem to be interested in any kind of education except engineering, and he never discussed education with me. I have always been a little amazed with that. Maybe it's because he knew what I wanted and I wasn't about to get it, so that was that. I wanted to go to a music school and that just wasn't in the cards. And of course there was no proliferation of music courses the way there are today.

In Detroit, I remember very well being in a theater one Sunday in December 1941, listening to the Erskine Hawkins band with Avery Parrish playing the tune "After Hours." I came out of the theater and the country was at war. So that kind of changed everything from that point. My two oldest brothers went into the army, but my brother Phil and I were still in high school.

From Detroit, my father went to an engineering job in Reading, Pennsylvania, at a place that manufactured an alloy of beryllium copper. Now, beryllium copper is kind of a fascinating subject, and at this point the factory was very, very inefficient. Something like 85 percent of the raw materials were going up the flues in smoke. My father came in with new methods. He called it management engineering. In those days the pejorative for that was an "efficiency expert." They used to do time and motion studies and all that. Within not too many months he had the alloy turned around to where only 45 percent was going up in smoke, and the percentage kept coming down. He got it down to about 15 percent being lost, and they were improving it all the time.

Beryllium copper was a very important alloy in the war years because it has some unique qualities. It is nonsparking so you can use it around refineries or any place that you need to use tools that can't have electrical sparks. It's not affected by altitude changes or temperature changes, so it's perfect for high-altitude springs for aircraft.

Apparently, you could make the same things out of copper in alloy with beryllium that you could make just out of copper, the only thing being was that they hardly ever wore out. So as it turned out, the copper companies were a little more pleased to have 85 percent going up so that they didn't have to compete, and they still made enough to satisfy the War Department. It was kind of a terrible story because my father suddenly emerged as an enemy to the people who were the real owners of the corporation. These were owners that he wasn't aware of at all. I always felt my father was naive where business was concerned and thought everybody was honest like he was, and of course that's not necessarily the case. I think a lot of times successful business people look at honesty as kind of an incurable disease, but it's hell for the people who have got it. There's no cure.

They started some kind of a whispering campaign in the town and the next thing we know the FBI is coming to the door. They're doing things to discredit him in the whole community, and it's easy enough to do when you live in a town like that and the FBI starts asking questions about your neighbor. And being that my father was one of those people who had been for Roosevelt in 1932 and then for the Republicans thereafter, it was kind of ironic because he very much had that kind of right-wing authoritarian mind-set. And of course he knew everything as people like that normally do. I mean, he knew very well that Ravel wrote one piece of music, the "Boléro"!

This was always confusing to me because in some ways he was so smart, and in other ways he was so inflexible and missed the point. So it was a real shocker to him when he turned out to be the villain. They were just starting to build a new plant but they aced him out. He was history, gone. He never got over it, and it was a really sad thing to see a man who was in his forties, maybe going into his fifties, and now he was looking for a job on the kind of level that he'd always had. He was discredited by the company he was with and they can close doors on you anywhere they want to. He spent week after week going through the want ads in all the major newspapers in the country to try to find something where they wanted somebody with twenty to twenty-five years of experience, with a college education. But he never really found anything after that. He went to work for the government during the war years. He was with the Navy Department for a while, usually in something relating to materials or manufacturing, but he never really found a place for himself after that. It destroyed him.

Now the years at the Reading school were very good for me because it was a nice school, a good atmosphere, and they had, for the first time, a good band and a really good bandmaster who played interesting stuff. I won the first solo chair clarinet in the band, which, considering my limited education on the instrument, was pretty good.

One summer I had asked my father if I could work at the factory. I worked there as a mail boy, saved my money from the summer, and bought a clarinet. At the store where I bought it, they had a man teaching named Sam Correnti who I studied with. Sam was great! He loved kids and he introduced me to all kinds of things. He liked to take jazz solos off records, so I was playing things that Jimmy Dorsey played and that Artie Shaw played. Those were some of the exercises that we used, aside from the books. He had kind of an attitude of, "You can do it! Go ahead and try it!" After studying with him for a while, he brought in an arrangement of something that he'd written and said, "Here, re-voice this for another instrumentation," and because he assumed that I could do it, I did it. And that started me arranging in an enthusiastic way.

Another person that was very important and helpful was Mr. Muffet, who was the bandmaster at Central Catholic High in Reading. With him there was a kind of permissiveness that helped me build up a tremendous enthusiasm for playing. It may have led me down a garden path, because instead of learning how to read really well, I was busy improvising when there was supposed to be written parts.

Central Catholic High was a very nice school, and they had taken over the Luden mansion. The Luden family made the cough drops, and they were made in Reading. Eventually that became the Catholic high school. So they had pretty good facilities when they got their new building and all that went with it. They had a good-sized band and the band was good. Mr. Muffet let me play the first clarinet parts and he also used to take me with him on some of his professional dates. He'd go out and be the bandmaster for the Schumacher's Marching Band and the Ephrata Band and so on. He'd take me along as his first clarinetist. He used to like it when I improvised the solo parts instead of playing what was written. I was kind of in pig's heaven doing what I wanted and playing what I wanted.

One New Year's we marched in the Mummers parade in Philadelphia. You know I felt I had really hit the big time. Those are kind of exciting memories too, when you're a kid, to march in a big important parade like the Mummers. There was this thing that was kind of unique to the Mummers, and the first time I heard it, it was the eeriest sound. Sometimes these things outdoors have an incredible impact. This was a band made up of all saxophones and banjos and somehow it had kind of an effect like a bagpipe band. There is a kind of nobility to that sound. You hear those sounds outdoors and it makes your hair stand on end. This Mummers band did that to me.

There was a hit around that time that I didn't really associate with because it didn't have the same impact, but it was based on that. Art Mooney's band had a big hit on "I'm Looking over a Four Leaf Clover" that became part of the culture. But the sound of that was based on this Mummers band. Anyway, I heard that during high school and thought it was great.

An interesting situation at this time was that Pennsylvania still had the blue laws, which meant that Sundays were to be kept holy. You don't have entertainment on Sundays. The theaters had to close and the movies had to close and the bars had to close, and the only thing you could have were private clubs. Well, naturally, everybody had private clubs. So there were more jobs for musicians in the state of Pennsylvania than probably anywhere else I'd ever been. I started a little quartet with the kids at school, then I started another little band with a friend in town. He was another student of Sam's, and everyone called him Fuzzy, which his mother really despised. It drove her up the wall that all of the kids called him Fuzzy. His real name was Richard Helene. Both of us were alto players, and we became great friends and shared the band. It was like we were both the leaders, and we used to have an agreement. If I bought the stock arrangement, I would get to play the lead alto part and if he bought the stock arrangement then he got to be the lead alto! We'd have maybe two or three saxophones and a trumpet, and we'd be working all the time playing the Seventh Ward Democratic, the Polish American Democratic, the Six Ward Republicans Club, and the Irish American Club. You name it, we played it.

Then I got a steady job for a while with one of the big bands in town. Harvey Marburger had a band at the Orioles, which was one of the bigger clubs; the Orioles and the Eagles. The Eagles had the biggest band in town. They had about a fourteen- or fifteen-piece band with a full brass section and full sax section. The band I was playing with was more of a kind of stylistic band. Harvey Marburger played the Hawaiian guitar, the steel thing with the steel bar, the whooping and swooping music. It was a nice band, good players, and a good experience for me. I met a lot of guys.

One of the people I met was a piano player from Reading who had moved to Philadelphia and had worked there with Johnny Warrington at the radio station. When my family was getting ready to move to Philadelphia, he suggested to me, "Why don't you go down and see Johnny Warrington when you're there? Maybe he'll have something for you to do." So once I got established in Philadelphia, I took myself down to WCAU, which was the CBS radio station. I marched into Johnny

Gerry at WCAU radio station, Penfield, Pennsylvania, 1945.
COURTESY GERRY MULLIGAN
COLLECTION, LIBRARY OF
CONGRESS, MUSIC DIVISION

Warrington's office and said, "I'd like to write for your band." Johnny laughed and said, "Why not?" So he assigned some tune for me to do and said, "Here, take this and see what you can do with it for the band that we use for the weekly network show." So I did.

I took it and wrote an arrangement. It must have taken a few weeks to do, and I brought it back to him and he went over it with me. He said, "Well, let's see. You did this here, why don't you try this, and you could have done so and so in these bars here. No, this might be better here and why don't you voice this like this?" He went through the chart with me and made suggestions and some criticisms and editing and said, "Here, take it and rewrite it and bring it back." So I did and brought it back a couple weeks later, and he bought it and assigned another piece for me. So that was the beginning of my professional career as an arranger, with Johnny as a kind of mentor and teacher, helping me get started. He was the only arranging teacher that I'd ever had before or have had since. I always thought what it must have been like to be Johnny Warrington and have this high school kid show up and say, "I want to write for your band." I did a few things for him, probably not too much because I still had school to go to and it took me a long time to write things.

I didn't really like the school very much. It was this big West Philadelphia Catholic high school for boys. There were more than two thousand boys in the place and no girls. They had a band that was pretty dreadful, even by my youthful standards. You know, I had played with some pretty good bands by that point. This was just a sloppy band. The kids mostly went into bands to get a letter when they couldn't get on one of the sports teams. At least they could get a letter from the band and go to the games for free. I don't think I ever went to a game the whole time I was in that school. I think I was working on a large case of snobbery at that point, because I didn't want any part of any of that.

Luckily there were a couple of teachers that I liked, especially the homeroom teacher whose name I forget. He really acted like a human being and treated the kids like they were human beings. But the most important one was Brother Martin, who had charge of the band. Brother Martin realized that music was my main interest and that I was not about to be satisfied with this marching band. So he never asked me to join the band, but what he did do was make the band room available to me to do things if I wanted to. He gave me free run of the place so I was able to start really working as a professional musician, writing arrangements professionally when I was in high school. And I guess he didn't think it was a terrible thing because I got my school work done anyway, so it's not that I was neglecting my so-called studies. I had a great friendship with him. He was a wonderful man and he tried to help me. I think he was very proud of me, the fact that I had done those arrangements for Johnny Warrington.

Then I started a band with some of the kids in the school. I didn't have much choice of instruments because there were no saxophone players. One kid played tenor, Paul Schultz, and I depended on him heavily because he and I were the only saxophone players and we had to fill out the section with three or four clarinet players. We had a lot of clarinets and no saxes and a lot of trumpet players and no trombonists who could play. So I wound up having four trumpets, one trombone, and five reeds, which were two saxes and three clarinets. I had piano and drums but probably didn't have a bass player at all. I can't imagine what it sounded like.

Anyway, I tried to write charts for it that were something that suited the instrumentation and wound up with things that were more or less Glenn Miller style, leaning heavily on clarinet lead for the voicings. In a short while the band became the hit of the school. We played at the assemblies and I guess if prevailed upon, the school might have been able to give us a letter for our little dance band.

We went down to the girls' school and played for them. The girls' school was something else. It was two or three blocks down the street from us, and the girls had a symphony orchestra that started rehearsing in October for a concert in April. I used to go down there all the time to listen to them. I was so jealous because they were spending all this rehearsal time playing gorgeous orchestral music and I had to go back to the boys' school and I hated it.

Both photos: Gerry on clarinet, high school band, Reading, Pennsylvania.
COURTESY GERRY MULLIGAN COLLECTION, LIBRARY OF CONGRESS, MUSIC DIVISION

Well, I had hoped that some things in high school would at least be interesting, to take some of the edge off, because I really was not particularly happy there. One of the things that I had hoped for was my brothers had always talked about the fact that when you got into high school, certain classes were like college; elective classes and laboratory time, like chemistry. So I really looked forward to chemistry. I wound up with a teacher of chemistry who was a nice little man, but he was so boring. I mean, he would read a paragraph from a book and put you right to sleep. He had no enthusiasm. I didn't learn one bloody thing. Nothing stuck out of that whole year. Everything was just a blur and I started cutting, as much as I could get away with, more and more classes. It was such a big school that they had staggered lunch periods. I would have one of my buddies from my band come and get me and say, "Brother Martin wants you at the music room," and I'd take off and go down to the music room and work on my charts. So it was not exactly a mutual love affair between the school and me. But as I say, there were a couple of the brothers that I liked. They were sympathetic and I felt like I learned something from them. Other than that it was a dead loss.

3

ON THE ROAD WITH TOMMY TUCKER

IN THE FALL OF 1944, I started my senior year. I wasn't particularly happy about even starting this school year, but I went. The first class that I had was a lecture class in physics. I walk in and who have I got teaching physics but the same teacher that ruined chemistry for me. I had a funny sensation at that class because as this man read out of the book, I forgot the meanings of words. I was looking at them, I could spell them, I could pronounce them, but I didn't know what the hell they meant. I suddenly realized there are things that are so habitual that it's second nature. Things like tying your shoes or tying your tie just become automatic. You don't have to think about it. Around this time I went to tie my shoes and I couldn't do it. It was a strange sensation to just blank it out. I started having migraine headaches every morning. I guess it was probably close to the time I had the sessions with this teacher who taught chemistry and physics.

Well, after this one class I sat there so totally disassociated that I couldn't understand the words. I got up from class and went down to the principal and said, "I'm leaving school now. I'm going on the road with a band." He said "Well, you can't quit school. You have to have your father's permission." I said, "Yes, I'll have it." And I went home and my father came home and I told him I'd quit school. He tried to talk me out of it, but I said, "Listen, I'll be eighteen in April and the way things are now with the army, there's nothing for me to do that I want to do." And I said, "The last recruits may get stuck in some kind of a camp somewhere. I'll be a thirty-day wonder, and they'll ship me off to the South Pacific. So my future is not very bright, and I don't want to do it. But if I have to do all that then I'm going out to do what I want for this year."

I went to see Brother Martin and he was nonjudgmental. He understood what it meant to me. He didn't really think it was a good idea leaving school, but I think he may have had more insight into me than anybody else I was dealing with.

There is one area that I've purposely let go by, because I have only limited intentions of getting into more personal relationships with women since it's not sensation that I'm after here. But there is one relationship that I can't pass by. I mean, you can't really ignore your first love. A girl named Auga was my real first love—or maybe instead of love, my first real lust—because that's the feeling I've always associated with honeymoons and that's sort of like the process of falling in love. A honeymoon, whether it's accompanied by a marriage certificate, is still a honeymoon.

Auga was a beautiful girl and she was full of energy, vitality, and she was funny. At that age and falling in love, we couldn't keep our hands off each other. So it was about this time I was trying to study. I made a couple of attempts to study and I went to a teacher in Philadelphia, Cox I think his name was. He taught the Schillinger system, and I'd been kind of impressed with the things I'd read about it. So I was taking some lessons and then at the school they were letting me use one of the little studios at night to write, and I enjoyed the privilege.

Well, Auga and I, because we were so hot and heavy, she used to come up to visit me at the school. I didn't really encourage her to do that, but I didn't really discourage it either! Well unfortunately, Auga had kind of a penchant for talking about it to all of her friends. Before long we were the local scandal, and I was asked not to use the place at night to write, or anything else for that matter.

So about that time I left Philadelphia. I don't know what became of our relationship, but I guess the honeymoon must have been over at that point, although I can't imagine that stopping but there is also the possibility that Auga was a lot more sexually active than I realized and

I thought this was exclusively for me. Life often has little surprises for you in that area.

Now during the summer that year, I had worked at the Steel Pier with Alex Bartha's band. Alex had the band there for twenty years or something. It was a big band, well known in the territory, and Alex liked me. He was always talking about taking the band out on the road and having a name band. He really wanted to do it right this time. He didn't want to be just the house band at the Steel Pier. Well, I thought I'd found my star to hitch my wagon to! Little did I know that Alex had been saying this every summer for the last twenty years. But on the basis of that, I quit school and went down to the office of Jimmy Tyson, who was the manager of Johnny Warrington, and told him that Alex said he was going on the road and I wanted to go on the road with him. He laughed and said, "You know, Alex is always saying that, he's not going on the road." I said, "Well, he's got to, I quit school." He said, "You what?"

Jimmy had nothing for me to do, so I used to hang out in his outer office, and every band that came through town, they'd call up and say, "We need a substitute trombone player or a substitute trumpet player." He'd say, "Well, do you need a tenor player? Alto player?" And nobody did, until finally Tommy Tucker's band came through. It must have been about November or something like that, and we went through the same thing. Tommy needed a trombone player, and then Jimmy said, "Well, do you need a saxophone player?" "No, I don't need a saxophone player." Jimmy said, "How about an arranger? You could use an arranger?" And Tommy said, "Well, maybe. Tell me about him." So he told him about this young kid that wants to write and he'd love to go on the road with you. So Tommy said, "Send him around to the theater."

So I went to the Earle Theater and met with Tommy and his wife and he hired me; a contract for a hundred dollars a week for three ballads or two jump arrangements a week, copied. Oh yeah! So we left the Earle Theater and I went out with the band. I was off on the road. We were doing one-nighters and traveling by cars, and every place we showed up I was the first one out of the car and into the hotel, asking,

"Where's the piano?" So I spent all my time trying to turn out the arrangements that Tommy wanted.

When I first went to New York with the Tommy Tucker band I roomed with Dick Hilbert, who was a drummer friend from Reading. We used to spend hours together at night, just the two of us, and he'd be playing drums and I would be playing alto and we'd be playing tunes and we were indefatigable. It must have driven the people around us crazy. Dick was a very good drummer, but the atmosphere in the jam sessions finally put him off. He got tired of being in New York and becoming a machine for the soloists. We all wanted to play and stretch out and it was kind of a thing of getting control of our techniques, which is what we were doing. It was the beginning of the time, too, when soloists started stretching out and playing longer and longer solos.

Those jam sessions in New York consisted of . . . well, first of all, getting it organized, then we would chip in money to pay for the studio so it was our time to do what we wanted.

There were three or four places in New York where we would rehearse. There were Ringle's and Don Jose's, which was the inspiration for the swinging red door piece. We called it "The Red Door." Later on, Elliot Lawrence didn't think that was such a good idea in the days of Joe McCarthy, so it became "The Swinging Door"!

So in the jam sessions, people would start playing a fast tempo and the bass player and the drummer were keeping time for all of this fast tempo. And most sessions would have too many horns. You've got five or six guys and each one of them plays a long, long solo. You know that feeling. He plays a chorus and didn't quite get it so plays one more chorus and he'll get it this time and you don't get it so you say, "one more." And you find guys are playing twenty to thirty choruses. In the meantime, the drummer is still going ding da da ding. So these sessions would go on and on and after you got done with all the horns, then the piano player would get to play a solo. Well, a lot of the time, the horn players were quite selfish, and as soon as the piano player played a couple of choruses, somebody would jump in and they'd be back to the horns again.

So we started having our own sessions in order to avoid that. But this is the kind of thing that drove Hilbert out of town; probably all the other players too. From just the length of time he was doing it, sometimes with this little rhythm pattern on the top cymbal, and doing it for so long and so fast, he started to get a knot of some sort on the tendons on the back of his hands and his wrists, and that did it. He hated to do it, but he left New York and I guess he went back to school and became a psychology teacher.

Tommy had a very stylized, commercial band, or at least what people knew of him. The stuff that the band was best known for was very stylized, but they also had some very good charts written by some first-rate arrangers. There were a lot of good musicians in the band and Tommy was a good musician, so it was like they were very conscious of what they were doing. The musicianship was very high and they had a couple of arrangements by Ben Homer, who wrote "The Mexican Hat Dance" for Les Brown, and a couple by Eddie Finckel. Tommy had some good charts and when the band hit the jazz arrangements, the "flag work" as they used to call them, it hit, man. It was the first time I heard a brass section really, really hitting things together with some fire. I mean up close. Because you know, it was something else when you were standing next to the trumpet section and they would hit these ensemble things and just make my ears burn.

So that was a good musical experience, and from the road we went into what was then the Steven's Hotel in Chicago, and we played in their supper club for about a month and a half or two months. Bob Swift came on the band when I was there. He was the first of all the swinging guys that I met. Swifty was part of that trombone section, and it's when I first heard about people like Earl Swope and the players from Washington. And Swift used to break me up because we'd have rehearsals in the morning and I'd come into the rehearsal dressed as I normally would, and he'd call me Technicolor! I suppose between the reddish hair and liking colors, and probably wearing a variety of them, that was his nickname for me in the band, *Technicolor*!

Most of the time I was with the band I went to hear all the bands in town. It was the first time I heard Dizzy play. He was with Billy Eckstine at the time. So I heard those bands and all the other bands in town.

Of course, my arrangements for Tommy were getting a little wilder as time went on, and when the three months were up, he said, "Well listen, it's been great. You've written a lot of good things for the band and I like it, but I think your path lies in a different direction, but if ever you want to go into any kind of a business, you let me know. I'd be glad to invest money in you in anything, except a band." I laughed and said, "You know you're safe."

There is one thing that happened with Tommy's band that always kind of tickled me. He gave me an assignment to write an arrangement of a tune called "All of a Sudden My Heart Sings," a French song that ascends the diatonic scale and descends the diatonic scale. It was very much a French cabaret song. Well, I had no experience with this and no idea what it was. So when Tommy gave me the assignment, I went about writing in the way I would. I guess it was like a kind of embellishment you would do as a jazz kind of tune. It had a slow tempo. They wanted to record that while we were in Chicago. We went into the studios that are famous because of the sign that hangs over the control room; the big sign carved out that says, "Where's the melody?" This studio was famous among musicians; everybody knew about it. It's probably still there as far as I know. And the thing about it was that we rehearsed the thing, and we were playing it and the singers are singing and it sounded good. But then the guy from . . . I don't know where he was from. I'm not sure if he was the publisher from Columbia Records, or what his relationship was. I didn't know about any of that stuff anyway. They were just a bunch of faces to me. But this guy comes out and he tells Tommy, "No man, this is no good because there is no melody in it, and the thing is so simple." And I suppose I had done a pretty good job of disguising the melody. I think you've got to do something to create some interest in the diatonic scale. Some of the guys in the band and I were laughing because here I am, my arrangement being thrown out because I can't find the melody and here we are in the studio with the sign that said, "Where's the melody?"

As I continued to develop as an arranger, I picked up stuff from everything I heard. All those bands. My ears were constantly ringing with the ideas that guys were working on. Of course bands like Eckstine's, and another who came through was Earl Hines and his band. That was a good band with the two tenors, Wardell Gray and Kermit Scott.

I became more and more influenced by the things I heard, so it was inevitable. I'd started to try to incorporate these things and learn how to use them. So I understood what Tommy was saying. I wasn't sorry about that.

Then by the time April had rolled around, I had to sign up for the draft, and I went and took a physical. In the meantime, the musicians had told me all kinds of things to tell the draft board so they wouldn't want me. And by that time, they were listening to the psychiatrists because there had been incidents with young guys getting off a landing somewhere, you know the first out of the box, and they would freeze, and they'd shoot them down.

I'm not sure, unless you experienced it, that you could appreciate what the reaction was of somebody like me because I'm one of your shrinking violets. I'm your Ferdinand the Bull, who would rather sit and sniff flowers all day, man. I didn't like to fight in the schoolyard. I didn't like to play rough and get my clothes all dirty so I'd have to sit in my own sweat all day. I guess I was a little more fastidious than that. And to grow up on four years of newsreels of the war, by the time I became eighteen, man, I was scared to death! As it turned out, I didn't need any of the things the musicians told me because that whole experience of taking off all your clothes and going around with hundreds of naked guys, man, and being prodded, pushed, and punched and questioned, was the most degrading experience. It was quite obvious that I was not army material because I'm not about to be molded into anything requiring the kind of obedience they're depending on. Forget it! If they'd offered me a job in a band, I would have been off like a shot, because that's something that

I know, it's something I can do and feel useful. Carrying a gun, forget it, I'm not interested.

What happened was, as I went through this thing, I was literally scared to death. The psychiatrist was a self-righteous, pompous pain in the ass, sitting there with his fucking uniform on and you're naked in front of him and this bastard is asking you personal questions. I hated it and I couldn't talk. I later found out that it has a name, globus or some dumb thing! What it means is that you have a lump in your throat out of fear, and I couldn't even talk to the son of a bitch. His comment was, "Well, you're obviously a bad apple. If you have one bad apple in a barrel it will spoil the whole thing." Man, he made me so happy that day; that was the end of it.

So here's the whole thing; I'd quit high school in order to go on the road because they're going to draft me, and they didn't draft me anyway. I couldn't have been more pleased.

On the other hand, I was kind of sorry because I would have loved to have gotten into one of the good army bands, like so many of the guys who became my friends later were able to do. A lot of things about it were appealing, you know. There's one thing that's kind of by rote. We say, "Man really wants peace," and "We've got to have peace," and all that. And you know, "peace on earth," and we go on and on about it, but the trouble is that war is really great and people love war. I mean, there's nothing that makes men feel more glorious, with the camaraderie and adventure and just going through the hardships together. I mean, it's man's finest hour. If we could come up with anything nearly as appealing to the masculine self-image, we'd have a success on our hands. So you know, it's kind of like we kid ourselves that we hate war. We don't hate war at all! But there was no place in it for me and as I said, the guys I met later on who were in the first army together in Europe, or the guys who were with Miller's band, I mean, they had some great adventures. It's too bad that you have to have a war to go to, but after all, they're not doing things in the world for the satisfaction of musicians, are they?

4

ON THE AIR WITH ELLIOT LAWRENCE

AFTER I FINISHED with Tommy Tucker's band, I went back to Philadelphia and joined the band of Elliot Lawrence. Elliot and I became friends because we were both a lot younger than the guys in the band and we hung out together a lot of the time.

Elliot always had the attitude that he wanted to give the arrangers credit. In fact, this is something that was common to two of the leaders that ultimately I worked for: Elliot and Miles Davis. Miles had that attitude too. He always felt if you list the personnel, you should also put the names of the arrangers on the bill.

So I wound up becoming really well known because we were doing a weekly radio show featuring Elliot's band from Philadelphia. It was a half-hour show every week on Saturday afternoon or something, which was a very good time for us. He was always announcing that this is a composition by Gerry Mulligan, and then I became like a personality. He would do the same for Frank Hunter or whoever the arranger was. Wherever I went, they'd heard of me and heard my charts, so that kind of eased the way.

A distinct arranging style emerged while I was writing for Elliot and this is part of the thing of being self-taught. I didn't learn a system for doing things. It's like everything that I wrote an arrangement of, I had to solve my problems as they came, so I would approach each thing as an individual. I could never sit down and just duplicate the kind of harmonization I did with a saxophone chorus like I did in the previous chart. And I was always, to myself, very critical of arrangers who did that; you know, kept writing the same arrangement over and over and over again; you change the melody but everything else stays the same. I just couldn't bring myself to do that, and I always attributed a lot of that to being self-taught. The very restrictions of my technique forced me to find my own way, and often my own way would produce an individuality that wouldn't have been there otherwise.

But I wasn't really consciously trying to do that. I was just trying to come up with a fresh approach to a tune or an idea for a jazz piece that would be interesting to blow on, and try to make good settings for the soloists and exciting shout choruses and that sort of thing. So it was really just doing the job as I perceived it.

I started to realize that what I was doing sounded a lot different from what other guys were doing, but I never really knew why. I never really understood that, and yet it was the sort of thing that I could usually recognize of the arrangers who were the leading arrangers. I could usually identify their writing in short order. A lot of lesser-known arrangers I wouldn't be able to identify because they were writing by rote, doing the same arrangement over and over again.

But you tend to learn just from the doing. If Elliot wanted a jump arrangement or a ballad or whatever it was, I'd sit down and try to think the thing through and say, what's the best way to do this for the band, and so on. And Elliot's situation was very good for me because we had a lot of rehearsal time, and it was great being able to play the stuff and to try things and probably write things, and incorporate it into something else and allow things to develop. And as a consequence, because of that I was able to develop some kind of an individual voice.

Elliot was open to any things that I wanted to try. When I was writing for Tommy Tucker, he needed specific kinds of material for specific spots in his shows. I didn't have those restrictions with Elliot, and so I was able to try all different stuff, and I wrote a lot of originals for him.

While I was with Elliot Lawrence, Charlie Parker really started to emerge onto the scene. It seemed to be quite sudden. As soon as the first couple of records came out it became kind of widespread. One was on a label called Comet and it was Red Norvo's date. On it were Flip Phillips and Slam Stewart and I'm not sure, it may have been Teddy Wilson on piano and Red on xylophone, and Dizzy and Bird. Anyway, these were kind of swing band–oriented and not too shocking, but when Bird played it was like a new country had been heard from. It just was an altogether different atmosphere, and it was really striking because he played with such clarity. Then when the first quintet records came out on Guild with Dizzy and Charlie, they were very accessible to everybody, I mean, to hear and to understand, because they were arrangers.

This was something I hadn't really even thought about then, but not too long ago I was talking to John Lewis about it and he said, you know, the thing is that Bird first showed up and they always talk about Bird and Diz. But Bird and Diz were quite separate entities who, until they played together in Dizzy's small group, had very little to do with each other. He said that he thinks Bird was a big influence on Dizzy as soon as they got together, but Dizzy really was from another school altogether. You know he was influenced by Roy Eldridge, and the things that he did were really out of Roy more than anything and not really related to all of the things that were going on at Minton's, the famous sessions up there that Monk and a lot of other people were involved with.

So they were really quite separate, but in the context of the quintet, they were Dizzy's tunes primarily and they were Dizzy's arrangements and they were good. The fact that it made it kind of a showcase for Bird was wonderful. They were some of the best things that Bird ever recorded. And Bird, like any other soloist, needs a setting. I know that everybody went around and just recorded Bird for his own sake, but to me, that kind of misses the point of music. I can't just see music as being one soloist playing the thing and that's it. You know, too many guys approached it that way over the years. They only put up with what they call the head and whatever is going on in the arrangement until time for their solo. That's just introduction and it doesn't mean anything. You do without that; it all starts when they start soloing.

Well, I don't think like that and Dizzy didn't either. He always had a very, very good sense of arranging. In fact, Dizzy did a couple of arrangements for bands that I think most people didn't know about.

Gerry and Dizzy Gillespie, 1958. COURTESY GERRY MULLIGAN COLLECTION, LIBRARY OF CONGRESS, MUSIC DIVISION

He wrote a couple of things for Woody Herman's band and he wrote things for Jimmy Dorsey's band, and these were things that Elliot and I used to hear on these transcriptions because he wrote them at a time when the record ban was on, so nobody heard them. He was quite a good arranger, very imaginative and very individual. So that was where he was coming from. He was really a band man, an arranger, and a Roy Eldridge–influenced trumpet player.

Bird was just something else altogether. Bird was Bird. It seemed like he came along fully formed, but it wasn't quite that simple because of the stories about Bird's youth. He used to talk about when he was a little kid and he'd be down at the places and he could hear Lester Young play. He'd be out in the alley listening through the openings in the fans in the kitchen so he could hear Lester Young. And later on he took a job in New York dishwashing some place because Art Tatum was playing there, so he could hear him all the time. Not too long ago I was putting something together for a history course, and I was listening to a record of Art Tatum's that I hadn't heard, and I heard him play this really elongated line through a set of chords. It was very complex and fast moving and it suddenly hit me. I said, I think that Bird studied this passage or must have heard Tatum a lot because he used to do things like that—things guys hadn't done on horns before. The thing of making his melodic line running arpeggios on chords. Running them in a different meter. Not like 1-2-3-4, but he would go like 1, and then the third beat would be 2, and then another beat over here and so he would sail through this progression, hitting the chords, but not in the same place, and come out here four bars later, someplace else. Well, Tatum used to do that and then Bird did it. And sure enough, I found out not too long after that he did take this job as a dishwasher just so he could hear Tatum. It showed up in his playing. God, he had an incredible facility. The way he used the horn was marvelous.

Somebody sent me a tape of Bird playing at home when he must have been maybe late teens or early twenties. He was playing with a friend of his, a guitar player, and of course, he was playing "Cherokee." This was his number, man; he worked on that thing for years. Somebody said that when he did "Koko," it was not just a little accident that it came out the way it did. He'd been laying for that thing for ten years. The solo he played on that is like a masterpiece in itself. But oddly enough, the sound of him playing when he was very young with his neighbor, the guitar player, sounded very much like Bird. It was all there already. So Bird was unique in that, where it came from. It seems like a logical evolution, but even so, that's the mystery.

When I first heard Charlie Parker, it had a profound effect on me and how I perceived music altogether. And this was because Bird had a unique approach to rhythm, and it was so much in control. Maybe it's a misnomer to say rhythm in that instance, because his approach to playing in a progression was his own. I don't know how he arrived at it.

Oh my God, when I heard those records, it was like taking the scales off my eyes. It just made me see the possibilities very clearly. There was something kind of inevitable about the way Bird played and it was very direct and very melodic, and it transcended the limitations of the horn or playing things because it felt good on the horn, which most players had done, you know. You do things because they feel good on the horn. Bird didn't seem to care about that. He did things because they were in his head, and then putting these two things together forced the horn to react to what he wanted, he wasn't reacting to the horn.

But probably the main effect from first hearing Bird was to want to lighten up my time, to put things right in the time where they belong, to have a more immediate command of playing with a rhythm section. I was always fighting mouthpieces then. It sounds like a simple enough thing, but it's not always easy to find mouthpieces that work the way you want them to.

But hearing Bird gave me the model of what I wanted it to sound like. I finally heard that this was the direction for playing, and in playing an ensemble way as well. Because it meant having control of the time, and it meant having an attack—control of time and attack, and to free the player from a lot of what felt like restrictions of the progressions. He broke through the progressions in ways that he made much more open and flamboyant melodies through the existing progressions that guys had done before.

So it's obvious from that, then, that the influence Bird had was on all levels of listening and adapting listening to playing. And for me, it also went through the other cycle of the writing functions. I should think that playing, I guess, is a left-brain function and writing must be a right-brain function.

Well, things like that are fascinating to me because when they came up with these concepts, a lot of things became clear to me that were very hard to understand. And to have the understanding that different lobes of the brain have different functions in how we think made it a lot easier for me to try to put them together, because I've spent my life trying to do that.

My first experience with Bird personally was kind of remarkable. While I was arranging for Elliot Lawrence's band in Philadelphia, Bird came into town with Dizzy and they were doing a concert at the Academy of Music. We were on the show and they had their quintet, which included Sarah Vaughan. She was this shy, thin-as-a-stick kid. She must have been eighteen or nineteen years old with this big voice. She was wonderful.

We were having a Friday rehearsal for the Saturday show, and Red Rodney brought Bird by the studio to meet everybody and hear the band. Bird was great. Everybody liked him and he was very complimentary, and he liked the charts of mine that he heard. He invited me to come down and play with them. I said, "Well, I'm not playing the concert. I'm just arranging for the band." He said, "Well, maybe you can come over to the session at the Downbeat Club anyway."

So the next day, in the morning, I get a call from somebody at the station who said, "You'd better bring your tenor sax down because Frank Lewis, the tenor player, tripped on the stairs at home. His kid left his skate or something, and he broke his wrist and he can't play, so you have to sub for him." Well, I came into rehearsal that afternoon and the guys are all giving me kind of a fishy look like I was doing a little black magic here. So I wound up playing the show on tenor.

Afterward we went over to the Downbeat and Bird was going to sit in with Don Byas and the regular rhythm section. Jimmy Golden was the piano player, and I can't remember the other guys; it was a long time ago.

Anyway, I sat and listened to a set or two and by this time it's getting late. I am listening to Bird playing with Don Byas, I mean, two of the greatest jazz saxophone players I'd ever heard. The pair of them could tear it up. Don was something. He had a wonderful sound, great command, and he was a fast, really dynamic player. I was getting ready to go because I had to be up the next day and so I went over to Bird and said to him, "I've really enjoyed it, thanks a lot and I hope I see you again soon," and all of that kind of stuff.

He said, "You can't go, you've got to play." I said, "No, come on, play with you guys? Don't be ridiculous, I'd be scared to death." He said, "Now wait a minute." So he went to the checkroom and got my horn where I'd left it, got the horn out and put it together and blew on it and said, "Okay," and handed it to me. So I had to go play with Don and Bird. I don't know what the hell I played. I have absolutely no idea because it scared the living daylights out of me playing with these guys. I felt way out of my league. But Bird was complimentary and very nice to me and encouraged me, and that was great.

I had been writing for Elliot's band for a while and then I left Philadelphia. As I mentioned, Elliot and I both being young guys, we became good friends and spent a lot of time together. This created some resentment with most of the musicians in the band, and they started to pull some nasty things on me. So I just took off and went to New York, and it was at that period that I got a job right away with Ike Carpenter. He was a piano player and a singer from Georgia with a broad Southern accent. I used to love him, man. He would sing "I Don't Stand a Ghost of a Chance," and he managed to pronounce the words with two syllables, two or three syllables. So we worked some gigs with that.

I remember working up at a club in Albany, and it was a fairly small band, a couple brass and a couple of saxes and I don't even remember what we played, but it was a nice little band. Bobby Sims, Zoot's brother, was playing with the band, and I felt like I already knew Zoot because of the fan magazines there used to be for bands. In one of the fan magazines I had, there was an article on the Bobby Sherwood band, and it had pictures of all of the soloists and something about them. One of the people in the band was Zoot Sims. So when I met Bobby, it was great because I loved the way Zoot played on these records and I felt like I knew him already.

When Zoot finally came to New York not too long after that, we immediately became good friends and hung out a lot. Some of his California habits were a little hard for me to adjust to; like we would go have breakfast in the morning and I would pick him up. He was staying some place over on Eighth Avenue, and we would go out and he would look for a hot dog stand. He'd have these chili burgers and Coca-Cola and something else hot. I can't remember what it was but it was typically California. "Zoot, my God! How can you eat that for breakfast?"

Anyway, we hung out together a lot. Then, when he was going to be in New York, we rented an apartment up on the West Side. Zoot was about the only guy I ever knew that we used to practice together. I think because of Zoot, I became a much better saxophone player than I would have been otherwise. I never really felt like studying the saxophone after my initial lessons with Sammy Correnti. Not because I thought I was a great saxophonist; I think more than anything I thought I wouldn't be a great saxophonist. As much as I loved hearing Ibert's chamber orchestra piece that featured Marcel Moulet, I never really have had the patience to have the discipline to do that. It sounds simple, but it's hard to play. You really have to develop the technique involved with doing that. I always wound up working on stuff that related directly to what I was doing. To me, the horn was sort of a necessary evil. I felt if I could play in the ensemble well, I could write better for them. So Zoot and I would do that, practice together out of the Clouset books and the Jimmy Dorsey books, and we enjoyed a long friendship. During those years we were close, even when we didn't share an apartment.

Bobby Sims and I became good friends too. He knew all the group singers because Bobby played trumpet and sang. Among those was

Buddy Stewart and I think Dave Lambert was probably there, and Lillian Lane was the lead singer. She had a beautiful sound. So he introduced me to them and I used to hang out with them a lot, and we would sit around and sing the arrangements. I learned parts of the arrangements. I used to have a good time with them.

We all knew the things that Davey Lambert had written for the different vocal groups in bands that he had been with, like the Gene Krupa band. Some of those arrangements got very popular, like "I Don't Know Why I Love You." So we used to sit around and sing those things as group singers like to do. One of the people that was there and part of that whole group was Beverly Stewart, who was Buddy's sister. It was through Beverly I was introduced to the lawyer who was Gene Krupa's partner in the band. His name was Johnny Gluskin. His brother was a music director in Hollywood named Lud Gluskin. Gene and Johnny had an office at 1640 Broadway, and I used to go up there all the time. Beverly was working up there in the office, and they were hoping that Anita O'Day was going to leave the band and they were going to try out Beverly to take her place.

5

"DISC JOCKEY JUMP"

WHEN IT CAME TIME for Anita to be replaced, Johnny hired me to go out with Bev. I went up to the office at night and worked on charts to take out to California so I had some things ready when I got there. I brought this arrangement of "They Didn't Believe Me" and Gene liked it a lot, so that was all good.

We flew out to California to join the band. Flying out to California in 1946 was a little bit of an experience because we were flying on DC-3s and altogether it was a twenty-four-hour trip. It flew from New York to Buffalo, Buffalo to Cleveland, Cleveland to maybe Chicago, Chicago to St. Louis, St. Louis to Oklahoma City; you puddle-jumped across the country, and those planes didn't fly very high because they weren't pressurized cabins. I've often thought about how over the years my view of the country has gotten progressively higher. You know when you see it at 5,000 feet it looks one way and landmarks are still familiar and look on a human scale. Then the next kind of planes that came along went up to 10,000 to 15,000 feet, so that's a different view. I mean, the Grand Canyon at 5,000 feet is a lot different than it is at 35,000 feet. So now we zip back and forth at 35,000, and it's an altogether different view.

But it was a twenty-four-hour trip out there and, you know, I guess in the time that we spent in New York, Bev and I started to go together. You know, the young love syndrome. We were both very young and inexperienced, and we liked each other so we hung out together. Very innocent I must say. And so flying out together was kind of a romantic adventure as well. We enjoyed that.

So we got out there, and Buddy Stewart was singing with Gene's band at that point and, as I said, Bev was supposed to audition with the band. They thought she would take Anita's place. She was a good singer. But we got out there and the first thing that happened was that Beverly found out that they had already hired a singer, the girlfriend of the road manager. So that was the end of her career singing with the Gene Krupa band.

We were working at the Hollywood Palladium, and I'd only been on the band a couple of days when I ran into Charlie Parker, who was in town working with Dizzy Gillespie. He asked me if I had any pot and I said "Yeah, I guess I could get a couple of joints." So I go traipsing down to Billy Berg's, where he was playing, and promptly got myself busted standing out in the parking lot with him smoking pot. So that was a great way to join a band. Especially the Gene Krupa band. Gene had been through an earlier bust himself in Buffalo and had been treated pretty badly.

So I was arrested and taken to jail. You had to wait until you were arraigned or something to get out, get bail posted and all that. So I guess Johnny Gluskin bailed me out and took me under his wing. He had to be responsible for me because I was underage, and I'm sure that was a bad position for the band to be in because that whole bust that they put Gene through in Buffalo was based on the fact that there was this young cat who was working as a band boy or a roadie or something had claimed, when he got busted, that he was getting it for Gene Krupa. Guys in the band who knew about it said it wasn't so. They just set Gene up, and Gene was very resentful of the whole thing because he said that before the day of the hearing he was in the judge's chambers with lawyers, and they assured him that this was just a formality and they knew the kid wasn't telling the truth. So when he got into the court-room they not only found him guilty but sentenced him to six months, man; that was it. He felt like he'd been sold down the river and what it meant was, headlines all around. All those bastards wallowing in instant notoriety. I mean, those are elements that people don't normally think about. They really did society a favor there, putting Gene Krupa in jail for six months. You know that was really an important move. But that's the way they think.

More respect to Gene the way he responded to it and recovered from it and rebuilt his career, because it was a very destructive thing to have on your record in this country at that point. But everybody welcomed him back and the band was very successful. A good band. Gene was a lovely man. I always had been kind of impressed that all the leaders I worked for were such good people. Gene was a sweetheart. Elliot was great, and Thornhill was unique. And Stan Kenton was remarkable in his own way. You know, basically a very nice man.

When my bust took place, well, they just made a lot of trouble for me. It was expensive and a lot of moralizing went on. The police and the district attorneys can all be a pain in the ass with all that. They're always right there with a moral for you.

Nothing happened to Bird because I had it in my pocket; he didn't have it in his pocket. They said they found a seed in his pocket and they all laughed and said, "Well, we can't hold you on a seed." Charlie left in good humor. So I got caught and spent a very uncomfortable night in the drunk tank.

When I first joined the band, most everything in the book featured Charlie Ventura on tenor. Gene said that he would like to give Buddy Wise and Charlie Kennedy more solo space, and since we were all interested in what Charlie Parker was doing, that I should write some solo space for them. Well, as it happens, there was one guy in the band who oddly enough I encountered later on in the Thornhill band. And this was the kind of guy that liked to sit back in the trombone section and he would go to the second trumpet player and say, "You know, I understand that the wife of the alto player has been saying that your old lady is so and so and so and so." Then he would go to the second alto player and say, "The wife of the second trumpet player has been saying some pretty funny things about your old lady." Then he would sit there and watch this thing develop. The guys would be cool for a while, but then the friction was there, and one day there would be an explosion. And this guy would sit there and chuckle. He-he-he. They called him "Black

Barney" and "Evil." A couple of names like that because he had gotten a reputation for this sort of a thing, but he still was always pulling things.

Well, I show up at the first rehearsal with my new charts and I'm standing in the band room talking to some of the guys, and Charlie Ventura came in and he was furious, man. His face was red with anger, and he said, "Where is he? Where is he?" He sees me and comes over and immediately starts throttling me. He has me against the wall and was strangling me. It took I think four guys to pull him off me. I said, "Charlie, what happened?" and he said, "You son of a bitch, what do you mean I can't blow? And you're writing all this stuff for these young kids." Sure enough, man, Black Barney had been at it again. And Charlie, who should have known better, went for it, man, because it hit him where it hurts.

The older guys were really upset with the way things had turned over when Bird came along. They were very vulnerable to criticism or being called "old hat," so that's what Black Barney pulled on them. This new arranger, this sharp new arranger, is calling you old hat. Christ, that's all I needed. But Charlie was a nice guy and a good player. He really had such a great sound on the horn.

I was with the band for quite a while; in fact, I spent about a year on the road with them, and most of that time I was the arranger. I filled in a couple of times playing, once when one of the tenor players got sick on the road and another time when we left New York and we had a new alto player, Harold Terrill. Gene didn't like him at all. He just figured he couldn't cut it so, unfortunately, I had my new alto with me and got pressed into service whether I could do it or not. It was only a couple of nights after I started playing alto in the band when we played someplace where the first set was going to be a radio broadcast. We were getting ready to go out on the stage, and Harry Terrill hadn't shown up. Harry was the lead alto player, and he didn't get there on time. I don't know what happened because it was very unlike Harry to be late. But for whatever reason, he didn't show up and I had to play lead alto. Man, I was scared to death because they had some tough stuff in that book and suddenly to be trying to play lead with a section was a bit much for me.

I must say though, there were a bunch of good saxophone players in that band and I learned a hell of a lot because I had to. I really had to dig in because they were power players.

So anyway, I kept writing for the band and traveling with them. During that period I guess Beverly was there in Los Angeles, and we were all living in the house together. Buddy and his wife, Jerri, and Beverly and me. There was somebody else there, I don't remember who was there now. It might have been someone else in the band or a friend of theirs. Anyway, I was tied up between arranging and my new job and all the details of this damn bust that I had gone through.

Beverly didn't get the job singing, and somebody took her out to see Benny Goodman's band that was playing in Culver City at the Meadowbrook Gardens. She met Stan Getz, and the next thing I know I'd lost my romance to Stan. On the one hand I couldn't blame her, because of the disappointment of not getting the gig and also the disappointment of my getting all hung up. But the next thing I know, she married him. She married Stan. And that was the end of her singing career and just about everything else because poor Bev had a very rough life. I only saw her a few times after that. Eventually she got strung out on heroin and then I suppose that they split up. He left her, and then not too long after that she died. I don't know how long it was. The times are all kind of encapsulated, and I don't really know anything about them because I wasn't around them at that point.

There were times when they were married when I remember seeing them and I'd always hoped for her that things would go well because I liked Bev very much. She was a very, very sweet girl, and very considerate of me also. Really, she got me the job with Krupa's band. So I was very, very disturbed to see her wind up in such a bad position.

The band headed back to New York on a long train trip that went first up the coast, and we played in Seattle or Vancouver, one or the other—Seattle, I suppose. We got off the train and got on an old Greyhound bus. I discovered where the old Greyhound buses went, man. They wound up in Saskatoon, Saskatchewan. We were on this bus a couple hour's drive from the main line of the railroad up to Saskatoon in the wintertime and the bus broke down. So we show up at this place a couple of hours late and the audience is all sitting around huddled up shivering, because we were playing in an ice rink that has been covered with wood. It's cold. One of those gigs where the guys get in and immediately get the horn out and start playing. Forget about the uniforms. And from there we went to the next province over, Regina, I guess, and then to Winnipeg, and finally we got back into New York.

There were a couple of important lessons I learned on that trip. One was I never was really very fond of sitting for long periods of time playing cards. They started a poker game in Los Angeles that included Gene and Joe Dale (the road manager), the lead trumpet player, Charlie Ventura, and a couple of the other guys, and this game went on every time we were on the train, which was a long time. I think it was about five days we spent on this train. Gene and Joe had been the winners, and the other guys had lost an immense amount of money. Why in the name of God would you sit and bet your salaries, man, and wind up doing all that work and all that travel and end up with no money. I couldn't see it. Not only did I never take a chance myself, but when I had a big band and the guys started playing cards, I put a limit on it. You want to play small stakes, fine. If anybody starts being big losers, that's the end of the game. I won't stand for that kind of stuff. Prez (Lester Young) never got a salary the whole time he was with Basie, according to Sweets (Edison). You know those guys would sit and play cards all the time and blow their entire salaries into the future. So I had a terrible reaction to that.

That reminds me of an incident with Buddy Stewart. Buddy was a small guy. He was built like a jockey. In fact, when he was younger, he had been a jockey. He really would have liked to have continued, but he got too big and heavy for that, but he still was very slight.

So one time we arrived in Asbury Park and checked into our hotel. It was the afternoon or the morning I guess, and Buddy and I went for a walk on the boardwalk. We're walking down the boardwalk, and we hear a guy in a diner or cafe along the boardwalk and he's having trouble getting his order. They're starting to raise their voices and they sounded Cuban. We looked over and he was a little guy, so Buddy immediately figured this guy's a jockey. So he went over and tried to help get things smoothed out and get the guy what he wanted. We got into conversation with him and we had a good time. So he said, "Well listen, I'm not riding today, why don't you come out to the track with me and see the horses?"

So Buddy said, "Yeah, that'd be great." Now even though he wasn't supposed to go up into the stands, he did, you know. He went up in the stands with us, and I think Buddy and I each put up about five or ten dollars based on the jockey's choices. He picked the horses for us in each race. That's obviously why they don't want the jockeys to go into stands like that. The jockeys know what the horses are running, what kind of condition they're in that morning, whether they are in a good mood or a bad mood.

We just bet very, very conservatively, and we left with like a hundred dollars apiece because he picked winners in just about every race. Except for one race that he picked; Buddy second-guessed him because Buddy had become a father just a couple of days before that. So he was a new papa and there was a horse running at sixty to one called Proud Papa and he said, "We've got to play that," and by God, it came in. So that was my one experience. I figured we were lucky that time, man. If I could always go around with a jockey, maybe I'd be a gambler.

When we got back to New York, the band went into a place called the Aquarium on Seventh Avenue. It was a place that had a big plate-glass window in front. It was kind of elegant inside, and we played there for a few weeks.

It was during this period that Ventura decided to leave the band, so Gene needed a replacement. Well, I heard the record of the Randy Brooks band that Stan Getz played on. I never heard him when he was playing with Benny Goodman so I don't know what he was doing there. In fact, I don't know that he ever recorded anything during the period he was with Benny. I've never encountered anything.

Anyway, he played on an arrangement of "How High the Moon" or something with Randy's band, and he just sounded so terrific on the thing. Really sounded wonderful with the band. So I immediately started to try to talk Gene into getting hold of Stan. I thought he'd be perfect because the whole book was built around the tenor. The arrangers, George Williams especially, often used tenor saxophone solos like cadenzas for key changes or some kind of an interlude between choruses, besides being the main solo voice in the band.

He'd write these things where you play a chorus and then have to get to a new key for the singers or something. So he'd write these chords that really didn't go anywhere but it sounded nice because Charlie would play arpeggios or something and it was a nice filler into the next key.

The book was really based around the featuring of the tenor. So Gene did get hold of Stan and invited him to come out and play with the band. He came out and played a one-nighter or something, and then afterward the guys in the band told me that Stan was really great and impressive. Red Rodney told me that Stan said to him, "Do you think I should take these solos out to the microphone?" and Red said, "Of course." So the first time he's playing these things, he would look at the part and see what the progression was and then he would walk out to the microphone and play something beautiful. Like a composition, melodicizing these unrelated chords. I was really gassed to hear that because I thought that Gene would hire him for the band and we'd really have something great.

I had heard him play with a band once, but I still hadn't met him. So one day I was walking into Charlie's Tavern. I guess it was the day after he had played with our band, and I was really pleased that he was going to join. I'm walking in and Stan Getz is walking out, and I recognized him and I guess he knew who I was, because I said, "Stan," and before I got anything out of my mouth he said, "Listen man, if you want to keep living, keep walking," and I said, "What?" And he said, "Listen, I know you went with my old lady before I married her, and I hear that you only played (and then he put in a very distasteful vulgarity) with her but you didn't (a common Anglo-Saxon euphemism) her." He took off, leaving me standing in the doorway with my mouth hanging open. What was that? He's got to be kidding. I went inside and Zoot and the guys were in there and I said, "What the hell is wrong with him?" It was the most ridiculous thing I had ever heard. Well, in its way, that was to kind of color my relationship for all the years I knew Stan. I would see him and he'd be insulting and insufferable, and the next time he would be maybe apologetic or go along as if nothing had ever happened. Just being a nice guy. That would go on maybe two or three times, and then the next thing I know, he'd do something else. He was absolutely mercurial and he'd pull the dumbest things. He could just be so downright mean, and I never could understand it. So I was always on my guard with him. I never could trust him and never knew what to expect.

In fact, there were two episodes I can remember. One was in 1985 after Zoot died; I was to play a thing in Chicago at their jazz festival, and they had Herbie Steward, Jimmy Giuffre, Stan, and me. The date didn't stand out in my memory for anything musical at all, but we were supposed to play. They wanted us to do "Four Brothers" and "Early Autumn" together, and the promoters wanted me to do a set of a few numbers with Stan's rhythm section, who were playing for this whole segment.

I told the agent, "Listen, I'd like to do that for you and it's for Zoot's tribute, but I don't think that playing with Stan's rhythm section is a good idea, and I think that it's going to create a problem." They said, "No, no, it won't be a problem." I said, "All right, listen, I'll do it but I want your assurance that you'll tell Stan, because I want to rehearse with him. I don't want to walk on stage and just play because I haven't played with these guys. So I want your assurance that we're going to have a rehearsal before we do this concert and that they're agreeable and they know they're going to play with me." He said, "Fine, we'll cover all that."

So the day of the concert I show up, they have a rehearsal call, and I show up at the rehearsal, and his rhythm section comes in and they are really fit to be tied. They are furious. They had gotten in from some place, like at nine in the morning. They had a long, long trip, and they didn't know about it. Stan had never mentioned it and of course the agent didn't talk directly to the musicians, he talked to Stan. I could see Stan's fine hand at work. I asked the guys, because during rehearsal they were very uncooperative, very hostile, and so I took them to the side, one at a time, and I said, "Listen, I don't know what happened. It was my understanding that you guys knew about this thing, that you were playing for me today and rehearsing" and each one of them said, "I didn't know anything about it, man," and they all told me their sad story about how tired they were, which I sympathized with. I said, "In the meantime, they put me in a box because nobody told you and now I'm stuck and I've got to do it, so I really would appreciate it if you would try to be helpful because otherwise it's going to be impossible for all of us. I also want you to understand that I intend to pay you guys extra for playing for me. I didn't expect you to knock yourselves out for nothing." And they said, "Oh, okay."

When we did the show that night, they were great and Stan was fit to be tied. He was furious that the guys were playing well for me to the extent that when I went back on stage to do "Four Brothers" and "Early Autumn," I had barely walked on stage and put my stand down (I didn't have my music on it) when he kicked the thing off. He would do anything now to try to make me look in a bad light. I just laughed. I think finally I was able to give him some of it back again that he had laid on me all these years and the idea that I'd upset his plan, because obviously he was pulling this whole thing just to make a scene, you know. Such a waste of time. It felt good to be able to get around it and to be able to get with the other guys and have a good session with them. Why should we have difficulties because he's trying to do his number?

Years later I played with my quartet down at Fat Tuesday's when his son Steve was booking the bands. I thought, well, this will be nice because Steve was Beverly's son, and I was kind of interested, especially because of my relationship with Beverly. When I got down there, Steve was kind of hostile. Oh God, here we go again. I always tell clubs that when I finish a set, I don't want you to start tapes of anything. I would prefer not to have any music in the room. If you feel you've got to have music in the room, wait five minutes after we're done and then start playing your tapes, if you think that people can't stand to have a little silence for themselves, you know, talk to each other. But wait five minutes.

Well, we get done with the first set and sure enough, man, the tape goes on immediately. We finish holding the last note and the tape goes on. And guess whose tape it is he's playing? He's playing his father's tapes. I went to him and said, "Steve, I told you I don't want you to start playing music the minute I get done." He said, "Okay." So we do the next set and he does the same thing, and I went back to him and said, "Steve, I've told you once, I've told you twice, and I'm telling you for the third time, I do not want any tapes starting. I want five minutes with no music." And he says to me, "What is this vendetta you've got against my father?" I said, "Wait a minute, Steve, we're here for a week. Do me a favor. Don't come around me, don't talk to me, and don't play those tapes," and I didn't talk to him again for the entire week. I'd have nothing to do with it. He's going to take up the cudgel like I've got a vendetta out on his father. Man, I've been trying to protect myself from Stan's idiocies all these years and the number of things that he pulled. I always thought I was pretty even-tempered and fair about it.

It would seem to me that a lot of things Stan did were indications of the old low self-esteem syndromes and really bluster and brag and all that to cover up an inferiority complex. So I suppose those are the classic signs of whatever his problems were.

But he wasn't the only one suffering from that by any means. Most of us were going through some variation of that, and it had various manifestations. But Stan was kind of peculiar and he didn't seem to give a damn what anybody thought about him, and it was like he went out of his way to alienate people. I had some times with him that were great musically and personally but like I say, I never knew what to expect. And based on that meeting, you can see, that kept me off guard all my life.

When writing for Gene, what I found myself doing was trying to combine the things that I'd been learning playing with small bands with the big band. And that didn't seem so far removed to me because the ways that the big band swung in the 1930s, when it was five brass, three trumpets, two trombones, and four saxes, was light enough that the blowing could really be important. And in some of the arrangements of some of those bands it was indeed important. It became the lifeblood of Duke's band and Benny's band.

So that started to get lost because the bands got heavier and heavier and heavier and they kept adding to it, and the poor baritone saxophone became a tuba and everybody had to have four trumpets and they had to have four trombones. And, of course, every time you add another voice, man, it's not just another voice, you know, it's another carpet you've got to tote around. So everybody picks it up off their fanny and moves and it gets heavy, heavy, heavy. Sometimes the bands started to sound to me like maybe an underdone doughnut.

What I wanted to do was to make a band move in a way that didn't get in the way of the little band. That was pretty easy to do with Gene Krupa because he liked that, man. He liked a band that was sleek, that was up on top of the beat and none of this laying back and having the rhythm section keep time for you. He came from Benny Goodman's band, and Benny used to love to rehearse the band without the rhythm section. He'd do whole sections of rehearsals without the drummers. You know the band has got to swing by itself; it's not the drums swinging the band. A band swings, and the drums are part of the whole instrument. You know, it's another kettle of fish.

So the early arrangements that I did that were recorded were certainly successful with the leaders. I was writing other stuff that was another style altogether. But the things that the leaders liked were based on what I'd been learning from listening to Charlie Parker and Dizzy Gillespie in a small group they had; pieces like "Elevation" that I wrote for Elliot's band and "Disc Jockey Jump" for Krupa's band. I hadn't even thought about what I was doing. Gene pointed it out. He loved the idea and he said it was like a *concerto grosso* idea, with a small band in front of a big band.

I said, "Yeah, so it is. That's terrific, what a good idea!" And in fact, one of the titles that Gene considered for it was "Quartet in Bebop," because he decided if we put a good title on it then it would be a good record. And you know, that's not bad. Then he came up with "Disc Jockey Jump," and I said, "That's great, man, you call it 'Disc Jockey

Jump' and all the cats, all the disc jockeys all over the country, will play it 'cause that's its name."

Another arrangement I wrote was of some Gershwin ballad, it may have been "Someone to Watch over Me." I wound up doing a thing with it that had kind of a semiclassical sound to it, with two voices moving through it in kind of a classical way. Anyway, it wasn't a real obvious statement of a melody, and Gene was in a particularly bad mood for some reason that day. I don't know what happened, but he came to the rehearsal. He had already been rehearsing and he came in and he was steaming already. So we played this one arrangement of mine we'd been working on, and he stopped it at one point and said, "All right, where's the melody? What are you playing?" We all realized we were in trouble; Gene was not feeling at all well that day. But oddly enough, that was the day he pulled "Disc Jockey Jump" out of the book again. I had done that early in the stay with the band, and we rehearsed it and we never played it. And this must have been eight months later or more. So he finally pulled it out that day and played it, and that kind of made him happier because the band sounded really good on it.

Another piece that we did that day was an arrangement I had written of Mel Torme's tune "The Christmas Song," which came out really nice. I wish I had even some notes on it, but that's part of the book that burned. We didn't get to record it.

While I was on the Krupa band, we did a couple of films in Hollywood. There were two films, one was a feature called *Beat the Band* and the other was a short called *Follow That Music*. It was fun having the experience of being on the set of a big studio in Hollywood in the 1940s. It was an altogether different atmosphere, I guess, even than today. But you know, I was a young guy being able to see all this. I really loved it and Marty Napoleon and I were roommates in the band. In *Follow That Music*, they did a shot where we were supposed to be playing cards in the hotel room, and Marty and I threw in a couple of lines of dialogue. My deathless line was, "It's your move, Marty," and they had me write something. I wrote a piece of music that I suppose is used on the short. I've never seen it.

The short was the kind of thing where the band comes to town looking for its big opportunity but doesn't get the opportunity, and we wind up working as waiters in a restaurant. Gene is in the kitchen and does his bit playing on all the pots and pans with his drum sticks, and for some reason Red Rodney became kind of the star of the thing.

As I mentioned, when I played in the band it was always to help out for some reason. Somebody turned up sick or somebody didn't work out who joined the band, and so one period I got pressed into service when we were doing the split weeks in theaters in Ohio and Indiana and I was playing second alto.

Harry Terrill, the lead alto man, was very much in the mold of Marshal Royal, you know. Marshal had the perfect name for a lead alto player and the kind of sergeant at arms of the band. He always ran a tight ship. It felt a little military. Well, Harry was like that too.

Of course I was the arranger for the band, and I was impatient a lot of time playing the shows, four or five shows a day, playing these ballad things that I liked. In fact some of them I wrote, but I was always changing my notes or I'd make a line out of it, and it used to drive Harry crazy that I was always changing these things.

One show in Akron, Ohio, he got so mad at me; the curtain had just come down man, and he turned around, put his horn down and lunged for me. We went over the chairs and he was trying to strangle me. They pulled him off me, and I think after that Gene assembled the band and said something not apropos of that at all, but he realized there was a lot of tension in the band. So he said, "I will not condone these perfunctory performances," and I promised Harry I'd try to play the notes and not mess around with them and drive him to distraction. So I was good for a while.

I was a terrible side man because I just didn't know what my own boundaries were, and I was always stepping on people's toes. One time, after a particularly hard trip, we flew, I think, in a DC-4 from Winnipeg to Atlantic City. But this time we'd had this long, tiring trip and so we were all kind of exhausted. We played the job that night, and the band really sounded sloppy to me. When we finished up, I got up out of my seat and turned around to the band and said, "You know, the band sounds so sloppy, what's the matter with you guys?" And Gene is looking at me in kind of stunned surprise. Again he has a band meeting and reads them the riot act about the performance, because about that I was right. But he turned to me and said, "I'm sorry, old man, but your outburst was unforgivable so this is the end. We have to let you go." So that was the end of my playing career with the band, but I kept on writing for them after that.

The last time I saw Gene he was very sick. He had leukemia, and he had transfusions before coming out to Chicago so he would have enough strength to play. I hadn't seen him for a while, and he was going to play that night with Teddy Wilson and Slam Stewart and Benny Goodman. So when I walked in the room and we saw each other, and I'm glad to see him, and we get ready to hug each other and he said, "Gerry, I'm so sorry," and there were tears in his eyes and it broke my heart. "I'm so sorry, man, that all your music burned up in my house." It struck me as one of the more remarkable things that had happened to me. Here's a man who had so many problems, including his house and garage burning to the ground and being terminally ill, and he's apologizing to me for the loss of my music. That was Gene.

While I was with Gene Krupa, bandleaders were trying different things. I remember seeing Tommy Dorsey's band in a big place in Cincinnati. We were playing some place and had a night off and went down and heard Dorsey's band. They traveled in two buses. They had a string section, they had charts that were just gorgeous—charts that Bill Finegan had written and some of the other arrangers like Sy Oliver. There was a full string section, much bigger than anybody else had carried, and the vocal groups and all that. Man, it was beautiful, but it was big and that was a lot of people to carry. There were a lot of bands around. They were all still working and there were theaters going, so 1946 into 1947 felt like it was going to be really a prosperous time for the bands.

Then a number of things happened that changed everything. The recording ban, the entertainment tax of 20 percent, the gas rationing, and the deterioration of the ballrooms all became factors. Bands started to run out of places to play. You couldn't reach your audience. Things didn't happen fast enough to be able to take up the slack, even for the audience, because what was happening was the country itself was in tremendous transition. People were moving all over the place and guys were coming back from the service and going to school on the GI bill, so the whole country was in ferment. And the bands; nobody had enough money to be able to carry it long enough to sustain until things got reorganized.

Of course, at that point, people still thought that it would reorganize. They didn't see the abrupt change that was going to take place because there was nothing wrong with the music, and people loved the music. So what happened next was almost an artificial overlay. The change was from a superficial standpoint, not from the body of the audience at all, and it was an economic problem at the root of it.

Well, I suppose it must have been after the Krupa band that I started to play the baritone. I don't really know why I did it. I hung out sometimes with a baritone player named Johnny Dee who played with Frankie Carle's band. He was very interested in horns for their own sake. I don't know if he was teaching or buying and selling horns, but for some reason I made the decision. I don't know if it was anything that Johnny said, or if he had an influence on me or what it was. I can't recall. But it seemed like a pretty arbitrary thing to do. I took the old horns that I had—my alto, tenor, and my clarinet—and sold them, and decided I was just going to play baritone. Why I did it, I never really understood, because I hadn't really been playing it. I wasn't playing baritone with Ike Carpenter, I wasn't playing baritone with Krupa's band ever, so it was just one of those kinds of left-field decisions that I've never been able to rationalize in any way, but that's what I did. I was always kind of sorry that I did because I wound up never finding an alto I liked as much as the one that I sold. Later on I went and bought one, and I never played it much because I never liked it. Same thing with the tenor. So it was all of those things that kept me playing baritone. I wasn't even tempted to play the other horns. And that was the beginning of it. I started going to jam sessions playing nothing but baritone. When I worked with a band it was on baritone.

I had always been fascinated with the role the baritone played in the band. It wasn't just the bottom note, instrument or ensemble. But a lot of the bands, a lot of the arrangers that I liked used the baritone in a way that was very melodic. And, of course, Ellington's band, the way it appears is that Duke wrote the top line of the ensemble, the melody line for the trumpet, and he wrote a bottom line that was the baritone. There was a lot of contrary motion in these two lines, and then you could figure what the rest of the section is doing based on these two main lines. So that means the baritone line was essential to the ensemble, and I liked that very much.

There were other bands around that featured the baritone in unique ways. For instance, Ozzie Nelson had a very good band, a very musical band, and, as I mentioned, each band tried to develop its own style, something recognizable in the style, that when people heard it they would know that was Harry James or Ozzie Nelson or Will Osbourne or Duke, or whoever.

The sound in the Ozzie Nelson band was fairly straight-ahead kind of writing for the ensemble but with baritone sax obbligato wandering through it, and he used this device a lot and it really worked. It was a unique sound and I think that, as much as anything, led me to the possibilities of the baritone as a melodic instrument. Most of the bands when they added a fifth saxophone, a baritone sax, they stuck it on the bottom like a tuba, which can be boring to play. But if you've got something interesting in the ensemble, it's a great register. It's like playing the cello in an orchestra, which is a beautiful register in relationship to the whole ensemble.

In fact, I've often thought, when people ask me, "Why did you choose baritone instead of alto?" I said, "Well, if I had been a string player in my youth, I probably would have chosen cello over violin for the same reason." There's just something about the register that you are attracted to, that you choose to play in. The cello and the baritone are both very much human voice registers.

6

CLAUDE AND GIL

THERE IS KIND OF an irony about the Thornhill band, or a coincidence at least. I had loved the band as a kid still in high school, and I started getting Thornhill records because the sound of the band was beautiful. I always thought that Claude approached writing for a dance band as if it were an orchestra, and even though there were no strings, he always used, in the early band especially, two clarinets. A lot of the time people thought there were French horns in the band, but there weren't. In the early band it was just five brass and the four saxes plus two clarinets, and he managed to get those orchestral sounds that way. It was the clarinets that did it, not the French horn. Later on he did have French horns because that enhanced the thing and gave it more depth, but even so, as an orchestration device, you can get those kinds of orchestral, far-away sounds that they did so well. There was always imagination in the arrangements. They always came up with some kind of unique approach to tunes. There were some things they played that were just so imaginative and beautiful to me, and he had a great vocal group that they used in interesting ways.

At one period during the early war years, or even before the war, maybe starting in 1939 or so, Glenn Miller had a daily half-hour broadcast. It was a very popular show even though it was on at 6:00 a.m. or what seemed like an ungodly time, but it was, I suppose, before the news or after. It became like an important slot for a music program. It was very popular.

Then, after a while, they stretched the show and did another segment that had Claude Thornhill's band on it. So for a while it was Glenn Miller, I think for a half-hour, and then Thornhill's band for a half-hour. I loved the band. Then when Miller and his band were drafted into the service, Claude was given the Glenn Miller time slot, so he was really set up to become the popular band in the country. And it was popular. People loved it.

So things were really looking up for a while and then, after not too long a time, Claude got drafted and it wasn't a high-profile draft. He chose to go into the navy and Miller got into the air force; I guess it was still called the air corps then. Miller was made a major and was high profile. And you know, they made a big fuss about it, and it was something that everybody felt something about.

Claude, on the other hand, ended up being like a chief petty officer or something because the navy wasn't about to make any musicians into officers. They figured that the upstart air force could do that, but the navy was not about to breach tradition. So none of the musicians were made officers. Claude became the piano player in Artie Shaw's band, and Shaw was a chief petty officer. I don't know what rank they gave to Claude, but number one, it was low profile, and number two, it was really tough because they sent those guys out to the South Pacific and they had some hair-raising stories to tell.

Artie left after a while. I don't know how long he was out there. Claude took it over, and from all of the accounts that I've heard about it, Claude was really remarkable out there. He'd play a piano if they had one or he'd play accordion if they didn't. He proceeded to try to make good music for the guys, island hopping for God's sake, flying island to island and going around playing for the guys. I mean, it was really physically tough and I don't know how many years they did that; really something.

So finally, when the war was over and Claude came back, I heard that they were reorganizing, and I was back in New York staying at the Edison Hotel. I had a room that was on the back of the building, which meant it faced the back of all these other buildings. So it was like a great big, not just a little air shaft, but a big air well between the buildings.

The first morning I was there I hear music, and I open up my window and I say, "My God, that sounds just like Claude Thornhill's band. It must be somebody playing records or something somewhere," and I listen. They play the thing through and a while passes, and they start playing the thing again and they stop. I say, "My God, they're rehearsing," and it turns out my room was just about over where the rehearsal hall was.

I had this friend who was like one of my crazy Texas friends who just loved music. He was a guitar player, but he just loved to be on the scene and he was fun-loving. His name actually was David Wheat but his nickname was Buckwheat, and it fit him down to the ground. He was really a character. He showed up in my room and he had some good Texas pot or something, so we'd sit there and smoke and listen to Thornhill's band as long as they rehearsed. For the whole week, every morning and into the afternoon, the band would be rehearsing.

So I heard them when they were putting it together again. I was like the kid in the candy store. I never did go down to the rehearsals at that point because I always hated to interrupt some place if I didn't know somebody.

At some point I had gone back to Philadelphia and I was living there. One day I got a postcard from Gil Evans that said, "What the hell are you doing in Philadelphia? Come to New York where everything is happening. . . . Gil."

I had met Gil Evans, most likely when I was with Krupa's band. I remember going to some place in New York and I met Gil, who was there backstage, and we became friends.

I said, "Well, I guess you're right." I took off for New York and found myself a place to live and proceeded to hang out at Gil's place most of the time Finally, Gil talked to Claude and Claude invited me to write for the band, and it was just kind of a natural evolution.

My first arrangement was "Poor Little Rich Girl," which Claude liked a lot. So they used to use that as the opener from then on, kind of the warm-up piece. Gil and Claude always felt that Gil's writing and

Gerry and Gil Evans, backstage, Avery Fisher Hall, Lincoln Center, New York, 1982.
© FRANCA R. MULLIGAN

my writing, and also Bill Borden's writing, all kind of fit together. Even though there were different stylistic things, they were kind of complimentary to each other.

So that worked out nicely, and I wrote for the band for quite a while. I was very much in awe of Claude, you know. Claude was such a shy man and I was always basically kind of shy and reticent, so our conversations together were always a lot of hemming and hawing, and neither of us could talk to each other.

I never intended to play with the band, but they were going out on a tour and Gil and Claude wanted me to go with the band at that point. What had happened was we spent a lot of time having sessions in New York. Whenever the band was in town, the rhythm section, who were all kind of disciples of Gil, would always get together and blow with Danny Polo, the clarinetist, and maybe one or two other guys.

I was playing with them a lot in that way, so it seemed a natural evolution to go out and play with the band for a while. I was out with them for a few months, I guess. It wasn't a terribly long time and it wasn't the greatest period for the band either, because that was the time when things were starting to fall apart in the whole music business. I think they had a hell of a time keeping the band working and getting a price for the band. It started to happen in 1948. That must have been kind of a crucial year. The bands started to disband one after another because the guys just didn't have the money to sustain themselves. Duke, for years, sustained himself on his composer's royalties and ASCAP royalties and sank the money into the band and kept his band going. But not everybody had the means to do it. I remember Count Basie in the early 1950s went out with about a seven-piece band and he disbanded. Woody even, for a while, had a small band so it really died very quickly; going from having hundreds and hundreds of bands all over the country, it just sort of disappeared.

The focus was moved. I guess all of show business was in kind of a ferment; they didn't know quite what to do with themselves. It was also a transition from the important days of radio. Radio was still it, you know. What the family did in the 1930s, man, you had your favorite show, the Jack Benny show and the Fred Allen show and Burns & Allen and so on and everybody would sit and look at the radio set. But radio was great, and as a social focus I always felt radio was a healthy evolution and television was unhealthy, because radio did things that you still had to use your own imagination; you did your own visualizing. Television does it all for you, you know; you're just kind of a blob who sits and reacts to all of this. When you compare the stuff they do now to the science fiction things they did in the 1940s and 1950s, I mean, there's no comparison, and the 1930s even more so, though I must say the Flash Gordon and Buck Rogers things were quite satisfying when we were kids.

But musically it was a good period for me because the band traveled by cars most of the time at that period, and Danny liked to have his own car. Because I was young and strong, I always had the first gig of driving after the dance was over. Danny and I liked to take back roads instead of going on the main highways. We'd say, "This road looks good on the map." So we wandered around and sometimes wound up in the middle of somebody's farm in Indiana at six in the morning. We had some kind of eerie experiences that way.

Being with Danny was kind of a settling experience for me because Danny was very mature and gentle and kind of spiritual. There was a quality about the guys in Thornhill's band who were close to Gil. They all had this kind of spiritual quality. There were lots of almost religious-sounding theories that these guys were always into. When they were in town, Gil and Billy Exner, the drummer, would talk all night. They were very much into mysticism. In fact, the relationship with Danny and Gil was mystical to begin with.

Gil had known Billy for years apparently, and Billy had been a seaman all his life. He didn't start playing drums until he was about forty, and some place he was in—South Africa or Asia or somewhere—he bought a picture of a man with an Asian face. It was just a beautiful picture: a very serene, wise-looking man with kind of a wispy gray beard. He brought that picture back and gave it to Gil. Well, sometime later, Danny Polo joined the band, and Danny Polo was the absolute spitting image of this picture that Billy had brought back. Man, he looked like a younger version, not that much younger either, because Danny had gray hair and his mustache had turned gray. He was probably in his fifties, but he was just identical to this picture. There were lots of little things like that about those guys that made for a kind of contact between them that was unusual.

The guys in the rhythm section, like Joe Shulman, the bass player, loved Billy—and they just had all these theories about how rhythm should be played and its function in the band. They were very influenced by the Basie rhythm section, where Freddie Green was really the control center of it. Barry Galbraith, guitarist with the Thornhill band, was very much in that mold. He played with the band in a similar way to Freddie, and later on when I got to know Freddie, I realized that there were other similarities in personality, which often happens—that people who are of similar physical structure and similar personality often have the same kind of approach to music. And there will be something recognizable in the ways that they play. There are these basic structural similarities. I was always fascinated with the ways that people's physical presence related to their playing.

A good example was Lester Young, whose music, especially when he was young and playing with the Basie band, had such grace and a flying, soaring quality to what he played. It just came out so effortlessly, and he would stand and look so graceful and holding his horn up, man, he was flying.

Bird, on the other hand, who was very down to earth, had a hard, straight-ahead kind of time. He could swing but it was in another kind of way altogether. Bird would walk on the stand and plant his feet like a tree, you know; he was like rooted to the ground and so he'd play this stuff that was fiery and with that same kind of earthy, basic beat going on. The ways that they held themselves physically related to the ways that they played.

I'll never forget one time I was standing outside Birdland and I turned around and saw Prez's hat kind of sailing up the stairs, you know, a porkpie hat with the big brim, and he'd sail it upstairs . . . effortlessly, man. He floated, you wouldn't see him taking steps, he'd kind of float out of the place and down the street and right behind him a couple of minutes later came Charlie. And Charlie comes stomping up the steps and the whole place rattled—such a total difference in personality.

Several of the musicians in the Thornhill band were drawn to Gil Evans. I think they gravitated toward him because Gil tended to be a philosopher. He adopted attitudes that I think were his associations with, probably, Zen Buddhism. That seemed to be the direction that he was evolving. But his attitudes were very considered and nonjudgmental, and there was always this kind of activity of thinking and theorizing and talking. It was an ongoing thing. So it was a very rewarding experience for everybody to be part of something, and you'd feel like something is happening. Gil was very much the focus of it. He brought that out in other people.

He was a leader in a way, but he refused the conventional roles of leadership, and he was very happy to let Claude be the one who had to deal with an audience and with agents and with the musicians. You know, it suited him just fine that he didn't have to do any of that and he could just concentrate on writing, which of course is a very selfish way to be and he realized that. It's a hell of a lot easier to let somebody else do all the worrying and all the kind of work you don't want to do.

But if you want a band and you want the things that go with having a band—the music—somebody's got to do it. Bands don't just happen. They don't run themselves, and they have to be self-supporting or they can't function.

As a consequence, Gil was a kind of guru to everyone, even though he really refused the role. There are things that happened to me during that period that if Gil had really offered advice, it's quite likely that I would have done things differently. But he didn't, so I went my way. After the fact, sometimes he would get mad at me because of what I did. I'd say that it's too late and I wasn't smart enough to go and undo what I had done.

For instance, at one point all of us, even though we were writing for Thornhill, needed to write for other bands to make money. And George Russell, he was always looking for other bands to write for, and Johnny Carisi, you know, we had to do it. One time I got an offer to write some stuff for Herbie Fields, a tune that he wanted that was a vocal for the girl singer. Herbie had a band that was kind of a stomping band. There were a couple of bands like that. I always liked them but I never really thought for myself that I had a feeling for writing for them. I was always trying for orchestral things, the interrelation of parts and counterpoints and all that kind of stuff, and these kinds of bands didn't function well in that kind of situation. These were ensemble bands, and that's what you should write for them.

Well, I did the best I could on this thing and brought it in to the rehearsal and they liked it and it worked out all right, but Herbie wanted me to change the ending. Well, I was kind of stunned, not because I felt that it had been written in stone and that it couldn't be changed, it was because I couldn't change it. I didn't know what to do. I had done what I could do, and this was again my own limitations. So without saying anything to him, I collected the music and left. I'll never forget the look of astonishment on Herbie's face and on the musicians, like, "What happened?"

I went back and told Gil what had happened, and, you know, I was kind of being a little smart-ass about it I guess, like wanting somebody to give me a pat on the back or something, and he was furious with me. Well, I agreed with him, and I learned a little bit about being able to swallow false pride or to be able to overcome my own blustering, because I think we usually bluster, do dumb things in life, because of our basic inability to know the right way to do it. You make the worst mistakes trying to cover up what you're trying to hide. In this case, I was trying to cover up the fact that I didn't know what the hell to do, and I made a bunch of people unhappy. I really hurt Herbie's feelings. I never meant to do it and I didn't know how to undo it.

Gil, instead of offering any advice at all, was mad at me. That was no help. I really needed some direction. Somebody had to tell me because I didn't know how to deal with people. It was hard to get along because I've always, with my quick temper . . . things would erupt out of my mouth that were not what I wanted to say but then the damage would be done and I didn't know how to undo it. That led to a lot of personal trouble for me in dealing with people. I am embarrassed to this day to have hurt Herbie Fields' feelings when he had nothing to do with it. It was my inability to be able to do what he wanted with the arrangement. That was life. That was just one example.

7

THE *BIRTH OF THE COOL*

I HAD A FURNISHED ROOM in somebody's apartment over in the old Madison Square Garden area. In fact, I think it was in that building. It was a funny place because of the strange people there. They had card games going every night so I had really no contact. I mean, everybody was friendly, but I was kind of not there. So I didn't wind up spending much time there. I was over at Gil's place most of the time.

It finally got to the point where Gil and I were taking turns using the piano and taking turns sleeping, and there were people in and out of the place all the time. Day and night we'd have people over there, so there was no schedule like with normal people. When guys would come, we would be up and have breakfast or whatever, or eat something if you felt like it, and one of us would be using the piano.

This went on winter and summer and it got really cold down there, so we were bundled up in overcoats and blankets sitting at the piano taking turns writing. And more than anything, it was just an outgrowth of these endless, open-ended conversations that were always going on with guys who came down, like George Russell, John Lewis, John Benson Brooks, John Carisi, and occasionally Johnny Mandel. Blossom Dearie was a regular and Specs Goldberg, who was a drummer. Specs and Sylvia Goldberg were two totally undisciplined young musicians, and they were great. They were regulars there, and they were always kind of making things happen. There was also Dave Lambert and his wife, Hortie, and their little daughter, Dee, who was still a babe in arms. She was a year or two years old. They were kind of living out of their suit-case, living here and there trying to make ends meet, the pair of them with a baby on their hands. Also John Benson Brooks, who was an old friend of Gil's. He wrote the book for Randy Brooks's band. He was a good arranger and wrote a couple of well-known tunes, most notably "Where Flamingos Fly" and "You Came a Long Way from St. Louis."

Several guys from the Thornhill band came around when they were in town, especially Billy Exner, Joe Schulman, Barry Galbraith, and Danny Polo. Bird came by only a few times. He wasn't a regular by any means, but he would show up occasionally. Bird liked to spend time with Gil. Bird was always looking for a little serenity, and I think that Gil gave him the illusion of that. Bird liked to hear things too, and Gil would play stuff for him like classical and symphonic music that he'd never heard before. I guess he hadn't that much experience of it, but there were certain things that were his favorites. For instance, one of the things that he loved was "Children's Corner," by Debussy. I can't really recall now but there were other pieces he particularly liked—the French writers, the Impressionists—which is why I say that kind of longing for a more serene existence, which the French orchestral approach intimates.

So for all of us it felt like a transient existence. We were all trying to find some place for ourselves, and the theorizing was a natural result of that. We lived much more on our ideas than we did in physical reality. We'd walk out of the place, and, of course, you're right next to Fifth Avenue, and we had taken the kind of exaggerated bohemian attitude toward life, man, and living in the middle of Fifth Avenue and 55th Street—so out of place . . . it was funny.

Miles and I would walk down the street and people would stare at us, you know, like look at how peculiar we looked. Miles would get mad at people staring and I'd say to him, "Well, you've got to admit, man, we're a pretty strange-looking pair wandering around here." Which he had to admit and had to laugh at.

Miles always called me *Jeru*. That was his nickname for me. At that period all of my different friends had different names for me. Miles always called me *Jeru*, so the people around Miles always called me *Jeru*.

Gerry and Miles Davis.
© JIM MARSHALL

And Brew Moore always called me *Jeremy*, so around that band they called me *Jeremy*. So it's no wonder I suffered from an identity problem!

The thing that I found interesting then, and I still find interesting to this day: I can sit down with other arrangers and talk for hours about ideal instrumentations and why I would have this and why I would not have that, and what's practical to take on the road, and, you know, what an ensemble would cost you if you did. It goes on and on and it's fun! Well, Gil and I had this notion to follow through on the idea, the stuff that I was writing for Gene's band, for instance, where it was a little band and a big band ensemble, and Gil started to do the things, the Charlie Parker tunes for Thornhill's band. So we were applying small band principles to big bands.

And to do that, what kind of instrumentation do you mess with? Well, that became kind of a running thing with us. So then we started theorizing about how to put the elements together, a small band and a big band; the kind of setting that would give the arranger some scope for writing ensemble things, and writing stuff that had more density to it than just a couple of horns and a rhythm section. It had to be something that would give the possibilities to the writers and then try to combine that with the freedom and the settings for the horn players to be able to sound their best.

That's why we finally wound up with this thing with the six horns, because it seemed to offer a lot of possibilities. Our original thought was that we wanted Danny Polo with the thing on clarinet, but we realized that was impractical because Danny was always on the road with the Thornhill band and there wasn't anybody else that we wanted on clarinet. Part of that was, you see, Danny's sound was so much that wooden sound that I always loved. There was talk about Irving Fazolo and Barney Bigard and the New Orleans players, but Danny played our system and it was that particular sound that would really have been good in the band.

Whenever the Thornhill band was in New York we would have sessions, and we'd go to a studio up on Broadway and 51st Street. Danny would come to these sessions and he would get his horn out and he would sit there, and he would never play. He'd say he was listening and he would have his horn in his hands, and we never pushed him and said, "Why don't you play?" or, "Play something." You know, it went a couple of months like that. Whenever the band was in town it means we had time for at least half a dozen, or eight sessions that we'd play where Danny did this. At these sessions maybe Zoot would be there, or Al Cohn. All of the players that were around us were always invited to come in with us. Finally, on this last session, we were playing, and Danny picks up his horn and plays a solo on something and our jaws dropped because of what he had done by listening to all of us play; it was like he'd absorbed a whole other style of playing. I mean, it wasn't as if he were playing bebop clarinet, but it was like playing with an understanding of what had happened. I never thought of myself as a bebop player and was criticized for that. Although it was something that Roy Jones wrote and I was kind of glad because in comparison with a lot of the players, I thought Roy was very kind to me. It was complimentary. But you know, something he said that was kind of a criticism, he thought that with my connections with Bird that I should have sounded more like Bird but

I didn't. And I didn't want to. I couldn't for one thing, Bird was Bird. I wasn't trying to just imitate Bird or imitate his phrases.

Well, this was the same thing with Danny. He didn't imitate what was going on, but it was like he absorbed it in a way that had the feel and the understanding of what was going on. Which was the reason when we heard that, if we needed another reason, that Gil and I wanted him in the *Birth of the Cool* band because he really had absorbed the essence. At that time, the clarinet became the forgotten instrument. There were guys that played really good clarinet, and it was like they understood and encompassed the whole thing of bebop, and they were technically really incredible. Buddy DeFranco was a wonderful player, and Buddy was from another school, like the Benny Goodman school that had also encompassed what Bird had done. And he had the facility to get around the horn and do it, but what Danny did was something totally different than that. It didn't have the kind of angularity of bebop, but it fit the idiom perfectly.

So that was one of the more remarkable things that I experienced. To be there with a mature musician. Danny was no kid then, he was probably in his fifties. And he sat there until he had something to say. Then, when he said it, we all said, "Wow!"

We wound up holding it down to one trumpet because if Miles were to be the trumpet, his sound was so personal that we didn't really want to have to blend with another trumpet sound. Let the trumpet sound be his and it really fit. It became an easy thing for me to write for because I could hear Miles melodically much more easily than I could hear a trumpet player who was playing an open trumpet sound.

We tried to have enough low horns to be able to use the tuba. In some ways, I've always felt that maybe the tuba was extraneous. Especially when you realize that the amplified bass gives the bass another presence in the band, and a lot of times the tuba lines get in the way of the bass lines and vice versa because even though the bass line is walking, it can still serve the same function in the ensemble. However, we wanted to have the tuba because we wanted a continuous chromatic scale for the band, from the very bottom to the very top. Not having a clarinet or flutes or anything else restricted us on the top, so we only went as far as the trumpet went. Ideally, we would have been able to go above that and that was why I'd always thought to have a clarinet with it.

The French horn: we thought of the center section of the band as being the French horn and trombone. We could have done with a third voice in there, but we never considered having a tenor, ever. We didn't think that a tenor had the ability to blend into the ensemble; the sound is so disguised, you don't know it's a tenor. And that's what we wanted, you know, that the instrument loses totally its individuality and becomes part of the ensemble. That way, you can have a small ensemble with cross-voicings and do things that have the impact of an ensemble without having actual ensembles.

It's kind of, I didn't realize it then, but it's kind of the tricks that you would deal with a chamber orchestra when you've got an orchestra of maybe twenty-five or thirty pieces. I mean, obviously you're limited to how powerful an impact you can get out of it, but you do it the right way and you can get a lot of noise out of a twenty-five-piece orchestra. You can make things hit.

Well, this is what we wanted. How do you put these things together with the least number of instruments? The baritone was, of course, a flexible link, working with the second or third voice with the French horn and trombone, and it's the only instrument that really connects with the tuba. We could work together as a unit, where it wouldn't have the same kind of tuba blur if you put a trombone with it. The trombone clarifies the tuba sound so it loses a lot of the amorphous quality that's useful in a tuba in the low register of the ensemble. It's mainly ballads and stuff like that where you want it. So the baritone is perfect for that.

But as a basic instrumentation it worked rather well so that the overall ensemble of those six horns playing together had a unique sound and was a good ensemble sound. It also offered lots of possibilities that we didn't explore to any great extent. We didn't write that much for it. There were probably only fifteen or twenty charts that we contributed. That's from all of us who wrote for it. So it didn't go on long enough to really pursue it to the extent that we might have done. But you've got two high voices, two middle voices, and two low voices, so that they can be used in very different ways contrapuntally and breaking up different kinds of small ensembles or small unisons. So it did indeed offer the possibilities that we were looking for: the most latitude for the writer with the most freedom and best setting for the soloist. That was the basis of it, and it was the result of a lot of theorizing.

When we started writing for it, Miles was really the practical one. It's a little hard for people to realize that, but Miles always wanted something of his own, and he really had the desire to have his own band and make a place for himself in the music scene. He loved the sound of the Thornhill band, and when he heard this idea that we were talking about with the instrumentation, he thought that that could be it. So he was the one who started making the phone calls, getting the guys together, picking out the players, and reserving the rehearsal studios, and generally assuming the role of leader. And that's how we started actually playing together because I think if it had been left to the rest of us, we probably would have kept on theorizing and writing and never getting around to doing anything.

We were writing for the thing itself, not for any outlet. It was a figment of our imagination. It was Miles who took it out of the basement and put it in a rehearsal hall, which was kind of a mixed blessing because Miles was responsible for making that first push. But then when we actually got to work, he didn't have the ability to take over as a leader and to say do this, do that, and do the other thing. I'd say without emotion, without judgment, "This is what you do." Well, that's what a leader has to do.

As a consequence, there would be some friction that grew up in the band about interpretation or about who's soloing or whatever. And Miles would just let these things lie and next thing you know, instead of things resolving, they would fester and you would wind up having some kind of warfare, which happens with bands. That's what happens when you put talented people together, you've got to have a leader. He has to be accepted as a leader and he has to, as a leader, lay down the law . . .

"It's like this!" A band is no place for a democracy, it does not work. You can't have ten leaders in a band.

Now in this band, Miles was the leader and provided the sound of the band, but John Lewis and I did the bulk of the writing. So in that way we controlled the direction of the music, and that's kind of an ideal situation. In the best bands that I was with, the leader had the idea of what the music should sound like and what he wanted to do with it and usually was a writer of some awareness himself. But he had to have arrangers he could depend on and guys with imagination and guys who were focused, and not have to be focused on business because that's the complicated thing. How do you have a creative enterprise and take care of business too. It's very, very tough to do. It's like being an absolute split personality.

So Miles got the record date and at that time, because of the kind of interest that was going on, it was one of the two or three times that Capitol Records discovered jazz. There were some very good guys who started Capitol, like Johnny Mercer and some of the people he was connected with in California, like Glenn Wallachs. Anyway, they wound up signing various of us guys to different kinds of contracts. They signed me to, I guess, a writer's contract. Miles they signed to do these records and probably a publishing contract, too. Unfortunately, Miles had a kind of penchant for signing with more than one publisher to write exclusively for them. So there were a few times he wrote things that had other names on them to kind of get around that. They signed Buddy DeFranco, who was supposed to make some small and big band things for them, and Lennie Tristano, and I don't remember who else.

But because of that, it kind of gave a focus to us. It looked like we were going to find a place for ourselves in the music business. We worked one engagement of a few weeks at the Royal Roost. I don't recall, but somebody told me we were working opposite the Count Basie band, which may well be, but I don't remember that at all. I was totally focused on what we were doing. And as I say, Miles was very much in favor of the idea of the sandwich boards, or the billboards they had outside the clubs that had the personnel written on them and they also said the arrangers. He felt the arrangers should get credit.

I kind of enjoyed the Royal Roost engagement, but it was a very tense occasion. The band wasn't able to really relax and enjoy itself at all in the club. There was a tremendous amount of stress involved. It was fun playing that stuff in public and all that, but the band didn't really settle down and gel because when you get down to the club situation and the thing that we were trying to do, it really needed more concentration on how to do it. If you start stretching out too many solos on those arrangements, and to me this always happens in arrangements anyway, if the solos are too long then the composed parts lose their continuity. They lose their connection with each other and that's what Miles started doing in the club—playing more and more choruses on the things so the band never really solved those problems and Miles wasn't considering it. John Lewis used to get really mad at him because he wouldn't assume the responsibility and wouldn't consider the band because the band was a unique thing. It's not like going into the club with a sextet.

And Miles had strange ways of taking out his anger. It would build up. If problems grew up around him or if things were very tense, he'd get mad at the band, and his way of doing it would be really illogical. And without a word we'd see this happen and say, "What's this?"

For instance, neither JJ Johnson nor Kai Winding could do the date at the Roost and so we needed another trombone player. Well, he never discussed who to get on trombone with John or me or with anyone else in the band, but he encountered some kid playing trombone somewhere and he said, "Hey kid, do you want to play with the band?" Well, it turned out to be Mike Zwerin.

So he brings in this kid that nobody knew and also, I think we really didn't like him very much because he was kind of a little snobbish we thought, and not that good a player. I'd forgotten some of these things until somebody gave me the pirated version of the radio broadcast from the Roost. On one of the things, I guess there are a couple of those floating around, but one of them, the program apparently started out playing "Move," Denzil Best's piece that John Lewis wrote the arrangement to. It starts out, and we're on the air and the first solo is this kid playing the trombone. He got himself lost in the first eight bars and never got it back together again, and he played about four choruses.

I said, "Wait a minute!" So, you see, Miles had taken the thing and it was like he was punishing the band by doing this. But also, he was destroying the music because Mike didn't belong there and if he was playing with the band, he had no business playing those solos. I mean, he got solos; like there's Miles and Lee Konitz, John Lewis, and me to cover the lead solos and instead he's giving them to some kid who's never played with a band and who gets lost on "I've Got Rhythm." So we were all thoroughly pissed off at him for that. That's why the band never really could gel and function as a band because you can't do things like that. You can't do things just as emotional whims and expect to have a functioning social organization. You've got to really work at it.

So that kind of thing really just split the whole thing up. It functioned well as a rehearsal band because as a rehearsal band you're in an altogether different world, but when you're out functioning as a working group in front of an audience, that's different. It's an altogether different kettle of fish and it takes focus and concentration. It takes consideration. It takes awareness of what's happening on the bandstand and in the audience, and you have to kind of be able to nudge the guys toward each other if they are not doing it naturally. Of course, ideally, you get musicians who think like that in the first place. But we were like a bunch of guys each going in our own direction, and nothing was pulling it together.

The actual recording sessions were different because you're not dealing with an audience now. You're dealing with the music and you're dealing with your part in the ensemble, so everybody is doing their best to cope with their problems.

They sent Pete Rugolo in from Capitol to supervise the dates, and, of course, Pete hadn't been around the band and hadn't been around me or any of us, and he didn't really know what the hell we were trying to do. At one point when we took a break, he said, "Gerry, we're having a hell of a time in the control room, and I don't know what to tell the engineer. We're just really not getting it."

I said, "Well, I don't know what to tell you about how to record it because I don't know that much about the microphone and the techniques." He said, "All we are trying to do is get a natural balance between the six horns," which already is a challenge because the volume range of these horns is so varied that to be able to control the tuba in relation, for instance, to the baritone or to the trumpet or alto, is something that we've got to be considering all the time. So that's what we're thinking about. We're trying to blend with each other and we were set up in a way so that we were all facing in on the microphones, so ideally we should have been able to hear each other to a certain extent. But I think probably what they needed to do . . . I don't know if they had the facilities then before any kind of stereo, to have more microphones than we used. I don't know what the limitations were on the equipment but that's really what it seemed like it needed. It needed more control of the definition on the inside of the ensemble. I really realized that a couple of years ago when I was putting things together for the *Re-Birth of the Cool* album and the concert tour I did with it, and also, because Lee Konitz was doing something and he asked me to transcribe one of the things because none of us had any of that music. That was another large-sized error.

Anyway, trying to hear the inner voices and the lower voices, there's no definition at all. Now, a lot of those things I wrote; if anybody should be able to hear them, I should be able to hear them, and I can't hear any definition between them. It has the sound of the chords and so on, but there's no real telling who's playing what. Oddly enough, when I started to get into those things and tried to reconstruct some of them, I remembered why I did what I had done and made the choices I did, because a lot of times you have to make arbitrary choices about who plays what line and what you may choose to leave out of an ensemble if you've got too many notes you want to play and not enough horns. So, you've got to make choices about what makes the strongest chord structures and I couldn't hear anything on the records at all. They just had no definition.

Birth of Cool: *(from left) Miles Davis, Lee Konitz, and Gerry Mulligan.*
COURTESY GERRY MULLIGAN COLLECTION, LIBRARY OF CONGRESS, MUSIC DIVISION

But what they did have was the overall quality and atmosphere of the band, and it had the melodic sense of all of the things that were going on. So in a strange way there was kind of perfection about those original *Birth of the Cool* recordings, that with all of the imperfections, as far as the technology or even in the playing, the musical perfection is there because of the stuff that it was played on. Miles was brilliant on those things. Miles and Lee were both absolutely brilliant the way they played in and out of the arrangements. It was wonderful and made everything worthwhile.

Another thing that made it worthwhile was Max Roach on the first date. The first set of dates was really wonderful. He was far and away the best drummer for the thing because he really could approach it as a composer, and he took the kind of care with playing with the ensemble that showed his compositional awareness. I loved the way he played in the ensembles. He really understood them and knew just how to kick them so they would really move, and I don't think the band ever had that kind of accuracy and vitality again.

Gil Evans wound up writing only two things. One was like a reduction of an arrangement he had written for the Thornhill band, "Moon Dreams," and he did the arrangement of Miles's tune "Boplicity." I think it's quite possible that he didn't write more during that period because he was really busy doing stuff for the Thornhill band. He didn't really have the time to put into it. I, on the other hand, could kind of do what I wanted to do because if Claude gave me an assignment, great, but I wasn't on salary to the band and, you know, periods would go by where I wasn't writing anything for anybody else anyway, so I could afford to put the time into the things. That's probably what it was, more than whether he was involved because he wanted to be or not.

One of the things that happened in the years that all that activity was going on at Gil's place was that George Russell got an arranging job for the Buddy Johnson band. George was working on this thing but he was way behind schedule and it was obvious that he wasn't going to get the thing done on time. So, in order to help him out, we volunteered. I said, "I'll write a section," and maybe John Lewis wrote a section and Gil may have written a section, and George had a section. So there were at least four of us contributing to this chart. Then we wrote the thing out and you can imagine, these four totally different styles of writing in one arrangement. We took the thing up to Buddy Johnson's band. They were rehearsing at the Apollo in the basement and it was funny. I don't think Buddy Johnson had any idea what was going on. He was like, "What the hell is this?" It was a disaster. It was supposed to be one long piece and the sections didn't have anything to do with one another.

During the time we were doing the Royal Roost dates with the *Birth of the Cool* band, Benny Goodman called up Gil Evans and asked him if he could go down to the Royal Roost with him to hear the band. So Gil brought Benny down one night. Benny sat there and was listening to the band and he would say to Gil, "Who wrote that chart?" and Gil would say, "Well, that's Gerry's," and all the stuff that he liked were my charts. So he told Gil he'd like me to write for the new band he was going to start. He wanted a bebop band. Popsie (Benny Goodman's road manager), among other people, had been after him to put a new band together, so why not get a modern-sounding band.

Somebody in Benny's office contacted me and invited me to write for him. I talked to Benny but my problem was that I wanted to play. At that point I had started to really feel like playing, and I told Benny, "I'd like to write for you but I'd like to play with the band." Well, at that point, I wished that Gil had been a little of a different personality, but Gil was so laid-back he figured you do what you want. He wasn't about to offer advice, and because Gil was about fifteen years older than me, I guess I expected him to be kind of like a master and a guru, and he just wasn't about to assume that role.

If Gil had said to me, "I think it's much smarter for you to just write for the band and forget about playing," I think I would have gone about doing that, in which case, I probably would have written a lot of music for Benny Goodman that I would now be glad was written, and not go through the things that I did with the playing.

And so he never said, "Well, I think the smart thing to do would be to write for the band and keep away from it because aside from being better for your writing, the guys playing with Benny have a lot of trouble." Well, I didn't know any of that and I wrote a few charts for him, and I must say, the things I wrote for Benny, he played beautifully. The stuff just sounded wonderful! It was the best kind of thing to have a soloist like Benny as the main voice and the whole feeling of the band, because the feeling that I liked and was after, and was able to get, was kind of the feeling that Eddie Sauter got from the band. That was the one thing about playing in the rehearsals that I liked because we played some of the Sauter charts, and the saxophone parts were lovely things to play. I was only there two weeks. The first week Lee Konitz was playing lead alto.

We played some of that stuff, man, and it sounded so gorgeous, like "My Old Flame" and "How Deep Is the Ocean?" We never got into the heavy, long things that I wish we had, like "Superman" and "Clarinet à la King" or stuff that Mel Powell had written. I mean, there were such wonderful charts in that book.

But I was a very depressive kind of a person at that point. It was hard to picture me as the same person as the happy kid in Ohio. And, you know, it was thousands of dollars and thousands of hours into analysis to try to figure out what happened to me. What did I get so upset and angry and depressed about? But depressed I was, and angry I was, and Benny wasn't having any of it. I don't blame him. He finally took me aside one day and said, "You look unhappy. What are you unhappy about?" I said, "You really want me to tell you?" He said, "Yes." I said, "I can't understand how you can play the written music, interpret it the way you do, and can stand the band playing the stuff so sloppily behind you." Well, my problem was kind of particular because a lot of the old Fletcher Henderson charts were written for five brass and four saxes, so somebody had added a baritone part and a third trombone part and they doubled. And this poor little guy playing third trombone was terrible and just drove me nuts.

I ended up writing a few things, but it was funny because the next day at rehearsal when I walked in, Benny wouldn't play when I was around. And then it started a thing. I kept coming back because I wanted him to give me my music back, or pay me. Finally he pulled some dumb thing like I would come in and he would see me and stop the music, and he wouldn't give me any money. So I finally said, dig this cat with two million dollars and he won't pay me for my damned arrangements. I don't know where I got that figure of two million dollars but it sounded like a lot of money.

The only arrangement that he kept was something I had written for the vocal group. He had Buddy Greco on piano, and Buddy was also going to sing in the band, so I had written an arrangement for Buddy and the vocal group. It was the only thing he had for them, so he bought that one arrangement and gave the rest of them back to me. And it was a shame because he sounded so good on my things.

The return on the playing, I mean, the insights and the pleasures and the joys of playing those charts of Eddie Sauter, hardly make up for the music that I would have liked to have written for them. And I also feel that if I had written for that band, the band might have had much more musical success.

As it was, Benny was not and could not be a bebop player, and to get arrangements that were indeed bebop arrangements was like trying to fit a square peg into a round hole. It didn't work. But the stuff I wrote for him was very influenced by what Bird was doing, plus the other things that we as arrangers were taking from the influence of Bird, writers like Neal Hefti and the guys who were in the 1945 band of Woody's. Neal in particular, though, had a real grasp, and Dizzy was a big influence on what Neal did.

So I was writing more in that vein, and more fleet-footed, not the heavy-handed stuff that was coming out of the bands called bebop. Those bands were all hard, hard, hard-hitting bands, and Benny needed something that flew, and I felt I could have given it to him. So that, I regret. I wish I had written that music for him but that was the end, for me, with Benny Goodman.

My life went into total turmoil at that point. I started a long spiral down. I was gigging around town, and the kind of gigs we got as jazz soloists were very low. I remember one time Max Roach was trying to get the guys organized at Birdland, to get them to make a $25 minimum for going in there on an off night, or something like that. They were getting $12 or $15, something like that, and we'd play from ten at night until four in the morning. Max was trying to get the guys to get together on it, but I don't think he ever could. If one bunch of guys said, "No, we'll go on strike," another bunch of guys were there ready to jump in because they wouldn't have got the gigs otherwise. So that didn't work.

8

UTTER CHAOS
HEROIN AND TURMOIL

IT STARTED WHEN I was writing for Claude Thornhill's band. I was messing around with heroin but hadn't gotten myself firmly strung out yet. But the thing that I always notice is every time I see a photograph of myself during these periods, man, I never see a photograph of myself smiling. I guess maybe that was verboten then anyway. You know you're not supposed to smile. But I always looked pretty grim. I think music was my one joy and the rest of it was very difficult.

The whole thing that happened, you know, I started out around people using heroin, including Bird, and for a long time I never had any inclination to use it. Bird did one of his numbers that he often did with young guys, which was to let them witness him giving himself an injection and seeing the whole disgusting thing that he went through. I understand they used that in the movie. I think that was something he did on a regular basis to try to turn guys off the idea of using it because of the physical disgust. So he had done that, and even so, I had no desire or reason to get into it. I was able to function just fine on my own.

But the longer I was in New York in this period, and life was such a turmoil, constantly moving and there was frustration involved, that I started not having any idea of what the hell I was doing or where I was going. Somebody I knew was using heroin and I got hold of some and I said, "What a great thing, man." I could sit for eight or ten hours at a stretch and write without being distracted. So it started as an aid to keeping down all of the unwelcome emotional feelings and my real inability to react to people in a constructive way. It was a way of withdrawing into my own writing, so I could spend as much time as I wanted.

Well, that lasted for a while, you know, some months. Once you build up a habit then you have to have a source and it becomes a full-time occupation, just keeping supplied. So that became a whole new way of life, living in a kind of underworld because it's illegal, but nothing like the way it is now. I mean, it was small potatoes in those days and we didn't have the terrible scene around drugs that there is now. In other words, compared to the way it is now, it was relatively innocent. And, of course, I think if the powers that be, the politicians, the leaders, and the police, and so on, had been more realistic about what was going on, they could have controlled it at that point. They weren't talking about big profits, they weren't talking about big gangs, and mostly organized crime didn't want to mess around with drugs. It was kind of a petty thing to let the small fry do it. But it was relatively small. Once it became big profits, then it became the cancer of society, and now we've got international multibillionaires who make more money in a year than was made in the eight or nine years of Prohibition collectively out of bootlegging alcohol. So it didn't exist like that. And I still could feel relatively free to go all over the city.

The worst thing about it was that it was so time-consuming and my focus had changed. I didn't have time for the music anymore. The very reason that I got started using it, and then I didn't have time to write and there wasn't a hell of a lot going on; it was pretty hard to make a living. I was able to make something of a living by writing for some of the bands.

I was writing for Claude Thornhill and playing with the band on occasion. I continued to write some arrangements for Gene Krupa occasionally, and Elliot Lawrence had a band on the road so I also wrote for him. So there were things that I was able to do to support myself, but not well, because it's expensive to have a habit. Expensive, time-consuming, and demanding focus.

For a while, at that point, my main job was working with Kai Winding (pronounced Kay), or Kai as they say now, which is probably correct.

He always said Kay. I guess because everybody else did. He didn't care. He was a sweetheart, a very, very good man, and an easy guy to work with. He took care of business.

So, it was Kai on trombone, Brew Moore on tenor, and me on baritone in the front line. The rhythm section was George Wallington, Curly Russell, and Max Roach. It was a terrific band. We had a good time. Max didn't like Brew's playing for some reason so he would really play rough. He never would let the thing settle with Brew; he always kept him on edge. And then when he played for me, man, he was just a dream. I'm glad he didn't take out after me too, because Max could really be upsetting, but boy when he wanted to, Max could sure swing. He was great in that little band, for me. Brew might have had a different opinion altogether.

At that time we worked around a lot with the band at clubs in New York, and we did quite a bit of recording. At one point we went out to Kansas City and played Tootie's Mayfair, and that's where I first met Bob Brookmeyer. When he showed up there, he was a kid. I guess he was a couple of years younger than me. Well, this young valve trombone player came along and we hit it off right away because he was so bright and so talented and we had a great time. And that was the beginning of a long, long association.

I wrote some things for Georgie Auld when he had a little band. In fact, I wish that band had recorded, but it never did. It recorded in California with different guys. There are things in various discographies that say I'm playing on those dates that they recorded in California, and I'm not. I don't know who it was; I didn't recognize the playing. But I had nothing to do with that band except they recorded a couple of my charts. I wish they'd done more. There were some things that I wrote for the band that I really liked. I wrote an arrangement of "Across the Alley from the Alamo." It was really the first time that I had ever written a piece for a band and the band really swung the thing. They made it their own.

I got this illusion. I walked into the studio one day when Georgie was rehearsing the band and they were doing something else, and when he turned around and saw me at the door and the band there, no spectators, and he said, "Ah, wait a minute, 'Across the Alley,'" And they played the thing, man. I could see; it was like a bubble formed over the band. It was just so remarkable the way the thing swung and the way the guys made it their own. It was the first time I'd experienced that. I've experienced it since then, too, with different bands that had "that touch" that I've always thought about with that 1945 band of Woody's. There's just something incredible about this thing when it comes to life like that.

One of the kind of funny things during that period was Brew Moore and Zoot Sims, two of the Prez-influenced tenor players, and the two guys that I most often roomed with. We'd share furnished apartments together and in one period when I was rooming with Brew, he was pretty well strung out at that point and I was getting there, but Brew got a record date. He had this idea of getting all the tenor players together; all the young white guys who liked Prez: Brew, Zoot, Stan Getz, Al Cohn, and Allen Eager, and he sold this idea to Prestige. He asked me to write for it and so I started to write some things. Well, before very long it turned out that they made Stan the leader instead of Brew, because Stan was better known and all that and Brew liked the idea; he just wanted to do it. He said he didn't care who the leader was.

So Stan now takes over the leadership and I'm writing these arrangements, stuff for the date for Stan. He used to come by every day to the rooms where Brew and I were living and say, "How are you doing? Is it going all right? Are the arrangements done yet?" and so on. He was very concerned. I said, "Yes, Stan," and of course Brew and I would laugh. I wrote these things and Stan said, "Oh, I also want you to play piano on the date because you've played piano with sessions a lot. So you play piano on the date and do these arrangements and that will be great."

Comes the day of the date and I had come from another rehearsal or something and I had my horn with me. So I arrive at the date and I see Walter Bishop Jr. is playing the piano. I said to Brew, "Well, I see I'm not the piano player on this date." And at some point during the date, Stan asked me if he could use my baritone so he could play the fifth part

Gerry and Stan Getz, Germany tour, 1976.
© FRANCA R. MULLIGAN

rather than doing it on tenor, because it was kind of low. I said, "Sure, Stan." And so he used my baritone and I wrote two things for him, "Five Brothers" and "Four and One Moore." Well, to make a long story short, when it was all over, that was the end of Stan's soliciting into my well-being and my progress in writing. I started to try to get paid, you know. I left him a bill and heard nothing. So when I'd see Stan I'd say, "I sure could use the money."

I remember one time I went over to Zoot's pad over on First Avenue. Man, he lived in a five-floor walk-up and so I'm starting down at the bottom of the stairs, and I see Stan at the top of the stairs. He's just leaving Zoot's so we meet halfway, and I said, "Listen Stan, I really need the money." And he walked right by me and turned around and said, "I'll see you at the union." I thought, "Oh God." How do you deal with people like that?

So ultimately, I did indeed. I had written another chart for Buddy Rich's band and sent it off to California, where they were going to rehearse it at the Palladium. And of course it was not easy to make copies in those days. If I'd really had my wits about me or some kind of intelligence, I would have had a whole second copy made of the thing. Money was an object, of course, and you know it was expensive to do, but I should have done something.

Anyway, I sent this arrangement and the score off to Hollywood and it was not an arrangement that played itself; it needed somebody to rehearse it. It may have been a little too ambitious as a ballad for Buddy's band at that point, although I think that if it had been played right, he would have liked it. Johnny Mandel was playing with him at that point and told me later he remembered seeing some of the parts around the band room afterward. I said to him, "Son of a bitch, man, you saw those parts lying around and it never occurred to you to pick them up and save them and send them to me?" Johnny kind of rolled his eyes as he does and said, "Err, um, ahh."

The place was loaded with arrangers, none of whom would take the responsibility to rehearse the thing or to make sure that it was saved. And I had spent a month on this chart. It was "It's So Peaceful in the Country," an Alec Wilder tune, and it was one of two or three things that I wrote during that time that were very ambitious ballad arrangements. I wrote some beautiful stuff on it and that was the end of it. I never got paid and I never got my music back. Years later, Buddy apologized and he said they were remiss or however he put it.

Anyway, I'm owed the money for this arrangement and I'm owed the money for the two things that I wrote for Getz's record date, so I did indeed take them both to the union to try to get my money. Well, the day of the hearing I went down to the union all ready to tell my sad story and they said, "You can't bring these charges," and I said, "Why not?" They said, "Because you're not in the union. You've been erased for nonpayment of dues." Nonpayment of dues! I said, "If these people would pay me the money they owe me, I'd pay my damn dues!" And that was that. They wouldn't hear my case and I didn't collect the money. Stan never did pay for the charts.

Buddy ultimately did, and in the end he felt kind of bad about it because he realized that they'd been very slipshod. I think Buddy went through a period of expanding his ability to feel for other people. We became quite good friends for a while, because he seemed to have gone through a change where he was really concerned about how people felt and he seemed to understand then how hurt I had been by this episode with the arrangement. Nonetheless, the work was gone and I never heard the chart, but I got paid for it. But that was small comfort.

I took part in some rehearsals with Gene Roland in the spring of 1950. Gene had these grandiose ideas and he loved to have big, big, big bands. You know, with like twelve saxophones and twelve trumpets and nine trombones, and you know it was kind of fun but it wasn't really my kind of thing. He would try to put something together but nobody ever figured anything would come out of it. Gene was an arranger, but he was kind of a self-promoter. He was always trying to get something going, but he was so loosely wrapped that you knew he would never really get anything going; I mean, he was so laid-back. He would write arrangements for the different bands that I was with, and he was one of these fast, economical writers. By that I mean he wrote as few notes as possible, and he was always writing repeats and call this and repeat that, and often the arrangements just didn't make any sense at all because he would make mistakes with the repeat marks. Many times I was with bands that had some arrangement of Gene's come in and they'd try to sort out how the thing went because you couldn't figure out the sequence of the parts. I remember Bird showing up for at least one of those rehearsals, and of course Gene loved it because he sat back and there's this band playing his arrangements and he just let Bird blow. Everybody loved that.

I also wrote some arrangements for Bird with the strings for some specific engagements we did, like at the Apollo Theater and a concert we played at the old Knickerbocker arena in Lincoln Center—long gone. I was around a lot when they were doing the dates. I went down to Birdland all the time when he was there with the strings. Well, I loved the sound that he made with the strings even though it was a pretty sorry little string section. I mean, you can't do very much with five fiddles, or only like three fiddles and two violas or something. You know, it was very thriftily put together. Frugally, you might say!

What I tried to do in the things that I did was to be able to hear the strings and to do things with them that conceivably could be heard in the midst of the rhythm section, and Bird playing at his natural volume without having just to depend on the microphones to put it in the speakers, because you couldn't depend on that either. Anyway, treating five fiddles like a section, it can be done so that it gets a nice sound, but it usually is not done so that it gets a nice sound. You get five New York fiddle players and put this stuff in front of them and, you know, it didn't sound like much. So what I was trying to do was to figure out how not to use a lot of unisons. I used the three fiddles in unison and the two violas in unison to try to get some strength into the sound. And it was possible with the use of unison lines to get enough strength and sound to play off of Bird in the rhythm section, and that was the approach I used in the things that I wrote for him. I haven't even heard these. I know that a couple of those things have turned up on tapes and various records, but I haven't heard them yet.

Bird liked my tune "Rocker." I would like to have done more with it, but the problem with that particular project was really a lack of rehearsal time. And I didn't want to put any straight jackets on Bird. I maybe should have been more specific in laying out the progressions, but as I recall, I wasn't. So I don't remember specifically how I dealt with "Rocker."

The things that I remember best . . . I did one thing, it was a figure on "Out of Nowhere" that we used to do at the Apollo. It was part of the thing we did on the show, and I wrote the first chorus in one key, it must have been. I'm not sure whether it was G or E flat. Anyway, it gets to the end of the chorus and I had a four-bar break for Bird and it comes out in a new key. It's either G flat to E flat, or E flat . . . I can't recall. But anyway, Bird would pick up that break, play through the four-bar break, and go through these progressions that would just put me away. And then the new chorus came in and the rhythm section came in at the new chorus, which was the new key. But Bird didn't light until the first change into the tune. In other words, if it was in the key of G, the first two bars are G and the third bar is an E flat 7th, you know, like a nice rich-sounding chain. Bird would keep flying all the way through this thing and he'd light on the E flat 7th. And he would do something different on it every time. I would fall out of my chair laughing at these things that he did. Man, it just put me away.

Bird was a sweetheart. I always had a great time with him. But I knew him as kind of a fellow saxophone player and mentor that I admired a lot. A lot of things about Bird's attitude were like a big brother, an older brother. I saw how he could rub people in ways they didn't want to be rubbed. Unfortunately, I was an angry enough young man that I agreed with him anyway. So I'm probably not much of a critic on that one.

But Bird could be absolutely charming. You know, he could be the master of situations when he needed to be, and when he was, people loved him. He had all the qualities, all the equipment, to be a very successful concert artist. But unfortunately, he hadn't mastered his life and it ran away with him. But he sure had the equipment. A lovely man, I liked him a lot.

I suppose it was somewhere in there that I played with a band that Chubby Jackson put together. And the band, although I wasn't with Chubby's band, had a date at the Apollo Theater. It was Georgie Auld's date, so he took that band and called it his. We worked very, very hard up there. We did four and five shows a day. And, you know, you'd come off stage and in a half hour be in for the next show and play a short fill-in thing. And then Chubby had a record date and he used me on it with the band. He gave me a solo on "I May Be Wrong"—two choruses, which was unheard of. I was very pleased about that and to have that kind of push and recognition from the guys. Chubby always kidded me about that later on. "I was the first leader to give you two choruses on a solo." I said, "You sure were."

Around this time I made kind of a conscious decision to focus on playing more than writing, because writing was taking more and more out of me and in the days that I was using drugs, there was less and less focus. There was less time to focus on the music, so it defeated what I had started using heroin for, because I could forget about everything and sit and concentrate for twelve to eighteen hours at a stretch on writing. And then of course, the concentration of being able to get a supply ruined all of that and it became harder and harder to concentrate. So it was an easy thing to fall into playing more and writing less.

I also had a couple of unfortunate experiences. Buddy DeFranco wanted me to write something for a record date that he was doing with a big band. So I worked my head off and got this chart together for him and finished it up a couple of days before the record date was to take place. George Russell knew a young guy who'd been doing some copying for him, so he said, "Why don't you use so and so," I've forgotten his name. I said, "Okay," so I gave this guy the score to copy and proceeded to forget about it; it's out of my hands. It's in the copier's hands and now I can relax. Usually, you know, very seldom do arrangers get done two days ahead, man, we're usually struggling with the last part when you start to rehearse. So I show up at the studio on 5th Avenue, I think it was at the old MCA studio or something. It was kind of a little theater, a good-sized little theater, and it was a good place to record.

They record one piece, I don't know whose it was, somebody else's arrangement. I'm there early and I'm listening to all of the things, and I see the kid across the way who had copied my chart. Buddy calls, "Gerry, let's do your thing." So I walk down to Buddy and reach over to the kid who's coming down the other side, and he's got the score, and I think the parts. He gets up to the podium where Buddy is and says, "Listen Gerry, I'm sorry, I was kind of sick the last couple of days and I didn't get your arrangement copied."

Buddy was fit to be tied, but what can you say? I mean, he was mad at me because I'm supposed to bring a chart in. I'm looking at this kid and I must have gone totally ash gray, but there was nothing I could do. I said to this kid, "Did it ever occur to you that there are other copiers in town. Did it ever occur to you to get in touch with me and tell me you couldn't have it done? Did you know this was for a record date and what you've just done to me?" He said, "Gee, I'm sorry, man. I didn't know." I said, "Give me my score and get out of here." I would have killed him.

It made me very, very loathe to take chances after that. It just had a very bad psychological effect on me. It is a terrible amount of strain writing pieces and even today, to start playing a new piece, you know. The stomach drops and there's that moment of anguish because this may sound as bad as you think it does. And then if it sounds decent, you say, "Phew," and I think a lot of us go through that.

Things went from bad to worse at that point and I guess I became more and more strung out and really unhappy and depressed about the whole thing, and this time I went to my family. My mother and father lived in an apartment in Washington, D.C., so I took off and headed for home with my tail between my legs in a state of misery. My father rented a room for me around the corner from where they had their apartment and I proceeded to try to kick, cold turkey, for a week or two and went through those miseries.

My father got me a job at a bank. It was funny because it was the most depressing kind of job I could have had. My job was to register, in this branch bank, every check that came in and every check that went out. I was dealing with all of these thousands and thousands and thousands of dollars' worth of checks, and, of course, I couldn't rub two nickels together.

And so there I was in Washington, and I lasted about a week or two in this job. I remember it was autumn and I went out for the lunch break, and I'm walking around the town kicking through all the leaves and saying, "What the hell am I doing here?" So I went to the musician's side of town to the club where I knew they were featuring jazz groups and started to try to find a connection and get started all over again. I had a first-class case of the miseries.

9

GAIL MADDEN AND CREATIVE RESEARCH

WELL, IRONICALLY ENOUGH at this point, there was a woman named Gail Madden who had shown up in New York. Now I didn't know anything about this because I had left town, and I was fairly much off the scene before I left. So she came to New York with this kind of grand and glorious idea of a thing she called "creative research." She wanted to get a place, a house that was big enough, and she had backing with a friend who had saved tens of thousands of dollars.

This friend had gone to Gail for some kind of help to get some meaning out of her life. She had been a call girl and had saved an immense amount of money and was a very nice person. My recollections of her and that whole period are very hazy because, well, because of the forthcoming. Gail came and she had the idea that the three people she really wanted, as the kind of center attraction for this house, were Max Roach, George Wallington, and me.

I guess she'd gotten in touch with Max and I think probably found herself in some competition for the affections of our friend the call girl, who had the money, and George, who she didn't realize was a total recluse. George had grown up in the bosom of his Italian family, on about 37th Street and 1st Avenue, and I don't think he even went to school. It was really the Italian version of *The Little Prince*. His sisters looked out for him and whatever education he got, he got at home, and he did pretty much what he wanted.

He really didn't much like to go out. He just liked to stay home. I spent a lot of time in those days at George's house. But George didn't have the kind of outgoing personality that Gail would need for this.

And then, me. She had no idea I was in such bad shape but she persisted and tried to find me. She found out, I guess through my friends, that I had gone home to Washington. Well, she started calling my father. My father never told me about the calls and wouldn't have anything to do with her, figuring that she was just going to take me back into this scene of sin and degradation.

He knew that Gail was looking for me and Gail was telling him, "Well, I've got work for him to do and things for him to write," and my father had answered for me and said, "He doesn't want any of that. He's happy here at the bank." Finally, Gail turned up in Washington. I guess she went to see my parents and I still didn't know anything about it, but apparently she just kept going until she found me. I think she found me at the jazz club, because I don't think that my father ever told her.

She told me what she was trying to do and that part of the thing that she'd been working on was how to help people kick their addictions. She told me about her relationship with Bob Graettinger, who was somebody I had great admiration for. But she told me that Bob was such a mess as an alcoholic that he just wasn't able to function. He was dying and she got him straightened out. So I was more than willing to be a guinea pig for anything that she wanted to do because finding some way of dealing with an addiction, especially in those days, was very, very difficult. I had done all kinds of things, and later had the same experience of going to a psychiatrist and having him tell me, "Well, you stay off of your use of heroin for six months and come back and we'll talk about going into analysis." I said, "Listen, if I could stop using heroin for six months, I wouldn't be here." But they were scared to death to take on anybody because the police attitude was so intransigent and foolish.

Their attitude was "once a junkie, always a junkie." Well, it's not only that they treated you criminally, it's that anybody who used drugs was a second-class citizen and didn't deserve the rights of an individual. You see that kind of treatment institutionalized in the attitudes of police toward the people being arrested on today's television police shows. I think that there's probably been too much of that, with the movies and television showing the police being rude and mean to people. It's like nature imitating art. Then they figure that's the way you've got to be. As a consequence, it puts the whole society out of kilter of what a free society is supposed to mean. I mean, you can be free to do things as long as it fits into my conception of what is right. And of course they have been trying to do that here all along, to legislate morality, and then they get things mixed up. The whole thing about drugs started out as a tax problem, not as a problem of morality. All the first laws passed against the use and sale of marijuana and heroin were tax laws. But it was in the days of J. Edgar Hoover and his pal, Dr. Anslinger, from the Public Health Service, who wrote the book on it and made that shift, which Hoover did in a lot of areas. It became not only something illegal; it became a moral issue and a sin. That was an easy sell in this country, because our Puritan base has always latched onto the idea of morality.

So how to cope with a drug habit was more and more problematic, and then Gail finally found me and brought me back. She had her hands full to help me to kick . . . and she was into all kinds of things. She told me what she was doing and it all sounded like a good idea. To have somebody putting that focus on me, individually, really was a help. I learned later in analysis that a great deal of the problem with almost any addiction of any sort is low self-esteem. So to have somebody concentrating on my emotional problems was a big help.

If she could have come to New York and had the cooperation of the three people that she wanted to focus on, then I think she could have done something really remarkable. She did things like sleep conditioning. As I slept she would say things like, "you don't need this," and so on and so on. She tried to change my attitude from looking at the world as depressive to taking an optimistic view, and it worked. The cloud of gloom started to lift and I became ten years younger.

I tried to help her at that point but there had already grown up too much turmoil, and I think the focus it took to try to get me straightened out created jealousy from other people. I'm only saying this as I surmised a great deal of it because I wasn't that aware of what was going on. My focus was on Gail and me, and I thought everybody was pulling for Gail in this thing. I didn't know that people were trying to pull it out from under her. But that's an important lesson too. Whenever there is money involved, there's competition.

But then, as I started to brighten up my view, I played the piano. I always played the piano hard and she'd say, "You don't have to play the piano so hard, just easy." And in a lot of simple ways, she opened up my own perspective about music and more than anything, my approaches to music. I think in some ways I was probably a disappointment to her because she thought once I was somewhat healthy, I would dive right in and be writing a whole bunch of new music. But I wasn't ready for that.

I remember going around looking at buildings. She was looking for a place that would be a headquarters, a studio, the focus where we'd record and teach and live and conduct this whole thing. I realized, too, that it was such a good title because there's some outfit now that makes high-quality radios and stuff. I think it's called Creative Research or something. I don't know what it is but that was her name for it.

I remember one place we looked at on Riverside Drive. It was a mansion with probably four or five floors and on the top floor was a ballroom. The whole thing cost forty thousand dollars. It fell apart at that point, and I can't really go into it because I don't know what the ins and outs were. I just remember there were very strange confrontations and goings-on with Max. He got Bird in on it against Gail. Bird had originally been very enthusiastic about her ideas because she wanted to help him too, and he was a man who needed and wanted help. He would have loved to have been able to have some way of seeing that he could get away from drugs and the whole life of total dissipation. But it's very difficult to learn how to be a beginner, especially when you're so good at doing something. Bird had devised this whole thing that he was the best player around, but he needed to be a beginner again. He had to find some new direction for himself because he had, in a way, gone as far as he could musically. That was the reality of it. The whole thing with Gail got pulled apart because of internal tensions and competition and so on.

You know, an odd thing happened a couple of years ago. I got a phone call from Hank O'Neal. Hank lives on South Broadway in Manhattan, right next to a bookstore that he goes into all the time. It was one of those great old bookstores where all kinds of odd things turn up. He said one day he got a call from his friend at the bookstore. He said, "Listen, somebody brought me a box of stuff and I see the name 'Gerry Mulligan' in it." He said, "I don't know who brought it in or anything about it and I thought you'd be interested." So Hank took a look at it and among other things, there was a partial letter written by Gail to somebody in New York that had probably been written from California after we went out there. I didn't recognize the name of who she was writing to. I kind of got the idea that it was maybe a lawyer friend or something.

It started out with a sort of very direct statement of what she was doing and what happened. And as it progressed into the second and third pages, the writing kind of deteriorated, so I guess she had been smoking or drinking or something at that point, and the letter was incomplete. But in it she said some things trying to describe to him what had happened in New York. I said this was the biggest coincidence that I could imagine, that this letter turned up from nowhere.

I've made a lot of attempts over the years to try to find some trace of Gail because she was a brilliant woman, and for me, she helped me in ways that are just immeasurable. It sort of started me thinking about my relationship with some of the important people in my life: the long lesson of what we learn, who we learn from, who we help, and who helps us, and the learning process that goes with that.

So anyway, in this letter Gail says that the pressures of the concentration she had to put into me really distracted her from what she was trying to do, and it invited all kinds of dissension and ultimately exploded in her face. We were left, the pair of us, to fend for ourselves in New York. I had to try to make a living playing and that brought about a whole new period. With her prodding, I went on the scene and tried to do things with my own groups.

I remember talking to Monte Kay one time at Birdland. Monte was booking the room and he thought, yeah, sure, he could probably bring me in on an off night and have it be my band. He said, "Who do you want to get?" I said, "Well, I want to put something together with Miles." So he called Miles and Miles said, "Yeah, I'll come in there, but I want to come in with my own band."

It created a whole new level of resentment because I was a lot easier to take when I was a junkie and somebody was messing up, but to come around with some ambitions and to be a leader and bring my band in, that didn't sit too well! So I started new areas of dissent.

I remember another thing he said, "How would you like to come in with a group that Bill Harris is bringing? No, I guess you wouldn't want to come in with Bill Harris, too much soul." I never answered him; I started to say, "Bill Harris; yeah. I like Bill Harris." I remember him getting a kind of puzzled look as he went on and I never did do the gig. He really didn't know what the hell he was talking about.

So I did some things but they didn't really pay any money. I wrote some arrangements for Elliot Lawrence at that point. In fact, those were the only things I wrote without a piano, and they came out well. I always wished I had done more without the piano, because taking the piano away as a writing crutch opens up more freedom to write for the horns. So a couple of things that I wrote for Elliot during that period I liked a lot.

It must have been during this period there was another band that came along, and it's another one of those opportunities—kind of a screwy one in a way, especially then, that I wish I'd made better use of. Rita Hayworth was a dancer from a Spanish family of dancers, the Cancinos. Of course they changed her name for Hollywood, but her uncle, whose name was Cancinos (I can't remember his first name), had a wife who was a lot younger than he was and didn't look unlike Rita Hayworth—a beautiful woman. The uncle, the husband of the woman who was going to be the bandleader, was suffering from arthritis and couldn't dance anymore. They had always functioned as ballroom dancers.

So they decided they'd try putting a band together and she would sing and dance in front of the band in some kind of way. I don't remember how I got hooked up with them. This is the sort of thing when you tell stories like this with New York musicians, somebody would probably say, "Yeah, I remember that, he said so and so and he called Gerry, but I don't remember."

Anyway, they made contact with me and asked me to write some arrangements, and I said I wanted to play piano with the band. I wrote some arrangements for them, also without using the piano as a writing crutch. The stuff came out really well. I liked some of the things I wrote. I even remember two of those tunes, an Irving Berlin thing, "It's a Lovely Day Today" and "Falling in Love Is Wonderful," both from an Irving Berlin show.

Well, they liked me and they got the bright idea of me being a dancing partner for the woman who was the leader. I wish I could remember her name; they were lovely people. Just the idea scared me. I mean, today I see the kinds of things that people do, like Harry Connick with his singing and all that. I didn't have the guts to do those things, and some of those things I could do but I was way too shy and introverted to do it. But there was one part of me that really wanted to do it, man, because I had always wanted to dance and felt that would be great. It would have been really something. They were so nice and they really wanted to teach me to dance and have the show band. I finally chickened out. I don't remember how I left it and I don't know how the whole thing worked out, which I felt kind of bad about. If I had been a little bit different and able to go along with it, I might have been able to help organize it because musically, they made me music director and it was a nice band.

In one of the biographies that somebody wrote about me, they said that I wasn't interested because the woman couldn't sing. Oh, man, why do people say things like that? If that woman is still around, or her family, then it's not fair, because that wasn't it at all. I thought she was terrific! I really admired them, but the problem was that I was scared to death. It was as simple as that! And it would have been a nice thing to learn how to dance. That's an opportunity life presents that you just can't deal with. And life seemed to be like that, always offering something and there had to be a lightning decision. Can you do it or can't you do it, and where do you go from here?

10

LEAVIN' TOWN
NEW YORK TO LOS ANGELES

WELL, THINGS GRADUALLY DETERIORATED. During that period though, we did a lot of things because Gail was always working on me to build up my enthusiasm and optimism. We became kind of active in odd ways. It seems especially odd now I suppose, but I went around to city, state, and federal agencies trying to get various kinds of interest in a rehearsal band I had going. There is a picture that somebody took during those years, that turned up later, of us rehearsing in Central Park. We rehearsed one day and it was fine, and we went back another day to rehearse and the police came and chased us out. Gail was all for making a scene—get the papers to show photographs of them running people out of the park for playing music! We chickened out at that one. I'm afraid some of us felt a little too vulnerable. It was all right for me because I was clean at that point, but I couldn't vouch for everybody.

That was a whole other kind of band. It was like a jumping band, not a swing band. I can't really explain that band except that it reflects where I was in my own life and that was a period of extreme transition. You know, it was my survival period, because I had just about finished myself in New York with the drugs and the whole thing, and left. And then, when I came back, my views on lots of things had changed. I was trying to find a niche for myself, some way of functioning. The big bands had gone. And so, what to do? That was the kind of band I put together. It was just six horns. There were two baritones with me and Max McElroy and Allen Eager on tenor. It was kind of an odd little band that was a stopping point along the way.

Gerry rehearsing big band, Central Park, New York, with Gail Madden, 1949.
© BILL CROW

Gail was from the Northwest, and I think she had kind of a pioneer spirit that I've encountered in some people from that part of the country. She was very much an individualist. I gather from the stories that she would tell that she came from a very spirited family that gave her this feisty kind of background. She was willing to take on the world to do what she wanted to do. She was a musician and played the piano, and then she started to get into these scientific theories of hers about how to deal with addiction and problems like that, and how to organize creative people into profitable occupations that would at least be important in the community and make money to support us, and build something. How she really came to all that, I don't know.

Before that she spent time with Bob Graettinger, getting him straightened out. And, of course, thanks to the fact that Gail saved his life, he was able to write what he did. I mean, it's a tragedy that he died not too long after that from cancer, but he wouldn't have done anything had it not been for her. She used to tell me stories about Bob, listening to stuff that I'd recorded when *Birth of the Cool* came out. They'd listen to it together and it broke him up because when he heard my solo on one of my own pieces. She said he laughed because he doesn't know the piece either; meaning when he was playing with bands, he'd write something and then go play on it (he was a saxophone player) and he didn't know it. Meaning you have to learn it from another standpoint. And he laughed because he recognized it in a way that a writer would. The way I was tip-toeing on eggshells through this piece, it was obvious to him and to me that I really didn't know the progression, and it's always been a challenge: how to try to combine the two facilities because one doesn't really have much to do with the other. But how she arrived at that I don't know.

If it hadn't been for what she had encountered in New York, my destroyed condition, George Wallington's reclusiveness, and Max Roach's, call it what you will, self-centered desire to do what he wanted by himself without being bothered with anybody else. That just didn't work.

As I mentioned, I went around to various agencies including the police, and I'd say to them, "We've got a bunch of musicians who really don't have anything to do with themselves at this point and you've got kids with time on their hands who are starting to get involved with drugs, and if somebody could come up with a place, we could go play music for them after school; maybe accomplish something." I think I probably had more organized ideas of what to present at that point, but it fell on uniformly deaf ears, and the irony was that the police mentality, whatever department they were in, would say, "Well, listen, as long as you're here, maybe you would like to tell us a few people who are selling the drugs!" I said, "No, I wouldn't like to do that." That was kind of an ongoing disillusion but it was all part of a learning process, I guess, going into my computer and becoming part of my experience.

At times the police could be really difficult. Some cities were especially dreadful. In those days the Philadelphia police were just unbelievable. They liked nothing better than to hound the musicians. Traveling bands would come through, and those guys would be there shaking everybody down. And in those days that was part of the reason for the cool attitude, the cool way of dressing, man. Trying to be invisible so these people would let us alone because they were atrocious people with a destructive mind-set and were doing this for their own sadistic pleasure, and, of course, if they busted somebody, it's printed in the paper to show what a wonderful thing they're doing by cleaning up society.

I remember one episode in particular when Woody's band was in concert, I think at the Philadelphia Academy of Music. They busted one of the guys for having dope of some sort and they took him to the police station but didn't book him. But what they did was they called up, probably Joe Glaser in New York, and got him to promise to give them a couple thousand dollars. So one of these guys gets on a train, goes to New York, gets the money, and comes back and they release the musician.

That was about as bold a case of that kind of corruption as I've ever encountered. But there were some hateful guys on the narcotics squad in Philadelphia.

That kind of covers the period in New York and my do-good phase and trying to get some kind of help and involvement in the community. We ran out of money and we ran out of prospects. I guess we took whatever small amount of cash we had left and took off and came to Los Angeles in stages. There was nothing to do. There were no opportunities. New York was in a real decline at that point so there was very little work and not enough to support Gail and myself.

Gail had friends in Los Angeles. Bob Graettinger was there and he wanted to help us. She knew that Stan Kenton was re-organizing a band, and she thought there might be something for me to do there. She thought I should write for the band. But we didn't really just take off to Los Angeles. As I said, we went there in stages.

We stopped off for a couple of days in Newark, but it was obvious there was nothing for me down there so I took off for Reading, which is where I had been during the time I was in high school. My brother Don was there. He had lived in Reading all his life with his wife and family, who were little kiddies at that point.

Gail and I rented a room and, boy, the musicians and everybody in Reading were so glad to see me until they found out that I might stay. Then I felt that they all kind of froze up. They didn't need another musician in town, especially one with any kind of fame who might be the leader who was replacing them.

So about that time, I guess my brother told my father that I was there because I hadn't been in touch with him. And the first thing I know, a couple of FBI agents show up at the door of our room and haul us downtown and search us and go through the whole number. We had nothing.

Then my father showed up with my brother and my mother. The FBI at this point was a little put out with my father because he had assured them his son "the junkie" was there, and of course he was just doing this for my own good. They had to let us go and I was really pissed off about that one. You ask people for help and this is the help you get.

So I realized that Reading, Pennsylvania, was not the answer. We were not welcome there. So we went out and started hitchhiking. At this point I had no horn and very few belongings—a couple of shoulder bags of what remained of clothing, music paper, books, and such—and we hitchhiked our way across the country.

In the early stages of hitchhiking, the long-distance truckers were great. It was a lonely life for the guys who traveled by themselves and even though they were not supposed to pick people up, we'd meet them at the truck stops and they'd say, "Well, come on, I'm going to Pittsburgh or something—I'll give you a lift that far." And we'd ride with them and some of the guys were just great, you know, helpful and friendly.

I remember a guy driving a tanker or some kind of a big semi, and we rode with a crew who were big movers, Allied Vans or something. They had gigantic trucks. We made it mainly with trucks across most of the country into Oklahoma or thereabouts and then we started picking up rides with individuals, and that's when it got a little scary! Some of these cats we ran into were such cowboys driving. You'd ride with your heart in your mouth!

Nothing happened that was threatening to us but it was scary nonetheless. There was one family we rode with; it seemed like it was a couple of full-grown sons and a mother in this rattletrap of a car and they drove fast. It felt like Ma Barker! They were rough people. But that got us into Albuquerque.

Dick Hilbert, the drummer I had roomed with early on in New York, was there. After he gave it up, he left New York and became a clinical psychologist and then a teacher of psychology. And he was teaching at that point in Albuquerque. So we got to Albuquerque and he tried to help us. He tried to help us and he did, and through some contacts I made with him I wound up getting a job with a kind of a country and western band. You know, country and western music, especially, a lot of it is the kind of stuff that's played in the Southwest—swinging little bands. They really kind of hark back to, not exactly the Dixie days but, you know, the swinging two-beat or stomping four-beat. So musically it was fun!

They got a horn for me and I told them about the union thing, and they said, "Well, that's okay." I was able to straighten it out with the local union and I played there for a couple of months. We were able to get on our feet a little bit as far as money was concerned. Hilbert was a good friend and we had a good time with him and other musicians and guys that he knew from the college around there, so it was a good period. It was a rest between big-city life.

And so Albuquerque became a lucky destination. I was doing all right in Albuquerque and had a steady job but not much in the way of prospects. I liked it there, but what finished me was being erased from the union for nonpayment of dues. So the local union couldn't turn a blind eye to me anymore. The band had to let me go.

11

"YOUNG BLOOD"
WRITING FOR STAN KENTON

So Gail and I took off for Los Angeles and looked up Bob Graettinger. I don't remember how we finally got to Los Angeles, whether we hitched a ride or somebody drove us there or we took a bus or what. It's just a total blank. But when we showed up there, we saw Graettinger and some of Gail's friends. She felt at home because she was now among friends, and we got ourselves kind of settled and got me in with Kenton. They were in touch with Stan Kenton, and I wound up getting the opportunity to write for the band, which, even though it wasn't my ideal band or style or anything, I was very glad to have the job to write for them and did my best to try to satisfy Stan as a leader. I wrote a lot of charts for him at that period. I remember the first thing I wrote for him was very contrapuntal. I was trying to do a thing that built an ensemble sound out of all unison contrapuntal lines, and it built up to a nice solid ensemble chorus.

Stan didn't really like it very well, so he said if I rewrote it, he would take it. So I did. I took it and put the tune "Walking Shoes" on the first part and used the out chorus from the piece that was there, and that was all right. But I was always kind of amused by the fact that I felt Stan had kind of gotten stuck with me. He'd had all these various bands that were experimental or the large orchestra with strings, which was the thing he was dealing with when I was first around the band. It was a whole orchestra, and we were always governed by some kind of motivating principle. So this time he was he going to have a band for the musicians. This was going to be a swing band.

The fact that the musicians liked my charts and they enjoyed playing them, he sort of felt obligated to buy them. But he made sure that I understood that the other guys were to do the concert stuff and what I was writing was like the dog work, which was the dance arrangements. It was all right with me because I liked the tunes. I did the best I could with them. I'm not sure how much he liked them. Then I threw in a few originals along the way and he had the idea for me to write a piece called "Young Blood," so I did.

It's funny with that one, though. Gail and I had a little apartment in Hollywood, close to Hollywood Boulevard. It was a big walk-in closet and I had this little sixty-six-key studio upright piano. I wheeled it into the closet and stayed there for three days while I wrote "Young Blood." Just stayed there, man! It was the only arrangement I ever wrote in anger.

And I realized something else, too, because this has happened to me on a number of occasions, where I do something, a piece of music, a composition or arrangement or something, that kind of boils in my head. A sort of incomplete state for a long time, and I'll turn around and rewrite it and come up with something that's altogether different, but based on the original idea.

So it's a way of developing an idea, and that particular chart came about because I guess it was 1947 that Woody Herman re-organized his band. In the years that I was first with Tommy Tucker and then with Gene Krupa, the Woody Herman band was far and away the best band I'd ever been around— that I'd ever heard. Every time I heard them, the band was exciting and there was something in every chart that would make my hair stand on end. I loved that band!

The band had Bill Harris, Flip Phillips, and Sam Marowitz on lead alto, and the trumpets were Pete Candoli, Sonny Berman, and Neal Hefti. Later, either Conte Candoli or Shorty Rogers came in. Ralph Burns was such a good arranger. He wrote beautiful arrangements for that band. And Neal wrote great arrangements for the band. Davey Tough was on the drums. And then, kind of the spirit of the band was Chubby Jackson. Every time I saw that band it excited me! I loved it!

I learned so much from all of them. Mickey Folus was the other tenor. Mickey was later with Thornhill's band when I was with them.

So that band used to make me feel so good. Then during that period, I guess it was about 1946 that Stravinsky wrote the "Ebony Concerto" and Woody took the band on tour across the country and featured it. I'll never forget playing at a theater, or a dance, or something with Gene Krupa's band in Columbus, Ohio, and I went over to the auditorium where Woody was doing a concert playing the "Ebony Concerto." John LaPorta was doing the clarinet part, most of it. What Woody couldn't do, John did.

There were about seventy-five people in the audience. I couldn't believe it, man! It was such a great band and they were doing this great piece of music that was a knockout. I mean, Stravinsky writing for Woody's band and that can't muster up any interest in this bloody country? It was a wonderful concert they did, but the most disheartening thing was to see this little, tiny audience with a spectacular concert going on.

Well, not too long after that, Woody broke up the band and I guess he took a vacation for a while, which was very unusual for him. Then he re-organized the band in California.

By this time I was back in Philadelphia, and I'll never forget—I saved it for a long time—I went through so many changes in my life and traveled around so much, that I never really had a center where to keep things. I got a two-page telegram from Ralph Burns, who I had become really good friends with. I admired him so much. He was a great writer and a sweetheart of a player, a lovely man. And we liked each other! That was one of the things, I think, that made me feel like a part of it—because of the mutual respect I enjoyed from the men I admired, like Ralph and Gil Evans, Bill Finegan, and Sy Oliver, and people like that. They were older and experienced, and the fact that they accepted me was really important to me.

So I got this incredible telegram from Ralph saying, "Start writing!" Something like, "Pull out all the stops, man. Woody's re-organizing a new band." Then he told me some of the people who were going to be with him, like Stan Getz and Zoot Sims, Herbie Steward, Earl Swope, and Bill Harris and on and on and on; a lot of the names I didn't even know yet, but Ralph was so enthusiastic. I started to work on a chart of "Yardbird Suite" immediately. I worked on that chart. I probably spent a month on it. It was an interesting chart; it really was and would have been very good.

Well, it was almost a year before the band turned up in New York and had a rehearsal that I could go to. A lot had happened in the meantime. I don't think Ralphie was even there anymore because that band, in 1947, had such a rotten attitude.

Serge Chaloff used to do things that just infuriated me because he had such a bad attitude. Woody Herman's entire 1947 band infuriated me. I thought Woody was a wonderful man and I liked the way Woody played. He played the way he played. He expressed himself and was effective and I liked him. There was a quality in the 1947 band; they were just so full of themselves and they made life miserable for Ralph Burns. Serge was greatly responsible. They put Ralph down for being corny because he was influenced by Duke Ellington. Serge and the rest of them figured if it wasn't Count Basie, then it didn't swing and it wasn't music. Just really childish attitudes, but the worst thing was that Serge could be really cruel about it. He would ridicule Woody, ridiculed his playing while on the stand. I was always kind of mad at Woody for putting up with it. But Woody appreciated good musicians so much that he took a lot of crap from them.

When that band first started working, there was a place on Vine Street in Hollywood called The Empire Room. The band would start, and Woody would always be late. Sam Marowitz was playing lead alto and he always called the tunes until Woody got there. They'd play for half or three-quarters of an hour, then Woody would walk up and make an appearance on the stage, just so people would know he was there, and then he would go to the bar and get loaded. And he really had to get loaded before he could go on stage with the band because the band was so mean to him. Well, if you can imagine being mean to Woody, you know, he was the sweetest man I ever met. As a leader he was such an easygoing guy. He let the guys do what they wanted and if it had been one of the hard-nosed leaders like Tommy Dorsey, they would never have gotten away with it. Tommy wouldn't stand it for a minute.

I was at the Paramount Theater one time when Tommy fired the baritone player during the show and sent him offstage. Later on when I put my band together, I found out that the baritone player he fired was Gene Allen, my baritone player! Gene told me about it. He laughed because Gene was another guy who was such a nice guy that you couldn't imagine him doing anything to get himself fired. But Tommy had his quirks, man, and he was a hard taskmaster. Whatever it was, that was it. You'd see him point to him, and the baritone just picks up and walks off stage in the middle of the show. But Woody wasn't like that, you know. Woody would never ridicule anybody.

Well, Serge used to get my goat with things like that, and as years went on, he would always find something else that would get my goat because he was mean. He was also responsible for turning a lot of people onto heroin. I remember seeing that band on the road and going up to one of the guys' rooms and walking in the door and there's a lineup, like people waiting to get into a theater, or the checkout line at the super-market. Serge is playing doctor in the bathroom, man, and he's injecting these guys with heroin who couldn't inject themselves.

I said, "You son of a bitch, man. You're turning these guys on with a kind of glee," and it was a disgusting, negative thing. I wanted to kill him. What possesses people to do something like that? So Serge was a very negative guy. All that is a buildup to the fact that at one point, I got really mad and I said, "Serge, you've been winning the *DownBeat* poll, and I'm going to give you two more years and then you've had it." And by God, it was in two years, I started winning the poll and Serge never got it back again. That's a funny kind of a condemnation isn't it, "You've got two more years."

I used to say to Serge, "You know, Serge, you're full of yourself. You keep putting Woody's solo down on this record but his solo ain't the worst on the record by any means. It's you." Oh man, Serge would make me so mad. He was, in his evilness, a kind of happy-go-lucky person but he waded right through. When he came to Philadelphia, he moved in on me. When the band played at the Click Club he was a mess, but he invited himself in and what do you do?

And during that period, too, I used to tell Zoot how rotten I thought he was to join in. Zoot was a very fair-minded guy, a nice guy, and he always felt bad about it. But he was always one of the guys. Musicians do that, man; it's like they don't want to disagree with each other. So if somebody puts somebody down, they all jump on the bandwagon. It's like an easily led mob, and I've experienced that in so many different guises in my career.

One guy would start putting me down and everybody would jump in. Well, anybody that aspires to be a leader has got to accept that because one of the first things you've got to understand is that the leader is always a drag. That's part of being the leader. He's automatically a bad guy.

It was always difficult when guys made that distinction. I thought that in the early quartets everybody contributed. The first quartet we all contributed to the music and they accepted me as the leader; I mean, there was no question about who was making the decisions and who was calling the shots, but we were all pulling our weight. And we were all interested in the music so there was a feeling of unity and everybody playing a role in the group, because a band is a social unit and has to function in some kind of a way or else it falls apart.

I've had that happen, too, where guys either didn't accept their role or didn't accept my role or joined cliques. Imagine a quartet with two or three cliques in it? Well, it happened. And the only thing to do is either let things work out or get rid of the band and start all over again.

But in Woody's band it was really peculiar. I was always curious about why Woody let it happen. He was the leader. Get rid of the bad apples that are causing the trouble. But Woody was an admirer of talent, and he was always in kind of awe of the musicianship of the players and he really liked the band, so he let them get away with murder. And they were terrible, really terrible to him.

I'll never forget later on when they were back East, walking down 48th Street one time in front of the hotel on the West Side, where the band was staying, and they were loading the bus to go down to Hershey in Pennsylvania to play a one-nighter. Zoot and some of the guys said, "Come along." So I jumped on the bus and went on down and listened to the band. The funny thing was, that band in 1945 had something in every chart that interested me, something in every chart that excited me and made my hair stand on end. It was really an emotional experience being around that band. This band didn't move me at all. They were playing all this fast impressive stuff, but it was a dull band; just nothing made my hair stand on end. They played this little band thing that was way too fast and didn't swing. It was like showing off. They only played twenty-four bars during the whole night that made my hair stand on end, and that was an out chorus that Al Cohn had written on "Tiny's Blues." It was just one of those things, very, very simple writing that really did it. And that was the only thing that had fire; the rest of the night, forget it! It was just boring.

In a way it was a lesson, because there was a lot of excellent stuff going on musically, but the thing that was coming out of the band made it dull. It was a mean band! They were so busy looking down their noses at their audience with this superiority and generally bad attitude, like they are the greatest and everybody else is a square. They just spoiled it.

So that was the band that I took the arrangement of "Yardbird Suite" to. They were playing the Royal Roost. The Roost was down on 47th and Broadway. I went down to a rehearsal and they went through a lot of charts. I don't remember what they rehearsed now, but it must have been four or five charts and it went on and on and on. Finally they said, "Okay, that's it for the day, guys, see you tonight." I went up to Woody and said, "Hey, what about my chart?" He kind of rolled his eyes and said, "Okay," so they passed out my chart. They played it down and it really sounded awful, really dreadful. I couldn't believe it. Could not believe it!

So now the band packs up and leaves and I'm sitting by myself on one side of the club, and Woody then packs up with whoever he was with, his manager or somebody, and they start out of the place and he sees me sitting there and says, "Gerry, come here." We walk out together and start walking down the street. He said, "I'm sorry about your chart, man. I really didn't want to rehearse it. But there's something I hate to tell you and obviously you don't know." He said, "There are some of these guys who you think are your friends, and they pretend to be your friends. They're not your friends." Well, that hurt. I thought it was a very nice gesture for him to tell me what was going on, and it's true. I assumed that all those guys . . . individually they all, most all of them, came on as friends, including Serge. Red Rodney was with the band, but of course with Red I'd experienced that once before. I had gotten Red the job with Gene Krupa's band when Donny Fagerquist left, and after a couple of months Gene said to me, "Listen, you got Red the job on this band, and is he a friend of yours, because he's always bad mouthing you?" I said, "No, that's the first I heard about it."

So I think that's a lesson that often people, not only musicians, are surprised when they learn that when you say things about people it gets back to the people you said it about, so you don't live in a vacuum. Whatever the complaints against me, they carried into the music because the "Yardbird Suite" was a very, very good chart, and they just played it in the most half-assed, haphazard way. They didn't care. I had known all those guys a long time, so I could figure out who were the ringleaders and who were the followers, and who were the guys who were negative to the whole world and not necessarily me in particular. Some really surprised me, not only that they would join in the thing, but that they wouldn't stick up for me.

Zoot and I always had that kind of relationship. There were a few guys who were like brothers to each other, so to feel all this open hostility from the band, I really didn't know what the hell it was based on. I still don't know. I think it was just that thing of being an outsider, you know. I think I've always kind of given the impression to the other guys that I'm university trained and always tried to make a good appearance. So I looked like the enemy from the upper-middle classes, the educated elite, and I guess it never occurred to them that I dropped out of high school, was self-taught, and spent most of my years being wasteful and a ne'er-do-well.

But that image has, I think, confused a lot of musicians, black and white, and I've had a lot of antagonists because of whatever they attribute to me. I'm amazed though, when guys who know me join in on that, because I had some good friends in those days who weren't troubled by all those misconceptions. Zoot and Al were two guys I loved to spend time with.

And that's why I say, when it came time that Stan Kenton asked me to write this piece, I don't even know that I started out consciously to do it, but I drew on that arrangement of "Yardbird Suite" because I think that probably what I wrote in the out chorus was similar. I think that the anger I was expressing was the thing that had built up, you know. Because whereas I was glad to have the job writing for Stan, and it was a big help to me in a lot of ways, it still was kind of a pain in the neck to be relegated to writing just the dance charts, and looked down on as not being particularly important. Certainly not in Stan's scheme of things, and with the treatment that I got at the hands of Woody Herman's superhit four horsemen band. I was carrying enough of a load of resentment that I wound up putting into that chart.

The funny thing was the way Kenton's band ultimately played it. They played it really fast, and it sounded like I was doing my hostility number. But looking back on it and the way that I've had occasion to play it a couple of times recently—I played it last summer with Bob Brookmeyer's project in Schleswig-Holstein, Germany—I said to Bob, "You know, this thing is always played too fast. Could we try playing it one time at the tempo that I really intended it to be?" He said, "Yeah, I'd like to try that." And it became a different piece. It was a swinging piece and not loaded with hostility at all. I mean, it was a user-friendly composition that was actually about ten times easier to play at the slower tempo because everything swung and fit in place, and the brass in the out chorus wasn't trying to gulp big breaths, you know. The breathing was much more natural. It was kind of an eye-opening experience. Funny, though, that I thought I was getting my hostilities out, but what came out of it wasn't hostile at all, but it felt better. Sort of like why do you hit your head against a brick wall? Because it feels so good when you stop.

I always had a kind of reputation of hating Kenton and the Kenton band and all that. Stan and I always had a feisty attitude toward each other, which I think was kind of a puzzle for the other guys because of Stan being the leader and the older guy and I was always the kid. But I never had any qualms about speaking up for myself and I think that Stan and I had kind of a respect for each other. We knew we were approaching music from totally different places, and I always tried to do my best when I wrote for the band to do things that would please Stan. It wasn't easy for me to do because it was a different approach and he didn't really like my arrangements. So, while Kenton was organizing in California, I wrote for them and was around the band a lot. Then when the band took off and went on the road, I had to find other things to do.

12

THE PIANOLESS QUARTET

So I STARTED PLAYING MORE and I lucked into sitting in around town a little bit. I don't know whether it was through Shorty Rogers, it may well have been, because Shorty was one of the few people in Los Angeles who was really helpful to me at that point. He'd try to get me on record dates, and he'd try to get me on gigs, and if he was doing something with his little band, he would take me along. So I wound up down at The Lighthouse in Hermosa Beach. John Levine, who was the owner of the place, was very helpful because he tried to straighten the thing out with the union and got permission for me to play and set the wheels in motion to straighten all that out and get me reinstated.

Howard Rumsey was great because he had me down there for the weekends, and it was probably about this time that Gail and I split up. I mean, she really figured it was time for me to get off on my own, and she was trying to get herself back together because her life pretty much fell apart when she lost all of that stuff that she'd been building in New York. She had spent a lot of time and effort with me and she wanted to move on. So that left me by myself in Los Angeles, and I spent a lot of time going to sessions and looking for playing jobs. There were quite a few things going on in town so it was interesting.

But the main job then turned out to be the weekends at The Light-house. I played on Saturdays and Sundays. We would play long sets on Saturday then we were back again on Sunday, starting at two in the afternoon playing through to two in the morning. As the days pro-gressed, of course, and more and more people came in; it would get wilder and wilder. I swear, sometimes in that place, by the time mid-night rolled around, it was like playing in a high school gymnasium with a championship basketball game going on; just incredible chaos.

We'd start out in the afternoon with just me and the rhythm section with Howard and Shelly Manne. Frank Patchen was the piano player, and Frank and I became good friends. He was great; he used to pick me up in Hollywood, where I was staying, and we'd drive down there together. We'd play through the twelve-hour segments. As I said, it started out with me and the rhythm section but as the evening progressed, more guys would come in, so it would be like four or five horns by nine o'clock at night. We'd play through until two in the morning with the bigger band. It was good doing all that steady playing.

I did that for quite a number of months, and then one weekend it just really got to me and I said, "Frank, I can't do this anymore. I think I'm going crazy," So it just became more than I could deal with, but I did it for quite a while.

After that, at some point I met Dick Bock. I guess I knew about him because he had put together some dates for Discovery Records, but it turned out he was booking the room at the Haig, especially the off nights. He would bring in the guys to play on the night that the main attraction wasn't playing. So he started me playing there on Tuesday nights, and when I first was playing it would always be with Donn Trenner and the rhythm section. The main attraction was Erroll Garner. Of course, when Erroll was there, they had this beautiful nine-foot concert grand Baldwin on the stage for him, and it remained pretty much the same for the number of weeks while Erroll was there. Well, then they started to make plans of what to do because Erroll had been there for a couple of months and he was getting to the end of his stay, and they were bringing in Red Norvo and his trio with Charlie Mingus and Tal Farlow. They didn't use a piano at all, so they were now in a quandary about what to do on the off night, since Red didn't have a piano and they certainly weren't going to rent a grand piano just to come in and play the one night. So John Bennett, who was one of the owners of the place, said what they should do is get one of those little sixty-six-key studio uprights for the off night. Of course, in the meantime, Dick had said that he'd like me to put a group together to play the off nights—that I should take it over. I said, "Great," but when John said this about the piano, I said, "No, I don't think I want a studio upright. Thank you. Let me think of something else."

So then I started to try different things; maybe would put something into rehearsal and have something in there one night to try it. I tried a thing with a bass guitar, drums, and horn. You know, various ways of approaching a rhythm section without a piano. One of the things that gave me a lot of confidence to do that was from when we were still in New York and Gail and I were organizing some things. We organized that record date with Prestige with the six horns and three or four in the rhythm section. On that date we wound up using George Wallington just because we loved the way George played. Gail had been rehearsing the rhythm section because she was doing a thing with maracas, like a swishing sound that she had made go with the cymbal sound, and had done this whole number of rehearsing a rhythm section that had no piano in it.

So it was because of the things she had tried that gave me kind of an idea of what I might try, and what not to do and so on. Ultimately, I wasn't really pleased with it. It seemed kind of ordinary just having a guitar taking the piano's place, and it really didn't make much difference.

But Gail had been enthusiastic about Chico Hamilton's playing so I remembered that, and I went and got Chico to see if he was interested. He had been playing with Charlie Barnet's group on Hollywood Boulevard in a place called The Streets of Paris. I had played a number of sessions in the Valley where Chet Baker had shown up playing. So I played with him a couple of times and was very impressed with his melodic playing, which you don't usually hear in players at jam sessions. People are so busy playing their horn and playing techniques, but Chet was such a melodic player that I thought we could try it with no piano. We were lucky to get a bass player who had a good sound and good time but also thought like an arranger.

So each one of us brought something particular, adding to the group. It wasn't just playing the instrument; it was like bringing a point of view to it. And putting it together, it gelled. Everything was based on the bass because he was doing two things at once. It was like being part of the ensemble, plus part of the rhythm section. You didn't have a piano stating the chords, you know; it had to come from the combination of the bass, bass line, and whatever we were doing in harmonies, and Chico had his own unique approach.

All the time we rehearsed, we rehearsed with a small set. You know, we'd only have maybe a snare drum and high hat and a standing tom-tom and maybe one top cymbal on a stand. No bass drum, no set of tom-toms, so it was a minimal set.

I remember the first time we'd been rehearsing down in a house that Chet rented in Watts. We were getting ready after rehearsing to pack up to go to the city to play the job, and I look in the back of Chico's car. He's got a whole set of drums back there. I said, "What have you got your drums here for?" He said, "Well, we're going to work tonight, aren't we?" I said, "Yeah, but you're not going to use all that stuff, are you?" He said, "Certainly."

I said, "No, man; you must play with the same stuff that you've been rehearsing with." We argued for a while and he said, "Well, all right." I said, "Because you know this is the sound of the group. It's going to be different if you come in with a whole set of drums." So he capitulated and that's what he played on: the snare, the sock cymbal, one standing tom, and one standing cymbal, and played a good deal of the time on brushes. There were times when he played with Barnet's band when he was playing with sticks and, just because he felt like it, he would deliver some bomb in the middle of somebody's chorus that was just like from left field. I would see Charlie flinch and the guy who was playing the solo almost fall off the bandstand. I figured, I don't know, man, Chico could be a little dangerous with drumsticks sometimes. But he used to do things in solos that would put me away. It was one of those things that was, I think, a big factor in the appeal of the group, that Chico had such a good show sense that he brought that out in all of us, so the group wasn't as introverted as Chet and I were. There was a quality about the music that was very accessible. What we were doing . . . it was clear, you could see through it, and Chico brought this kind of extroverted quality to it that kept the thing alive so that there was some vitality there and Chet with his very melodic sense. I fell into a natural role of accompanying—being the bridge between the baseline and the solo line—and it worked. That was it. That's how the whole thing came about.

It's funny when I see the recordings that they've put out of all of the stuff we recorded; you can hear the progression of the things that I tried before it actually got to the quartet with Chet and Chico and Carson.

It was a phenomenal thing that even on the off nights we suddenly found ourselves with lines outside, people waiting to get in, and it happened so quickly that I was really unprepared for it. We played as long as Red was there with his trio. I don't know how long that was, but groups used to stay in a place for a number of weeks, maybe six weeks at a time. We played the off nights as long as he was there, and the audience built as we went along, so we were doing tremendous business in the place. We were amazed. We couldn't figure it out.

Dick Bock decided to start a record company. He just came up and said he was going to start a record company. He borrowed some money from drummer Roy Harte, who owned Drum City on Santa Monica Boulevard. We started the record company with Roy's $300 or $400, Dick's contacts and expertise in the record business, Phil Turetsky's Ampex, and my music. That was it.

The first records were recorded in the living room at Phil Turetsky's house. Phil was an accountant who was taking care of business with Dick on this thing and trying to get it organized. But he had an Ampex machine so we used to go up to his house. We did this whole thing without spending any money, actually. I guess the only money he spent was the money he borrowed from Roy Harte and bought tapes. That was about it.

I wrote mostly new material for the quartet, which you can hear in the way that it is written because it "wants" three lines: the top line, the harmony line, and the bass line. While many of the things that I wrote were worked out, a lot of the stanzas that we played weren't really worked out ahead of time. Chet and I could do things together where we would play tunes that we never even discussed. One or the other of us would just start playing it, and we would wind up doing something with it that sounded like an organized arrangement. So people couldn't really tell whether we had worked it out or not.

We were also able to do something that, to this day, I don't think many people are successful at: making convincing endings. We could go into some kind of a chord extension, a sequence at the end of a piece that sounded like we worked it out, but we could hear where the other person was going and wind up making sense out of it, and it sounded like it was written. Sometimes a whole night would go by and we wouldn't discuss what we were playing, and we would hardly play anything that we would normally play on other nights. We would just play a whole bunch of different things. That was one of the joys of playing with Chet; we were able to work together so easily in that way. It was a compatibility that I'd never experienced before and not really since. I've played with other guys that I have been able to establish a rapport, like all the years with Brookmeyer. We were able to anticipate each other but still not in the same way and not with the same ease as with Chet.

There was kind of a general movement to do more obvious things with counterpoint; I mean, the contrapuntal idea had always been there. It existed in the early days, especially with New Orleans music, with each one of the lines and each one of the instruments having its own function in the ensemble so they're playing separate lines, and that's counterpoint. And what we were doing was merely another application of the functions of the instruments, where in the Dixieland kind of thing you had the clarinet riding on the top embellishing chords, the trumpet playing around the melody so he's establishing the lead line, and the trombone playing in an accompanying way that's establishing a chord relationship that connects it with the rhythm section and with the trumpet or cornet line.

Ours was different because it was a different kind of rhythmic approach and the horns that we were relating were different. We did not have the clarinet riding high; it was another function. The trumpet was playing different kinds of melodies. He's still playing the lead line so that function remains the same. I was still playing the harmony line in place of the trombone, but the kinds of lines I was playing were structured differently because the rhythm was different. We weren't playing a Dixieland two, we were playing a much smoother kind of four.

My whole job, because we had left the piano off, was to establish always the sound of the chord progression that was moving through the piece, and to do that with my harmony line in relation to the bass line, which always had to be able to state something basic about the way the rhythm line moved—didn't have to just play roots of the chords that you always had to do on the bottom, but you could move through them in such a way that the implication of the chord was always there. So that then the thing, even though it wasn't obvious to the ear and it wasn't spelled out, the impression was there, and what we were doing was giving the impression of chord progression because of the way we were touching on those notes.

So we were even doing the same kinds of relationships as far as the counterpoint was concerned. What we were doing was changing the actual function of those lines themselves, so the counterpoint had always been there. There was this period in writing for the big band where, in fact this was something I was talking to Bill Holman about the other day, that was something that a lot of us from different directions were working on: ways of making a smoother kind of counterpoint and making counterpoint a more important element in band writing, instead of it being up and down ensemble stuff.

Now, Duke's writing incorporated a lot of contrapuntal ideas because he didn't write so much straight up and down ensemble things that you associate with so many of the bands—or like Count Basie, but especially Count's later bands . . . was more counterpoint in his earlier bands, like a lot of the unison saxophones against the punctuation of the brass, or the unison sax as the punctuation to the trumpets, and the trombones doing another function, that's all contrapuntal.

Bill Holman was saying that that was why he was taken, and I think Graettinger too, with the first arrangements that I brought in to Kenton's band because Bill said he had already been leaning in that direction, trying to open up the contrapuntal way of approaching it. So when I brought my things in, he said he really liked what I had done because I had achieved that in these charts.

There was probably more talk about counterpoint at that point. There was also the thing that when journalists write about something, they write about it in a way . . . I mean, the quartet was a new thing so they harped on the fact there was no piano and the fact of the counterpoint. Well, any of these ideas were not necessarily an original idea of mine, or that nobody had ever thought of it before. Of course people did, but it was a point of interest and something that they could make an identity of the music in words. It was also something that we were all, all of us as arrangers, were conscious of in orchestrating for a big band. I think many of us were working on the idea of making the big band more orchestral, rather than band-like.

13

ADVENTURES ON THE WEST COAST

ABOUT THIS TIME, they wanted me to bring the quartet up to the Black Hawk in San Francisco, because apparently Dave Brubeck had been talking about our group up there. I don't know who got in touch with me because I didn't have an agent yet. Fantasy was the company Brubeck recorded for, and he told them that they should get me to record. Well, the guys from Fantasy came around and to start with we went up and played at the Black Hawk. That was our first steady engagement with the group. I think Whitlock couldn't make it because he had something else to do, so Carson Smith became the bass player.

I tended to be sympathetic to Fantasy because Dave and I had become friends and I was glad to have Dave's interest, and I would have loved to be able to record for him. But I didn't feel I could because I had started this thing with Dick Bock and felt that my first commitment was with Pacific Jazz. But I got so much pressure from the other guys in the group because they weren't looking at it in terms of a record; they were looking at it in terms of income. You know, here we're offered an album and it's real money and I'm turning it down. So they really pressured me and I finally knuckled under to their demands. I always felt very wrong about it and doubly so because in the end, I think that was the best album that we did. That was the first album, a 10-inch LP that they pressed on red vinyl; very high-quality stuff. It was kind of too bad because that was the best album we did with the quartet, and it was not really good for the relationship with Dick and Pacific Jazz. But when we returned to Los Angeles, we went back to recording with Dick and did a lot of albums with him. And then of course he recorded Chet with his own group, so all these pressures were splitting everything up before we really even got established.

I never really had a contract with Pacific Jazz. I just was always available to record, and it's too bad I didn't have a contract because Dick ultimately sold that company for a lot of money. The people he sold it to never bothered to pay royalties, and I had a hard time even keeping track of who owned the thing. He had a royalty agreement with me because, after all, they started that company on a small investment and my music.

Well, Dick had given me like a 15 percent royalty because we were doing it on spec. We didn't get paid for the date. We may have had to put some checks through the union to make it legal, but if we did get anything it was scale, which was very low then. So he was going to make that up; if I'm doing it on spec they'd give me a 15 percent royalty, which is very high, and I got that royalty on all the early stuff from him as long as he had the company. But the other companies that bought the thing never bothered to honor any of those agreements, even if I took after them with lawyers. Also, I didn't have any contracts so I was just out in the cold. As a consequence, I've never really gotten any royalties, and to this day I probably don't get any royalties from them. I say probably don't, because I gave up keeping track of that stuff. It's too depressing that people are not honest and don't pay what's due. Most of my records, or a good percentage of them, have been in print since they were made, including those records. They've always been in print and I suppose it's the kind of thing that could become a career in itself, trying to chase down the royalties from people that owe you. I've spent time doing that and I find it very unrewarding; it's expensive and you spend so much time talking to lawyers, and lawyers are talking a language that's different from the way I look at things.

When we came back from San Francisco we went back into the Haig, only now we were the headliner working six nights a week. Musically, things continued to gel and the compatibility with Chet continued. That compatibility didn't really extend through to our personal relationship very much, though. We always got along and had a pretty good time together, but we were such totally different people with different kinds of attitudes of how we wanted to live. For instance, I was kind of a loner. I always had a handful of friends and liked to hang out with friends where music was usually the focus. Chet, on the other hand, always liked to travel with a pack. I can never remember him in those Los Angeles days that he didn't have four or five guys with him. They used to travel everywhere together and Chetty was kind of the leader of the pack, which always made it kind of hard for the guys traveling around with him because they would come around—I mean, Chet was their leader, but he would come to the quartet environment and I was the leader. That kind of confused these guys, who I don't think ever quite figured out what was going on.

They used to do amazing things, because we would finish playing with the quartet around two in the morning, something like that, and they'd pile in their cars, maybe six or eight of them, and drive up to Big Bear Mountain to ski. They'd spend the morning skiing and spend however many hours driving back, then go down to the beach in the afternoon to surf and swim and play on the beach and be beach bums. Then Chet would come into the gig at night. He would do this sometimes two, three, four days in a row with whatever variations. I mean, those are just the things I knew they did, but they did all of these highly energetic sporty things and it would just go on and on.

Finally, after a number of days of this, Chet's lips started to get dried out and chapped and he was missing notes all over the place and generally playing sloppily. And when he would play sloppily, he would get mad at himself and just complain and bitch and say, "Well, what's going on?" I finally said to him, "Chet, there's a remedy for the problem you're having here. It's called sleep. If you'd sleep once in a while, you wouldn't be having so much trouble playing." So, in this regard we were quite different.

Chet liked to drive fast and he liked fast cars. I guess as soon as we made some money at the Haig, he immediately went out and bought a Jaguar. During the period we were together, from the time we started rehearsals and played the off nights, I think he went through two or three cars and they usually wound up smashed up somewhere. It's a wonder he wasn't killed, he and his wife both.

One accident he had, he was driving very fast down all of those winding roads through the Hollywood Hills and came around a corner and of course thought he could do it, except that there was a car parked in the middle of the street, and he smashed right into it. He destroyed his Jag, and the ultimate result was he was finally in so much debt with all of these cars that he had smashed up and owed on, that he and his wife didn't have any place to stay. Well, by this time I had rented a little house in Hollywood, a kind of nice little conventional house in a nice conventional neighborhood; you know, a little space around it. It was comfortable.

So I let them stay there for a while, hoping that Chet would get himself on his feet and get his own place, because I didn't really like living with people too much. Well, not only did Chet move in, but the next thing I know I've got all the pack hanging out every day. I told him, "Chet, I appreciate these guys are friends of yours, but I really can't live with four or five, six, seven, or eight guys under foot. I just can't deal with that." So what they wound up doing then was, they'd wait until we went to work and then they'd come and hang out there until they knew it was time for us to come home. I didn't even know about this.

Well, Chet always had a thing going with this one narcotics cop who was a pain in the neck. He liked to ride Chet and Chet liked to ride him back again. They had this whole kind of contentious relationship going and I kept telling Chet, "Will you please cool it with this guy because he can make a lot of trouble. I mean, after all, you are carrying pot around and we are a little bit vulnerable around here so it would be a good idea to cool it." He kept on with it.

Around this time there was an article in *DownBeat* magazine about me telling the audience at the Haig that they had to be quiet while we were playing. The Haig was a small room. It only seated about 90 people and if you really crowded them in, maybe you could get 110 people in at the tables and at the bar. So if you got one noisy table, they'd make it impossible for everybody to hear. And since the people were paying an admission to come in and listen to the music, I thought it was unfair. I thought I was doing it in ways that weren't angry to the audience. People may have perceived it as being angry, but I wasn't. But the thing was, it's already going to appear angry if you say to people, "Listen, if you're looking for a place to hang out and talk, you picked the wrong room. There's a bar up the street where you can sit and talk until your heart's content and nobody will be bothered. But in here, everybody is trying to listen except you."

It was certainly unusual for a performer to tell an audience how to behave. But also, most of the people that came in there, who made any comment to me at all about it, thanked me. So I didn't feel like I was doing anything wrong and as far as what they wrote about it, they weren't there and I don't think they understood what the hell it was about. Also, writers love to pick up on something to hang a story on. It's the kind of thing that Jack Tracy said. It's the kind of thing that Gene Lees said when they were editors at *DownBeat*. They'd heard before they ever met me that I was going to be one of the really difficult people to talk to, to deal with, and both of them were amazed. We became great friends because they never had any problems with me at all, because these guys came to me and they didn't talk like idiots and ask stupid questions and treat me like a thing.

A lot of those things grew up because people like to talk, and of course there were episodes when I had done things in anger. My temper would flare up and I would do some dumb things, so I guess people expected the worst of me anyway. I mean, the relationship with Benny Goodman, the way that blew up, and my telling off Gene Krupa's band because I thought I was the leader. I was a kid and I didn't know any better. But that whole thing of being angry was also somehow typical of the time. So it didn't seem so outrageous because I was just another angry young man.

Around this time my haircut became a recognizable personality thing that it hadn't started out to be at all. The reason that I wound up with the hairstyle I did was that by the time I was nineteen or twenty I noticed that my hairline was receding. It was getting very high up on the temples on both sides, and I was starting to wonder if I was going to be bald by the time I was thirty like one of my brothers was. He lost all his hair by that time. A big traditional bald head.

So during the period early on with Gail, the whole experience with her kind of turned my imagination loose. She really freed me up in lots of ways, taking the cares of the world off my shoulders and the load of anger and defenses. I started to find all other kinds of ways to express myself. I started drawing and painting again, which I had liked to do when I was younger, and one of the things was that it freed my imagination about a lot of things. And because of what was going on and my body was getting rid of the drug addiction, it was like looking at the things that were going on in the body in a different way.

So here it was with kind of this looming baldness going on, and I realized one day when I was rubbing the fingers in the bald areas of my forehead, that there were little bumps. Instead of scratching them as if they were itches, because they did kind of itch, I would just sort of massage them and hairs came out of them. So I realized that what was happening was the hair was re-growing and I started to get a theory on why it was falling out. Since I had been a kid, my mother was always trying to train my hair to grow backward. She put those gels that they used in those days to plaster it down in some kind of a conventional style.

I started to think that by combing the hair, if the hair is not basically tough hair, which my hair wasn't—I've always had very fine hair, so it's easy for it to break and dry up and all kinds of things—so it occurred to me that by forcing it back, it was ultimately killing it off and that if I kept on doing that then the hairline would keep receding. Ultimately, what I did was cut my hair short. I didn't get it into a crew cut, or a brush cut, or whatever they call it, the military short haircut. I wanted it long enough so that it would lay flat, but instead of combing it back, I brushed it forward and it always felt like, just the thing of brushing it forward, it stimulated the re-growth of the hair. You know, it was like these little hair follicles started growing up and uncoiling themselves and the hair all grew back again! So I felt I had a theory that worked for me at least.

I've suggested it to other people that I know that had been suffering from the pangs of going bald early on, and for some people it worked. It helped the hair to re-grow by combing it in a way that's more natural. What I was doing, what I felt I was doing, was allowing it to grow and brushing it in a way that followed the natural line, so that the hair would grow if you let it alone. Because the hair doesn't grow backward, the hair grows on our head in a way that its function would be protection. The only way it can be a protection is if it formed some kind of a helmet over the skull. Which happens if your hair is cut short and brushed forward.

Well, the next thing I knew, I didn't even really realize it, somebody told me quite a few years ago that my hair became the style of the day and all of the young guys were cutting their hair like me as a style thing, not having any idea why I had done it or if there was any purpose to it at all. That's what happened in England, I think probably much more than here. It became kind of a thing for a while, the Mulligan haircut.

One of the other things that Gail did: she gave me a book that turned out to be a very important book for me. Later on I met Gerald Heard, who was part of the California group that included Aldous Huxley. He was somebody that Dick Bock admired a lot. Dick wanted me to meet him, so we went out and spent the day with him. While I was there I told him about this book, *The Martyrdom of Man* by Winwood Reade, that for me was like a breakthrough book. He kind of brightened up and said it was for him too. It had the same effect and he felt that it meant very much to him what it did to me. It gave me a terrific insight into him, to feel that influence in common with him.

But it was a fascinating book because it offered another point of view altogether on the evolution of Western civilization and how the Western and African and Asian civilizations overlapped in ways that our history books didn't cover at all. They weren't even aware of it.

14

THE TENTET
FURTHER EXPLORATIONS
WITH THE *BIRTH OF THE COOL*

DURING THE EARLY MONTHS of the quartet, I formed a tentet. The tentet was based on the nonet—the *Birth of the Cool* instrumentation—the main difference being that I added a saxophone, so I had two baritones. I had a baritone playing with the ensemble and I was freed up for more of a solo role or could do more things like the quartet: the trumpet and baritone, because that gave an extra dimension to the possibilities of arranging. The changes I made in it, I thought about making anyway with Miles if we had gone on with it. If that band had played other kinds of venues, if we had done theaters, and so on, we should have had a second trumpet anyway. And having a second baritone was a big, big orchestration advantage, which I didn't really have time to pursue to any great extent with what actually came out of the tentet. But the possibility was there. It really was a terrific moving voice to have in that. You know I would love to have had that with Miles. And what you can do with one baritone working with a tuba and one baritone working with a bone and horn, you know. Like all kinds of ways that it opens up the instrumentation. They really only could do it with a baritone.

I always felt that in the *Birth of the Cool* band we could have used a second trumpet. Miles was always able to carry that off, but he had his horn in his face a lot during the course of a night. You know, he'd play solos and he would play lead and he'd play backgrounds. It really is an awful lot for one player to do. So I wanted to split those chores. Also, at that point I didn't really know that much about Chet's ability to play in an ensemble, because there were always these rumors around that Chet couldn't read notes. I never talked to him about it and if I put a piece of music in front of him, he played it, and the same thing with the tentet. I put parts in front of him and he never had any trouble. So it's part of the legend that people put together about somebody; that even if someone never practices, and if they're a great player, you know they practiced at some point in their life. You don't get anything for nothing.

It wound up being that Capitol wanted to record it, and it was a very nice man that I met who came down to the Haig to talk about it. But he was a very ethical man and as it turned out, Gene Norman had said something to them even before talking to me about it. He went to Capitol and said that he'd like to record this tentet thing that I was talking about, and he'd like to record it for Capitol on their recording license.

Well, that being the case, the other producer didn't feel free to come down and have me record directly for Capitol, which was what he was about to do. So that was kind of a mix-up in a business way, and it became Gene Norman's production rather than Capitol's. I don't know how that affected the later evolution of the thing. I sometimes felt that we might have done another album if I'd done it directly for Capitol, but I don't know. There were too many other factors that ultimately got in the way.

This is one of the difficulties of doing things on my own. I'm good at starting things but it's very difficult for me to take care of all the details and see things through to their conclusion. So even getting that one album done was kind of a monumental task, putting it together. Doing a second one at the same time that I was getting rolling with this new quartet and working every night was not so easy to think about.

But that one album came out very well, and I've always been kind of pleased with that, especially keeping in mind that we didn't have the possibilities at that period of either over-dubbing or inter-cutting to any great extent. We didn't have much rehearsal time, and often there wasn't that much recording time. You know, I had a couple of three-hour sessions and I had a certain number of things that had to be done, so by God, they had to be done whether there were mistakes or not. And there are weak places and out-and-out mistakes in the playing in a few places that bug me when I hear it. I think mostly when people hear it, they don't probably see that there's anything wrong, so I had to let it go. I had no choice. You can't always be idealistic about those things if you want to get it done.

One of the lessons you learn as an arranger or composer, or a band-leader or soloist, is that everything costs money. Rehearsal time is a luxury; it costs money and that's why when I get into rehearsal, no matter who's paying for it, that's a luxury. You never see me wasting time schmoozing or hanging out. I'm always like nose to the grindstone. I think most professionals are that way because they know damn well how expensive it is and rehearsal time is the hardest thing to come by. I think the bigger the ensemble, the more expensive it is.

After a while, Chico got a call from Lena Horne, who wanted him to come back on the road with her. He had been part of her accompanying rhythm section before, and he needed to make more money. I mean, he could make a lot more money on the road with Lena Horne than he could playing at the Haig with a quartet in a small club who were paying peanuts.

He was very apologetic about it and sorry to do it but, you know, he had a wife and kids and responsibilities and home and family, so he had to take off. I was really upset with that. That was the beginning of a kind of rough period. I got very angry about that and ultimately I think what happened was I got so mad I tossed my horn across the room and stomped out of the place. Something very demonstrative, and that night driving home I was still fuming, and the streets were a little wet and some car pulled out in front of me. I hit the brakes too hard in my exuberance and they locked and the car slid into a light pole. When I realized what was happening and saw the light pole looming, I said, "Oh my God, I hope these electric wires don't land on the car." You know you see a replay of the last couple of weeks of your life.

Well, as it happened, I demolished the car and broke my nose and laid myself up for a while. They were all set to charge me with the cost of the electric light, but somebody had been on the sidewalk and had seen the thing and said this car had cut me off. So they decided I was the victim of a hit-and-run and I didn't have to pay for the lights, which was lucky. It was lucky that somebody was watching, because I wasn't.

So we needed a sub for me at the club because I couldn't play for a couple of weeks while my nose was healing, so we called up Stan Getz to help out. He came in and played with the band in my place for a couple of weeks, and you know, the thing with Stan, as I said, was always up and down. Somewhere around this time, probably after that, we got together because Stan had a group that was very much modeled on the quartet, you know, the contrapuntal relationship between the two horns, and the other horn with him was Bob Brookmeyer.

I remember we had a session, again I think it was at the house that Chet was renting, and the four horns were Chet, Stan, Bob, and me. What a great four-horn front line it was, and the four of us together were able to improvise ensemble things that were just wonderful. Then Stan tried to talk up the idea that we should go on the road and it should be his band. Brookmeyer and Chet and I looked at each other and kind of rolled our eyes. I guess we all decided we really didn't want to be in Stan's band. So that was the end of it, but musically it was too bad that we didn't at least make some records.

But the relationship with the four of us . . . I mean, you've got individuals who are, each one, wrapped up in his own ideas and ambitions and it's very difficult to put them together. And we didn't have anybody kind of helping with direction. If we didn't figure it out ourselves, it didn't get figured out. But it was something to remember—the four of us playing together.

What happened with Chet? Well, one of the things that happened at this point was because I was laid up, Stan used to make the announcement on the microphone at the club. He'd say he was taking my place because I was hurt in an accident and I broke my nose and they were having to do some plastic surgery on my nose. So he advised me, "Gerry, as long as you're getting a nose job, why don't you get a Jewish nose?" That was his introduction to subbing in the quartet, but he took my place and helped out for a while.

15

THE SHERIFF'S
HONOR FARM AND
GOODBYE CHET

WELL, BECAUSE THESE GUYS in Chet's pack were spending time at the house every night when we weren't there, the neighborhood sees all of these guys around and God knows, I guess they're playing music loud and smoking pot all over the place, and generally made it their own and making a mess. So I come home from the gig one night with Chet, and the police are there. The upshot of that whole thing was Chet, with his always riding the narcotics police and this gang hanging out, I got busted because it was my house. Everybody denied ownership of the pot, but it's my house so I got stuck. I wasn't any too pleased about that and I wound up being sent to the honor farm, which is part of the county jail system, for I guess ninety days or something, because Chet got himself a sharp lawyer. I had gotten a really rotten lawyer. He was really the reason I was in jail because he was so bad. I mean, he was so busy trying to impress the judge that he said, "Yes, I think it would be good for that boy to spend ninety days in jail!"

Then, of course, Chet had gotten himself a sharp lawyer who was very ready to blame it all on me because I was older. Chet with his damn running buddies. As soon as we left the house for work, they descended, eight or nine of them, who sat around smoking pot all night and the neighbors complained. That's how this whole thing exploded.

I unfortunately got a really dumb lawyer. So again it was my fault because I'm the older guy. I led him astray. Oh great, man! When I was first busted, they made a big fuss about it. But I don't think people pay much attention to that; one person's tragedy is another person's one-day news ingestion from the newspapers, and the next day it's something else again. It certainly was no circus like they did to Bob Mitchum. Luckily I was well-known in a particular area, and the people who were interested in music or interested in jazz knew about me from the club and all that, but nobody was paying attention to me. But it looked good for one day. You know: Jazz Musician Busted! That's certainly great for circulation for one day, isn't it? The one-day wonders.

The peculiarity was, finally, when all the smoke cleared, I found myself getting off the bus at this minimum-security compound in Castaic, California, or wherever the hell it was, somewhere up there. But it turns out that they were really waiting for me because there was a big kind of a battle going on about what the attitude should be in the state prison systems. There were people who were for punishment. That's what jail is for, punishment. And people who were care and treatment–oriented who would say that jail is for rehabilitation and trying to help these people adjust socially to being able to live in society.

I found myself caught in the middle of this because the care and treatment guys thought, well, I am a well-known musician and I could come up there and they've got a lot of musicians doing time for smoking pot, you know, so I can put together a show for them. It was perfect. I could put together a show for Christmas. They said, "Will you do it?" and I said, "Well sure, why not?"

They said, "Well, in order to do this, though, you have to go through at least a week or so with the labor gangs picking up rocks in the river-bed or something, because we can't put you right into this thing because the punishment guys will be angry about that." And they made me the head man in the dormitory so that I didn't have the same chores to do. I had chores to straighten up the place in the morning and then I could go off and write while the other guys had to do the labor details. Well, that created a lot of resentment from these guys and from one guard in particular. One guard was fighting for the care and treatment thing and these two guys were kind of in competition. The other guard was a mean bastard and he was just waiting for some kind of an opportunity to come down on me.

What happened was I started to work on this music for the show, and the role that I had in the dormitory building, the barracks building, was called mother: the mother of the barracks. Well, I was mother and the mothers were supposed to go eat earlier so that when the other inmates came over there to have breakfast, the mothers could straighten up the place, you know, so it all worked out. Well, one morning I show up late for breakfast and the guard who had been laying for me took one look, man, and off I went to maximum security. Oh Christ, what was I in the middle of. Maximum security was like being in San Quentin for God's sake, only it was overcrowded. There were three guys to a cell and they had this really horrendous thing, man. I'm telling you, it's an experience to go through because you realize what tens of thousands of people go through every day throughout the world. You know what it feels like to be penned up in a prison like that. It was a very hard learning experience and I feel sometimes that it would have driven me right out of my mind because you wake up every morning with lights on, I don't know, six or something like that. You have to roll up your beds, and the beds go up so you don't have anything to sit on. You're not allowed anything to read, you weren't allowed any writing materials, and they had music on all the time. It drove me crazy. It was pop music, kind of dreadful stuff. Luckily there were some pop tunes going then that weren't totally atrocious, but still, you never could get away from it.

One thing that saved my sanity at that point: there was a funny little Mexican guy in the cell with me, and he was one of these people who was just full of stories and he told stories endlessly. It was like being locked up with a Mexican raconteur. So he really made it possible to get through this. I wound up there for seventeen days.

Most of the guys I was around were in there for drug use. They segregated people. They had a homosexual compound—a barracks that had a fence around it and so they were kept to themselves. Next were the narcotics violators, and so on. I never paid enough attention to find out what everybody had done. It was none of my business, really. So most of the guys that I had any contact with also were in there for some kind of narcotics violations, maybe using or selling, one or the other. Of course the scene then wasn't anything like it is now. I mean, now it really feels like gangsterville all around, wherever you are. There is so much money involved. It wasn't like that then. It was kind of all pretty much amateur.

But that was a shock—getting out of maximum security. During the period that I was in maximum security, Gene Norman came up there once because he was a friend of the sheriff and he got permission to come up to see me. He was the only visitor I had when I was in max and, you know, not being allowed to read anything . . . it's not even punishment, it became torture. To take a civilized person and suddenly take everything away from him. It's like a musician's version of hell. Take everything away and play nothing but pop music for him. Great! It's a form of ongoing purgatory.

Gene came up with the idea of doing a concert in town. He wanted to come out and get me and bring me into town, and we would rehearse and play a concert downtown in the theater and get back in the car and bring me back up to maximum security. I said, "I don't think I want to do that. Thank you very much, I appreciate it, but no thanks." I could just see the advertisements for the thing: Like One Day Only! On leave from the Los Angeles penal system doing a one-nighter! The management has brought to you with great trouble and expense, fresh from a tour of Castaic, California!

In the meantime, Arlyne (Brown), who eventually became my first wife, had come out there to get a lawyer for me. She got an outfit called Narcotics Anonymous interested, and they realized that I had really gotten a dreadful lawyer. They used to talk about this lawyer and his brother, the different people he had represented, and the things that they did to him when they got out of jail, like putting sugar in the gas tank of cars. I remember reading in the paper while I was in there that the brother was beaten up by somebody. I could readily understand why, because he was just incredible. In order to make points, he was trying more to impress the judge with himself than he was trying to present my case, and the judge was a man they used to call a "hanging judge." He had put his own son in jail, who was caught joyriding in cars with some other teenage kids, and sent him to San Quentin. You know, like a first offense and not even truly auto theft, man; the kids were joyriding. He sent him to San Quentin, and the kid got in a fight and he was killed. So it was a terrible story and made one rightfully afraid of this judge's whims. But as it turned out, the judge was much more fair than one would realize, and when I found out after the fact what this lawyer had said to him, then I could understand what happened.

From there, because of Arlyne and this man who was a former police captain who had started Narcotics Anonymous, the things that they presented to the judge got my sentence modified to a short sentence, which mine was considered in any prison system, ninety days, man. They figure that's a drop in the bucket; six months was nothing.

Well, to me it was something. It seems if you're not institutionalized that seems like a long, long time, and I'm not institutionalized. So they got my sentence modified to time served, whatever I had served at that point. And all of the people in the place, including the guards and everybody else, figured that I wouldn't get modified because it was unheard of that anybody was modified on such a short sentence. But they came and got me out of maximum security and drove me into town to the hearing. Well, we were late getting to the hearing and by the time I got there, the hearing was over and I was free. So I was brought in from maximum security, man, and I was out of it. Just like night and day, the sun suddenly came up. Talk about shocks!

When I got out it was around Christmas. Arlyne and I were walking down Hollywood Boulevard, I guess that night, first night out, man, and walking around all bright-eyed and bushy-tailed and wouldn't you know it, walking toward us on Hollywood Boulevard is Chet Baker and some of his gang. Chet came up to us and I swear, he never said, "Hello," or "Gerry it's great to see you," or "Gerry, gee I didn't know that you were out," or anything. The first thing he said was, "Gerry, I've decided I've got to have three hundred a week," and I laughed. It was so outrageously off-the-mark and inappropriate. It just struck me as so funny that I laughed, and Chet never could figure out what I was laughing about. I tried to explain it to him but he could not understand. But in a funny way I kind of heaved a sigh of relief because, as much as it meant musically to have the group with Chet, I realized that being on the road with a group that was traveling by cars, I would be sweating blood all the time. Especially if Chet was driving, and even worse, if one of the guys were traveling with him.

I was able to get $1,250 a week for the band, and the expenses that I had to pay out of that were the commission to the agent, which was a minimum of 10 percent and often 15 percent, transportation costs, and the taxes and salaries, whatever that was. Well, by the time you get all this stuff added up, there's not a hell of a lot left. So that's why I was laughing. $1,250 for the band and Chet's asking for $300; it may have been $400. I'm sure it must have been $300, which in those days was a big salary. I mean, guys, the best-paid player in a band like Tommy Dorsey's or Harry James was $300 to $350 a week for a really great lead trumpet player. So that was a lot of money.

I was handling all the business myself; I had nobody else to do that. That's another thing: the leader, I guess, is just expected to do all that and take his time to do it and not get paid. If you got somebody else to do it, you'd have to pay him. But, I mean, if you've got a functioning organization it's got to be taken care of. That's one of the first lessons I learned around New York with guys trying to start bands. Buddy Rich had that problem. Poor Buddy started his band, and whoever was his business manager for the band deducted the withholding tax from the musicians' payrolls and never paid the money to the government. So the band wasn't even six or eight months old, and he owed the government hundreds of thousands of dollars.

So, man: pay the $2.00, whatever you do. When I figure a price like $1,250 for the band, that's not $1,250 of my money. Automatically, depending on what the tax scale was at that point, I would chop off a quarter from the top and figure that's the government's. $1,250, man, like $300 and something, knock off $300 to $350, that's taxes. Now you're talking about the money you've got to work with. And if you don't think like that, you're in big trouble. I always made sure the taxes were paid first, and always when I got accountants or business managers, I told them, "Don't be finagling around looking for the best deals, whatever the tax is supposed to be, pay it. Don't even think about it and don't be finding me any clever ways to avoid paying it because I don't believe in that." I carry my own weight as a citizen of the United States. I don't think anything is for nothing. This is the system they set up. I'll pay it, because anything else is a disaster.

You know it happened to Woody Herman, the same thing. The poor man, when he got to a point in his life when he wanted to retire, he couldn't because he owed so much money. The man was on his deathbed and the IRS had taken his house away from him.

That was a very important lesson and I've always stuck to that. To this day, if there's any question about something that an accountant can deduct, I say, "Don't play around with it." As a consequence, in all these years I've never had any trouble. I think maybe I've been audited once. My tax statements are always credible and they have a continuity to them, and obviously I'm not taking big deductions for anything. I never take illegal deductions and as a consequence they have left me alone. I'm knocking on wood while I'm saying that.

Not long after the exchange with Chet on Hollywood Boulevard, I started reorganizing the quartet and I'd decided I really was fed up with California, to the extent that I decided to get Brookmeyer to take Chet's place. I said, "Bring me a drummer and a bass player from New York." I was always doing dumb things like that because I flew them out to California, rehearsed, we played one date I think with them, and then got on a plane and flew back to New York again, except I drove because I bought a car, so I had to drive.

That was kind of the beginning of the end of my first marriage, because I remember very well driving back from California and we fought all the way. I don't know what the hell we were fighting about but we were just personalities totally unsuited to each other.

I've realized that in my relationships with people, the learning process that went on finally enabled me to become a person who could live with other people. I learned that life is not a one-way street and the whole idea of marriage is a cooperative venture. There are no rule books on it. You have to learn by giving and taking, and for me it was a long, long process to learn.

I think the thing that happened with Arlyne, my first wife, was that she wanted very much to help me and did help me, but we weren't able to help each other after the initial phase was over. When it came to living together and trying to function together, we just didn't know how to do it. I hate the idea of fighting but because I have a temper, it's easy for me to get angry at things. So it's like once you establish this atmosphere of war, it's like it never went away.

I'd met Arlyne in New York before coming to California. We were good friends there, and she was friends with a lot of the guys that I knew. She was kind of on that scene and had a lot of connections with the music scene in New York. She had been married previously to a musician, so she knew all the players with the bands and all that.

So I suppose that was how that came about. I probably called her up as one of the people . . . I needed somebody to commiserate with and that's how it came about; she came out and helped me out. But, as I say, with all the best intentions of helping, we didn't really know how to help each other. We stayed together for a few years—God, I guess it was five years—until our son was born. I tell you it was finally a case of leaving for the sake of the child. Usually people stay together for the sake of the child; I left for the sake of the child. Because of growing up in this atmosphere of tension, anger, and constant turmoil, the poor child was always with a rash and nervous and upset; it was just killing him. So, it couldn't work.

I remember her father one time—I kind of liked him even though he had sort of alienated everybody. He was a very, very well-known songwriter. He was Lew Brown, of DeSylva, Brown and Henderson. Lew was feisty all his life, always outspoken and apparently said a lot of things to people that he shouldn't have said to them. By the time I met him he was old. Well, he wasn't all that old, for that matter, but he was sick and much subdued, but lonely because he had driven everybody away.

I remember talking to him one time and he said, "You know, you should really think about it and try to get things straightened out with Arlyne because, after all, she'd fight the world for you." I said, "Lew, that's the problem: I don't want her to fight anything for me." Fighting is the whole problem. I don't want to fight. I don't want her to fight. And that's how that came about. It becomes part of a learning process of how to deal with living in the real world. You can't just spend your life with your horn in your mouth. If I could have kept my horn in my mouth, and kept my mouth shut, I would have been all right.

16

"WALKING SHOES"
LEAVING HOLLYWOOD

SO WE LEFT CALIFORNIA in 1954. We drove through to Boston, and the first engagement we had with the quartet was at Storyville. That's when I met George Wein and all his gang: George and Joyce and all of the people that worked with him all these years—Charlie Bourgeois. I really liked Storyville because it was a great club. It was almost like a dinner restaurant, very classy-looking on the first floor, the ground floor. It was a big room. Then downstairs in this hotel was another room, smaller, like an old wood, big saloon. And down there, he called that Mahogany Hall and had the traditional bands there. So we'd be playing upstairs, and downstairs would be, maybe, Jimmy McPartland and Vic Dickenson and Pee Wee Russell, and it was always like that. We met all these wonderful guys and used to have a grand time in the place. It was just a wonderful atmosphere.

I was never concerned about the acceptance of the new group. For whatever reason, people responded very well to it, and it was kind of an instant acceptance wherever we went. Brookmeyer fit right in. A lot of the stuff was written in the lowest register of the trumpet, so there wasn't really even the transposition problem on a lot of things. Brookmeyer was always conscious of the fact that we had to deal with the two low voices rather than having the high voice, so we tried to compensate for that in certain ways and mostly it worked. The thing is that it wasn't just a replacement for Chet, it was a different band. It was a good enough band that people accepted it on its own terms, and there was never any real comment about Chet not being there. It

(Left to right) Ben Webster, Earle Warren, Lester Young, Gerry Mulligan, 1957.
PHOTO BY MILT HINTON

(Left to right) Jimmy Cleveland, Gerry Mulligan, Bill Crow, Art Farmer, 1956.
COURTESY GERRY MULLIGAN COLLECTION, LIBRARY OF CONGRESS, MUSIC DIVISION

Gerry at a television studio, NYC, 1957.
PHOTO BY MILT HINTON

Gerry and Art Farmer, 1970s.
© FRANCA R. MULLIGAN

Gerry and Mel Torme, 1978.
© FRANCA R. MULLIGAN

to gerry

Ed Koch

Gerry with NYC Mayor Ed Koch and Benny Goodman, 1979.
COURTESY GERRY MULLIGAN COLLECTION, LIBRARY OF CONGRESS, MUSIC DIVISION

Hollywood mural by Richard Wyatt, 1990.
© FRANCA R. MULLIGAN

Gerry in Italy on Franca's home tennis court, 1976.
© FRANCA R. MULLIGAN

(Left to right) Zubin Mehta, Gerry Mulligan, Roger Kellaway, Jacob Druckman, and Earl Brown, New York Philharmonic concert, 1989.

Gerry in Milano, Italy, 1980s.

(Left to right) Joe Williams, Gerry Mulligan, Clark Terry, and Dizzy Gillespie at the White House, 1970.

© MILT HINTON

(From left to right) Jon Newson, James Billington, guest, Scott Robinson, Franca R. Mulligan, The Venerable Thamthog Rimpoche, Lodi Gyaltsengyari, special envoy of His Holiness The Dali Lama, inaguaration ceremony of the permanent exhibit of the Gerry Mulligan Collection at the Library of Congress, 1999.

COURTESY GERRY MULLIGAN COLLECTION, LIBRARY OF CONGRESS, MUSIC DIVISION

NEW YORK PHILHARMONIC

AVERY FISHER HALL
LINCOLN CENTER FOR
THE PERFORMING ARTS

ONE HUNDRED FORTY-EIGHTH SEASON 1989-90

ZUBIN MEHTA, *Music Director*

HOME OF THE NEW YORK PHILHARMONIC

Thursday Evening, December 14, 1989, at 8:00
Friday Afternoon, December 15, 1989, at 2:00
Saturday Evening, December 16, 1989, at 8:00
Tuesday Evening, December 19, 1989, at 8:00

11,452nd, 11,453rd, 11,455th
and 11,456th Concerts

Zubin Mehta, *Conductor*

GERRY MULLIGAN, *Saxophonist*
THE GERRY MULLIGAN QUARTET
(New York Philharmonic Debut)
Bill Charlap, *Piano*
Dean Johnson, *Doublebass*
Richard De Rosa, *Drums*
Gerry Mulligan, *Saxophone*

BEETHOVEN	Overture to "Fidelio"*
BEETHOVEN	Symphony No. 4, B-flat major, Opus 60*

    I Adagio; Allegro vivace
    II Adagio
    III Menuetto: Allegro vivace
    IV Allegro ma non troppo

Intermission

MULLIGAN	"Entente" for Baritone Saxophone and Orchestra

Works by the Gerry Mulligan Quartet

MULLIGAN	"K-4 Pacific"

*Recorded by the New York Philharmonic and currently available.

New York Philharmonic Program: Gerry Mulligan and the Gerry Mulligan Quartet with the New York Philharmonic.

Franca and Gerry wedding party (left to right): Dave Grusin, Gerry, and Franca.
© HANK O'NEAL

would have been nice to have had Chet during those early years, but I think the personal problems outweighed the practicality of it and I was afraid, really afraid, to have him on the road. I guess I had cause to be after all the things that had happened.

We started playing clubs around the East and Midwest and we were working all the time. Then we did what was the second and last Paris International Jazz Festival for Charles Delaunay. That was the first time to Europe. We took off from La Guardia in a Constellation and landed in Paris. It was a long trip, probably ten or twelve hours. We had played in a club in Atlantic City the week before, and there was an air conditioner blowing right on us the whole time. By the time we landed I wound up with a terrible head cold. So I'm taking this flight with a head cold. The plane was in sight of Paris and I could look out the window and see it. Well, it was like we dove into the airport. Man, we didn't come down gradually, we just dove down. By the time the plane got on the ground, I was writhing in agony with head pains from the cold and from the change in pressure, and they had to go and get a doctor for me. I was in terrible shape.

So we get to the hotel, and by this time, I don't know, something had happened and the guys were all mad. They were angry at everything. It was Brookmeyer and Red Mitchell and Frank Isola on drums, and they were mad. I don't even know what happened but it was one of those things, it was just chaos when we got there. It was like nobody was taking care of business and my guys got upset about it, and they present themselves and here I am with this head that's killing me. They present themselves in my hotel room and quit. *En masse* they quit.

I said, "Wait a minute, you guys. What do you mean you quit? We just got here!" and they said, "No, this is too rough, we quit!" I said, "Well all right, you quit. Go ahead!" They said, "We want our tickets." I said, "I'll give you your money back in the States, man; take me to the union. You're quitting here, that's it."

Finally, they came down off that and realized that I wasn't about to give them their tickets to take off and go back to the States. I don't even have any idea what they were upset about, and anyway I didn't care because I was in such pain from the thing I was going through. The other thing was that as we got off the plane, man, I'm staggering around with somebody holding me up on each side. When we got inside the airport, Thelonious Monk was there. He had been on our plane too. He's really nervous about playing this thing and was saying, "Well, you know, nobody here is going to be listening to me; they don't like me and I don't want to go play this." So, I told him, "Monk, listen, I'll be listening to you. When you're on stage you look over to the side and I'll be in the wings." He said, "Well, all right." And so I was there; whenever he played, I went and stood in the wings and made him feel better because he had a bad case of the lonelies.

We finally got all of that stuff ironed out and played a concert in Paris that first day. The next day we got on a train and it was an eight-hour trip to Basel to go play a concert there. Well, I was still miserable with this cold and fever and sweating and all that. When we got to Germany, I asked if we could get a doctor to give me a shot of something, even a narcotic, to cut down the shakes and the sweating constantly. But nobody from our party spoke German. And they couldn't find a doctor who spoke English or French, but they found a German-speaking doctor. They didn't understand each other at all. This guy gave me a shot of something that turned out to be adrenaline. So when I went on stage to play, my clothes were, literally, wringing wet. Every inch of my suit was soaked. You could take the sleeve and wring it out and get a puddle. I swam through the concert. I didn't play that concert, I swam it. But of such things are experiences made.

It was just a cold, and you know the worst thing you can do with a head cold is to take it into changes of pressure. I'm lucky; I don't think I did any permanent damage to my ear. I think that the hearing loss I have in my left ear was from the time I spent in front of Gene Krupa's bass drum. Now that I think of it, maybe it was that trip because it was horrendous and I didn't do any checking on my hearing at that point, so I don't know. But it's certainly not the best thing to do for your ears.

After Paris I began a long relationship with the Newport Jazz Festival. It started with the first one, which took place in the middle of the town at the Newport Casino. It was really quite a show because we had people like Peggy Lee, Billie Holiday, Stan Kenton, and so on. One thing I remember very well. While I was playing, somebody got into the place and stole Gil Melle's baritone and my saxophone case. Luckily, I was on stage playing so I didn't lose my horn; strange goings-on. Actually, that's one of the few times something was stolen from me at a place where I was working.

But Newport over the years was a lot of fun, especially in the early years. Musically it was a lot of fun. The whole idea of the Newport Jazz Festival was really Elaine Lorillard's baby. She had the idea and was really the moving spirit behind it. In those early years, she used to have big parties after the concerts were over. We had jam sessions and I'd find myself on stage with Coleman Hawkins and Vic Dickenson and kind of an unbelievable collection of players. I used to have a really good time musically there with them. I was always the lucky one in that department because I like to play all kinds of different ways with all kinds of different people. So George was always putting me with different groups that were maybe far away from the style of my band or the idiom that I was known for, and I loved to do that. But the thing was that we would go up there and spend three or four days. We'd be there from beginning to end and you wouldn't just play once at the show that you were on, but do other things, and it was also a great time for the musicians to spend time together that they don't normally get to do. We had time to spend together and hang out and talk about ideas, and I'd also rehearse new stuff with my groups, or guys would get together with musicians they wanted to do something with but wouldn't have time otherwise. They'd get together and rehearse and play. So in that way it was wonderful, and losing that really loses the meaning of festival and what the festival idea can give back to music, because now what it is, the festival takes from music and presents it, but it doesn't really give anything back. We're all on a treadmill and it's hard to conceive of where it goes in the future because the scene has changed so much. The people who were the prime movers of the festivals for all those years are dying off. We had people like Ellington and Basie there as regular performers, and Louis and

Mahalia Jackson and all of our groups; MJQ and Dave Brubeck. Well, as it happened, we're still around; we weren't the prime movers but we were there too. So we all enjoyed the outlet, but there was a tremendous spirit in these places. Jazz now is, in a way, much more commercialized in its presentation. The record companies are always trying to get their jazz into the charts and sell more records. I understand all that, but they become stylized in the process of doing that; relate jazz more to the pop music of the day and you'll sell more. So jazz naturally becomes more rock-oriented and you lose its connections.

So those early years of Newport were the kinds of years that showed great promise of what we expected the future to hold: the possibilities of getting things together and the opportunity to get musicians together, the give and take of natural social relationships. Of course I spent a lot of time with Paul Desmond. He was always a bad influence on me. I'd wind up hanging out with him and regretting it for days because I always drank too much when he was around to try to keep up with him, which of course I couldn't do. We were always doing nutty things. We'd get ourselves loaded drinking all night and hang out and thought we were having a ball, and wake up in the morning in a car and say, "What the hell are we doing here?" One time I woke up in my hotel room and he was sleeping in my closet, but the demon rum was my undoing, and his, too, I guess.

17

PRESENTING THE GERRY MULLIGAN SEXTET

I HAD THE QUARTET with Brookmeyer for a while and then formed a sextet. I don't remember what the impetus was to bring it about, but we played a couple of concerts in California, and I decided that I wanted the four-horn front line. Bob and I both liked the idea of that because it gave us more possibilities, and Zoot wanted to do it, and as long as I could have Zoot on tenor, then it was a good idea. I would really not have been as interested to do it if Zoot couldn't have made it. In my early years in New York, in order to defray expenses, I often shared a furnished place with one of my friends, and usually it was a tenor player. I used to share a place a lot with Brew Moore, and then later on Zoot and I were roommates. So we were buddies from way back. We spent a lot of time together when we weren't out working. To have a band, and Zoot with it, was like having my own family on the road.

I was always stuck for a trumpet player because it took me a long time to fill that chair because, ideally, it should have been Chet. I really needed somebody who played that style, and it was very, very hard to come by. And the guys that wound up playing for me didn't really play that style, but they played good and they found a function for themselves in the ensemble. So the band had its own individual approach.

We wound up doing a pair of high school concerts in California. It kind of tickled me because Dave Brubeck had his *Jazz Goes to College* album, so naturally I had to call it *Jazz Goes to High School*. We played up the coast at Stockton and then a date in San Diego. In Stockton we did a quartet date, and I think Chico came up to do that with us. It was kind of in a shifting period, I don't remember why it was, but it wound up—I had Chico on the thing, or at least part of it, and I think I had changed bass players then, too. I think Red Mitchell rejoined me. I remember we recorded that stuff, and then afterward Red didn't want me to put it out because he was trying steel strings for the first time and he didn't like the sound. I said, "Wait a minute, I can't not put this out because you don't like the sound of your strings." He was very put out with me because I went ahead and put it out. I said, "You may be very conscious of the sound of those strings and you don't like it, but I can't hear it. You sound like yourself to me and I have to put this out because, other than that problem you've got with your strings, man, there's no other problem with this album."

So it wound up, in one night, we did one of my favorite totally improvised pieces; Brookmeyer had left for some reason and I got Jon Eardley on trumpet. Then what was happening at this point is that Brookmeyer was going to rejoin me for the sextet with Zoot and Jon was going to be the trumpet player for it. So that's why there was all the shifting going on with the personnel.

But we did this thing in Stockton and we had this program laid out that we were going to do, and the people were late getting in, they really were. The place was only about half full and people were pouring in. In the meantime, we found ourselves on stage with an audience that wasn't ready. They were like fifteen minutes late. They probably thought it was an eight-thirty show or something. So I said, "Well I guess I'll play some blues while you get seated," and we started playing this thing and it just worked out. It was beautiful. It was called "Blues Going Up," and it was all kinds of devices that we started doing between the trumpet and the baritone line and the bass. The whole thing kept moving up and up and up, and it was one of those improvised gems that happens usually when there's no tape machine going. I mean, it will happen periodically with a band, especially like mine, where so many of the interesting things that happen are dependent on spontaneous combustion. So on this we finally got one on record and the whole way it came about was just so offhand, and it sounds totally worked out from beginning to end.

Then, two nights later, we went to San Diego and had a bit of a rehearsal to get some music together, and it was the first thing we did where we featured the sextet. There were things I did with three horns and things where Brookmeyer was playing piano. It was actually a good program and it worked out well.

From there we went back and put the sextet together, and I toured and worked with that for a couple of years. We used to play all kinds of things. We played a lot of concerts. The band was great in the theaters because we'd start out with the four horns in the center of the stage. As the tunes progressed, and as the evening progressed, we'd start spreading out and by the end of the night, we'd be across the front of the stage, each of us with a spot. We really spread all the way across. I would be on one end, and five feet away would be Zoot and five feet away would be Eardley and five feet away would be Brookmeyer. And the band would fill these places up. It sounded like a big ensemble just blowing our heads off. We never planned it like that, it just evolved. It turned out to be a tremendously effective presentation and a wonderful thing to be able to stand at the front of the stage and blowing out into the theater so the sound of the band was all reflected inside the shell of the theater and not depending on amplification, nothing, man, and it just sounded immense.

We also worked clubs and all kinds of stuff. We worked a club that was right across the city line of Baltimore, in the county. This place was so funny because it was a place that was kind of unlikely to be a jazz club, and quite possibly it didn't feature jazz all the time. I have no idea. I don't remember the name of the place or anything. We drove up and this big sign out front, says, "Tonight Gerry Mulligan Sextet featuring Brooks Meyer and Soot Zims." Too bad we didn't get a picture of that. "Soot Zims"; nobody ever dreamed of that as a nickname in all the novels I ever read about jazz musicians, or movies where the poor trumpet player has to play one more high note before he dies. Nobody ever dreamed up the nickname Soot. I said, "Well this is an original, man, really worthwhile. Soot Zims and Brooks Meyer, that romantic zinger of zongs." Zinger of zongs did I say?

Gerry Mulligan Sextet (left to right): Bill Grow, Oliver Beener, Zoot Sims, Bob Brookmeyer, Dave Bailey, Gerry Mulligan.
COURTESY GERRY MULLIGAN COLLECTION, LIBRARY OF CONGRESS, MUSIC DIVISION

It reminds me, one night they were doing a radio remote with the Stan Kenton band. They had one of these announcers who was a real radio announcer and talked in that kind of pseudo hip, poetic way, and he said, "Now for this next number, the musical question 'Why Was I Born' is going to be asked by the lovely Kai Winding, the lovely Kai Winding," he said. I guess he couldn't resist that, "The lovely Kai Winding steps mic-side and asks the musical question, '*Why, why am I here?*'"

We did two or three albums with the sextet, and I got in kind of bad with Mercury at that point. I had signed with Mercury previously and then let the contract run out because what happened was, a band goes through life cycles because a band can't keep playing week after week after week after week and have the same level of creativity. There has to be highs and lows. So with that band I could feel it, you know. I'd say, "Okay, this is going to be a slow week. It'll be all right. It's there, but it's not on fire." And maybe a week would go by, and by then I'd hear it was starting to get back again and I kept after the record company. I said, "Man, I need to record next week."

They'd say, "Okay, okay, okay, next week," and comes next week when the band is hot I'd say, "Okay, when is the studio time and we'll get in there." And they'd say, "Oh, we can't do it this week, we're recording Maynard Ferguson," and I blew my stack, man, because, you know this kind of frustration I didn't need. As a consequence, the records often are not an indication of what the band was really like. It's only an indication of the music and the possibilities. Man, when that band was on fire, it was really something. In other words, any kind of group that can transcend its own limitations, then you've got something special and that's what would happen with that. The band was of a caliber and did the kinds of things in concert that did transcend the limitations of the instrumentation of four horns and two rhythm.

It was frustrating as hell not to be able to get that onto a record. There were some records we did that did have enough of it there, so I'm not totally frustrated. But a lot of the stuff was the best we could do in studio circumstances. You could say, it's okay, it's terrific, but it's not great and like so many things, you have to live with it, you have no choice.

I was enjoying good success and not only were we doing good gigs and getting better money for it, but other things had opened up too. You know, the agents, the booking agents, really missed the boat on the demand for the modern jazz groups in college. So many schools would call up Joe Glaser's office or one of the other booking agents that were then handling our groups, and they just kind of ignored it, fluffed it off. It happened, Dave Brubeck told me, at one point it finally happened that these people at various schools would come to him and say, "Listen, we've been trying to get your group to come play a concert but the agents don't pay any attention to us."

So Dave started booking this stuff himself directly, saying, "Contact me directly, and go right around the agents." If you have an exclusive contract, you'd still have to pay a commission to them, but at least we'd get the dates. And because schools did that with Dave and Dave made the effort to do it, it started to open up the school market. Well, I found out even after that, that schools and various universities and colleges around the country had been in touch with ABC, Joe Glaser's office, my agency, and Dave's, to play concerts at their schools, and they ignored them.

Now the reason for ignoring them, more than anything, was that Joe had an interest in a lot of the clubs around the country, and he also had an interest in keeping the rest of the clubs busy. So if my band is a good drawing attraction in these clubs, he wants me to go service those clubs, he doesn't want me off on college campuses, which I found to be to our detriment. I wanted to play the college concerts and I thought it was really kind of rotten of them and a lot of the practices of agents, especially Joe.

Joe did a thing in Chicago that just spoiled it for all the clubs. Frank Holstein had a club out there called the Blue Note. He'd had this club for years, and he was a man who all of the musicians liked. He was really a nice man and very considerate, and he loved the musicians and he made life pleasant while they were there. They really treated musicians well, which was not always the case. You go to a lot of places and you're treated, in the hierarchy of things, just below the busboys. So you learn those places and if you can build yourself enough of a reputation, you don't go back. Or places like the Basin Street East in New York. I took the Big Band in there one time and they said, "Well, the band has to come in through the kitchen." I said, "No, they don't. If you think the band's coming in through the kitchen, then you get yourself another band." I wasn't having any of that.

During this period the multipackage concert tour scene evolved. It was kind of like topsy, it just grew. After the success of Newport when it was in Rhode Island, various people got the brainstorm of taking these shows out and touring the country with them. That was a success, too, and I was on some of those, every year that they did it. They could have been an even bigger success but they all wound up going out at the same time every year. If one show had gone out in the month of August, another show had gone out in December, and another had gone out in March, it might have developed into a kind of market, like building an audience. Unfortunately, it didn't work out like that. The first year there were a couple of shows. I wound up in shows with Duke's band, so it would be Duke Ellington, my quartet, and Dave Brubeck. One year it was Stan Getz and his group and another year it was the Australian Jazz Quintet. I mean, that's a loaded show. It was too long and too loaded! A group like mine gets to play a half-hour or twenty minutes, the same thing for Dave, and to try to get Duke to play three-quarters of an hour or an hour or something, I mean, you can't do it. So just mechanically, it didn't work. But they were successful shows and usually went way over time.

Then there'd be another show out with us at the same time and they were hitting the same cities often in the same week, or within a two-week period. Then also, Norman had Jazz at the Philharmonic out and the second show may be Count Basie. Then they'd have a Birdland group with Zoot and Al or somebody and Sarah Vaughan or Billy Eckstine.

They did all right in the first couple of years, but then, of course, the profits of one would eat into the profits of the other. You can't do it all at the same time. People don't have the time and they don't have the money to do all of this stuff, nor do they want to dedicate their lives to going to all of these shows. I mean, I'm going to see Duke and all these

Gerry and Sarah Vaughan on tour, 1979. COURTESY GERRY MULLIGAN COLLECTION, LIBRARY OF CONGRESS, MUSIC DIVISION

guys on Tuesday and I'm going over to see Count and all those people on Thursday. Forget it.

So by about the third or fourth year of these things, there were four shows out that included most of the big names. We were all out on shows at the same time and it killed it. The last year of them, in order to protect his show, Norman brought our show. That was Duke and Dave and me. So he tried to route them in ways that we would be separated, and in ways to give our show a breather so we wouldn't show up in the same towns with these other people.

Well, there are only so many cities and so many halls and, wouldn't you know it, we wound up in Kansas City, where they've got an auditorium that's got two theaters back to back. On this side of the stage is Duke Ellington's band set up doing our show and we had a pretty good crowd. It wasn't full by any means. We had maybe a thousand or twelve hundred people. In the theater on the other side was Count Basie and his show, and they had about seventy-five people in the audience. Well, that show closed that night, that was the end of their thing, and for the rest of us that was the end of the whole thing of touring.

All these guys milked the thing dry. It's not as if they ever could get together and talk about it and say, "Listen, we've got a good thing going here. It will be good for the music and it will be good for the audience. Let's pace it in a way so that throughout the year we can service the audience by bringing them these shows and not kill the goose that laid the golden egg." Well, they did kill the goose that laid the golden egg. It took them four years to do it, and that was the end of the touring show in this country, the touring jazz show as a success. Any attempts after that have been mostly failures. So instead of that came the jazz festival syndrome.

The festivals today are not true festivals. They're big productions where, again, in most cases the music is kind of separated from the atmosphere. It's like the music is an excuse for putting on this big money-making circus. That's maybe kind of an oversimplified and cruel way to look at it, but they are hard work.

In the early days of the festivals in Newport, there was another element involved. We were going off to kind of an isolated town where the focus of the town was on this production and we were there for a few days. So the musicians came in and we had time to spend together. We talked to each other. We did things together. We'd get together and have jam sessions and, in that way, just because of the connections that the musicians could make because they had time together, something came out of it. Well, that at least is the spirit of the festival. This is what it's supposed to be. There has to be some focus on the music and all the things that went on around it: the symposia; the little afternoon demonstrations or unknown bands; it was all of these things bringing it together, even to the point where there was a counter-festival where Mingus and Max did another thing in another part of town. It was great!

It was really great and there was idealism about the music, and if there was confrontation, man, the thing that came out of the confrontation was some understanding and music that meant something. But most festivals are not like that. Most festivals are big promotions. The musicians don't have any contact with each other, and logistically they're killers. You come in, you do your tap dance, you get off, you maybe even get a chance to say hi to the people who were on ahead of you, but there's no contact so nothing comes out of it. There's no creative aspect for the musicians themselves, especially where jazz is concerned. If you're not putting something back into the music, then you're helping to kill it, and this kind of festival that we have these days doesn't really put anything back. It's work, and for that we can be grateful, because most of the other ways of making big money in jazz are gone in this country. If it were left to the American promoters, man, jazz would have died on the vine a long time ago. The only thing that saved us were people like George Wein and the other people putting on the festivals. They filled the gap.

So whatever I feel is the lack where music is concerned in relation to this whole festival syndrome; on the other hand is the idea that they've kept some interest going and they've kept going the ability to get to an audience that exists. I feel like the audience has always been there, but getting to them through the morass of pop music is very difficult. We can't get there through the radio, we can't get there through the television, so how do you do it? We're the poor sisters of the music business, something that's an amazing development to the Europeans and Japanese when they come over here, because they love the music and to them it's something important.

They come over here and see the American Music Awards and they look down the line and say, "Okay, who's in it?" And they don't even mention jazz. It's not there and they say, "It's American music, did we miss something here?" There seems to be something amiss.

18

ADDICTION
AND TREATMENT

AFTER GAIL AND I SPLIT UP, I started to get back into the bad old habits with heroin. Not ever to the extent that I had been involved in New York, but still enough that it was an ongoing thing and it was time-consuming and constant. At that point, I was in California of course; I started to look for some kind of medical help, which was very hard to come by. If you have a problem, then you always are on the lookout for somebody with a cure. You constantly hear about cures for drug addiction or alcohol addiction or whatever; of course, they seldom worked. One of the results of this was that doctors and psychiatrists were very loathe to treat any addicts, anybody who was a user of drugs, because they were afraid they would get in trouble. They would lose their licenses. Police could accuse them of anything they wanted. As a consequence, it became very difficult to get any kind of effective treatment for addiction.

I went to a number of doctors in Los Angeles and always got the same answer; it was kind of amazing. If I stopped using for six months then they would consider taking me on as a patient. I said, "If I could stop using this stuff for six months I wouldn't be here, I wouldn't need you." So it was a stalemate.

Well, when I got back to New York after the rest of my stay in Los Angeles, with all of the adventures that were inherent in that period, I still kept up my search for a psychiatrist and finally, through a doctor friend, was introduced to a man named Bill Haber. Bill was very helpful and willing to take me on as a patient and wasn't worried about the consequences, because he felt that what he was doing was more important. His attitude was that we would try it. Because for him, to take on a . . . well, let's put it this way; he had doubts about taking on a creative person as a patient because one of the fears of psychiatrists was, if they mess around to cure the emotional problems of a creative person, they might just cure them out of their creativity and they don't want to be responsible. Not only him, but other psychiatrists too. Well, it makes sense, because a lot of the time the creative urge finds an outlet, and is forced to find an outlet because of the frustrations involved in whatever the emotional problems are. You know, it's the release of the storms of the emotions.

He decided to take it on and try it, and he didn't make any kind of a demand that I had to stop using beforehand or anything of the sort. So I started in with him, probably two or three sessions a week, and a lot of those sessions I would go in and sit. He was very much based in the Freudian system, it was kind of a modified Freudian system; I think a lot of the psychiatrists then were. But it involved the psychiatrists occasionally asking questions. They weren't going to answer you anything. If they were going to tell you anything, you've got to figure it out for yourself, which is the whole idea. And a lot of the times I went and I'd work with him for a while and I'd fall asleep. This went on and on and on.

He said that he wasn't worried about that. He thinks that even when I'm sleeping we're making progress, you know, so that after a year or so it started to have an effect and I made the first attempt again to put myself in some kind of a hospital or a clinic. It was up in the city, near the river, north of New York. I really disliked it there a lot. So I didn't last long, a few days, and then I left and went back to my old ways.

Finally, I suppose it was after a couple of years, and I had gone out on the road and taken a group out. One of the guys that was playing with us on this trip wanted to try heroin. Well, I tried to talk him out of it, I wanted nothing to do with it. So I didn't. Anyway, he got it and he came back to the hotel and turned himself on and proceeded to pass out. Well, I'd had some experience with guys passing out and I must say that, between Zoot and me, we saved the lives of a lot of guys because we worked on them until we revived them.

There was one time in particular, we gave artificial respiration for about eight hours straight to keep him going, and we saved him. One time we had trouble doing it; we'd call an ambulance, whatever it meant. I never could understand that thing. There were cases of musicians that I knew that other guys had let die because they were too stupid to know what to do, or they were too afraid to call an ambulance, and we lost a couple of very good musicians that way. Anyway, this time I wound up spending the night giving this player artificial respiration.

The next day I'd simply had it. I didn't want anything more to do with any of it. I called the agent; we were in Detroit and we were supposed to go to Chicago next. I called the agent and said, "You cancel out Chicago; I'm not going and don't book me with this group anymore. If you want me, I'll be in the hospital." I put myself in a place in New York for a couple of weeks and that was it. It was a slow process of getting through my own emotional turmoil and whatever the collection of things were that made reality so unbearable that heroin was the desirable agent of forgetfulness.

It's one of those things that's turned into such a problem in this country, but with such a lack of understanding of what it's all about, that it's heartbreaking to see what's happening now. To see that the people don't want to ever face the realities that are contained in it. We have this kind of belligerent stance toward the world, and we think that we can be everything by making it a war. So the war on drugs should have some kind of effect on drug use and controlling drugs or eliminating drugs, whatever they think they're going to do.

Of course, the opposite is true, and one of the other qualities that we have as a nation, that's built into our psyche because of the Puritan background that was the foundation of some of the early colonies, is that you can legislate morality. That you can forbid something, and by forbidding it you're going to exclude it, you're going to eliminate it.

We had the example of Prohibition, which was a total failure. We never as a people want to face the failure of Prohibition, face that the failure was in the passage of Prohibition in the first place. The idea that by prohibiting the sale of alcohol, that you can eliminate alcohol, but the reality was quite something else. The drive for the prohibition of alcohol began, or had its first showing in this country, before it was the United States. It was still the colonies. There were people who were trying to get legislation to prohibit the manufacture and sale of alcohol. And all through the nation's history into the twentieth century, people, various groups, tried to pass laws that would forbid alcohol, and they were never successful. What happened in the twentieth century was they figured out what was missing and they injected the profit motive, and then we had Prohibition.

A very interesting novel that Richard Condon wrote—by the way, I met him once with Max Youngstein. I went to Max Youngstein's apartment and Richard Condon came in. I was in awe of him because he was such a great writer. This novel, called *Mile High*, was kind of—I bought it in paperback when it was already years old—it felt like kind of a throwaway for him, but in it he put forward this theory that sounded enough like, hinted at, truths, to engage my imagination. I always felt that this was in some way related to what really happened. The organized criminals in this country, after they were firmly established and started making the social climb up the ladder, sent their kids to the good schools—to Harvard business school, to Pennsylvania, to Wharton business school—and these kids were learning the best of current business school practice. They'd get out of school and their awareness of the economy was on a whole different level than their fathers and grandfathers.

So in this book of Condon's, some bright youngster, fresh out of Harvard Business School, has the idea that this could be a great idea. That Prohibition could be a great idea and the only thing that was missing was the profit motive. Now if you can inject the profit motive, he should be able to carry it off, and the underworld should be able to profit by it for at least a few years before the people got smart enough to see what was going on. So they were able to get, of course, the temperance people, the puritans who were already against the idea of drinking. They were easy to recruit and if you were going to put money to their various movements, they were delighted to get it. They didn't really care where they got it from.

On the other hand, he proposed to a group of businessmen his idea of seven or eight business tycoons making a proposition that sounds like you're doing something for the country, because you're trying to help people. Keep protecting people from themselves, you know. So each of these tycoons was supposed to put up a million dollars. That means they had seventeen or eighteen million dollars in seed money to work with. Depending on whether he was dealing with an unscrupulous business-man or the kind that was hiding behind his veil of glee, he was able to con all of these people.

Then, what they did, they bought up the output of the French vine-yards, the Scottish distilleries, and whatever other thing that they could use, Canadian whiskey and so on, and proceeded to buy it up and rent warehouse space along the borders of the United States and the borders of Canada and on the seacoast. They went into the business of selling speedboats, you know, like dealers in trucks. They would make small loans to the guys to buy trucks and speedboats. They went into business, the small loan business, for trucks and all of the equipment you needed, plus hiring people, your staff, the training to run the speedboats, the trucks, the whole thing.

They get this whole structure working and now they've gone to work on the legislators because now they've got all of these temperance people working together and they're getting along. Of course, a lot of the young men were away at the war and that helped. So one thing or another, before long, they managed to not just get a law against it but they put it in the Constitution. This is the strange part, man, to mess around with the Constitution on this level. That's what's going on today; they can't just pass a law about some kind of thing about balancing the budget, they want to change the Constitution. This mind-set is so peculiar.

So they got the thing passed and it went into effect. They never thought that they could make it last for a few years. Of course, it was an unenforceable law. People were ambiguous about it. Most of the people didn't take it seriously, but what it did was, it made for a new kind of power structure in the law enforcement part of the society. So it was a boon to the people who outfit and supply police and to the police departments. You had to have bigger police departments. It was a boon to the lawyers because they all of a sudden found themselves with a whole lot of work that they wouldn't have had otherwise.

Of course, the greatest boon of all was to the underworld. Because what happened was, even though, or maybe essentially because of, it was an unenforceable law and people didn't believe in it and it was that kind of thing. It was like the morality that you wear on your sleeve that you give lip service to because it seems like you're supposed to. You're not a good person if you're not for Prohibition. The same thing is going on today. People are denying the obvious in order to appear to be something that they're not. So the one thing it did was give a terrific capital base to the underworld so that they were able to buy their way into what we laughingly would call legitimate business. Establish themselves in the economy, and the culture of this country, in a way where we'll never get rid of them. This was their entrée to Prohibition.

Now we've seen the same spectrum happening with drugs, except it makes the kind of money that was made in the 1920s seem like a pittance in comparison. Probably the underworld was able to clear themselves about maybe eight billion dollars for the whole period. And it ran longer than they thought because it was nearly ten years, through the 1920s. What's happened now is we've seen the specter of whole countries being taken over by the drug lords, and these people are making a billion dollars in a week, not in a couple of years. You never get rid of them. And you certainly will never get rid of them treating the thing as a war.

We're stuck with the misapprehension, and of course it's very disheartening, because if anybody that's connected with government even suggests that there are other ways to pass laws and build jails, they're immediately ridiculed and often run out of office. And it locks us into a way of thinking that's self-destructive. All that's going to happen is it gets worse and worse and worse. Our cities are cesspools and there are countries in South America that have been totally ruined. I mean, if you take the drugs away, they will collapse anyway because they would have no economies. Their whole economy has been geared to drug production and drug sales.

So in my case, I was lucky to find a psychiatrist who would take me on and I stuck with him. You know, the odd thing is, I don't remember when I started with him and I don't remember how long I was with him. It just became a part of my life, and Bill Haber is one of the people that I've always credited and have been thankful for saving me yet again. As I tell my own story, it's kind of obvious that my life has been saved so many times by forces outside myself. I'm a lucky person.

Kicking the habit is physically a painful process. Even if you've got medical help, you're still doing it yourself. The motivation has to come from inside. It can't come from outside; it doesn't do any good. Aside from that, the physical part of it is something that simply has to be gone through, and there's only so much that you can suppress those sensations with. The reason for that is that you're suppressing feelings in your body all the time that you're using drugs. Anything that you suppress, when you take the mute off, it's exaggerated. This is one of the painful things about withdrawal. All of the things that you spent your time avoiding come back at you, maybe twice as strong. In a way, that's maybe kind of a picture of the terrors of withdrawal. Physically, your body has to adjust. The body gets used to having a substance in it every day that it gets used to functioning with. You suddenly take that away and all of the organs have to function on their own without this crutch. The crutch is the one that suppresses all uncomfortable feelings, wherever they come from.

Usually, somebody that's addicted has emotional problems; there's no real logical reason to go into addiction. There would be ways of using drugs that didn't involve addiction, but as a society, as a culture, we're a long way from that. You know, we don't know how to use things once, or once a year, or doing something in a rational way, because it's become more and more prevalent in this century that our culture nurtures addiction. Everything about the culture, the whole function of advertising, is to create addiction. People try to convince themselves that television, for instance, doesn't have any effect on the people. At the same time, the same people who are running the television are selling commercial time and are out telling the manufacturers that they can get the people to buy it by their influence. In other words, they're trying to create an addiction on the part of the audience for a given product, and they pat themselves on the back when they are good at it. How can you con people into buying things they don't need and don't want, even better. Then they turn around and tell you, "Well, of course people aren't affected by violence on TV. You know, it's just play acting." It's nonsense. Of course, in our time you do have it both ways.

Once I got rid of it, I was anxious to get to work. It was hard for a while because, you know, when you're used to being able to turn to some kind of a quick fix to take bad feelings away, you don't feel good or you're depressed, or whatever it is, and there's a chemical substance that you can take. Well, to get used to the idea that it doesn't exist is hard. That's what's hard about kicking any substance in the end. The physical part is one thing, but what it means in terms of re-evaluating your life and your outlook is something that's altogether different.

But physically I felt great. So it was time to go back to work.

19

1957–1959
A HECTIC SCHEDULE

In April of 1957 I started an album I never actually finished. The reason it never got done is because the band itself sounded wonderful but I had a hard time. I didn't really write the rhythm section parts as completely as they should have been, and the guys kind of suffered through it. I had Dave Bailey on some of the things, and it didn't really quite gel. I don't think it was really Dave's fault. As I thought about it as it went along, I think it was my fault for not being able to give him more clear-cut indications. Then Gus Johnson was on the other date, and the whole thing really didn't get off the ground and come to life the way that I wanted it to. So I wanted to go back and re-think some of the stuff, and I needed to write some more for it.

George Avakian, who was the A&R man for CBS, said, "Okay, let's let it rest for a couple of weeks and you work on some more stuff and we'll see what we can do." But he was pleased with what we had and some of the stuff we did came out very well, but what I'm talking about is the overall thing. I really didn't have it together, and some of the faster swinging stuff needed more definition to it, and I thought we could get it together. Well, the couple of weeks stretched into a few weeks and then at this point George's whole life changed. He left CBS and I forget what came up, but anyway he wasn't available anymore. Not only had he left CBS, he wasn't around. As a consequence, I never got back to finish it and there wasn't enough material for a 12-inch album, so that stuff lay in the can for years until Henri Renaud, the French piano player who was an A&R man for CBS in France, had the bright idea of compiling the stuff from the various bands I'd written for, and recorded for, CBS. I don't think he had access to the thing I had done with Tommy Tucker because, you know, a lot of that stuff they unfortunately didn't save, but the Elliot Lawrence things, the Krupa things, and the things from my 1957 band, they used two or three of them on that and in different versions of those records I think that came out as *The Arranger*.

I did a lot of writing for that. I did an arrangement for "All the Things You Are" that I was very pleased with because it was a great-sounding band. Some of the stuff in that was just gorgeous, beautiful-sounding ensemble things, and Lee Konitz played really well on it. He did lovely stuff. And then we did it in a way, like I played a chorus, then I brought my chorus down to an accompanying thing and then Lee came in and we did kind of a duet chorus, then went into an ensemble thing with Don Joseph playing. I don't know if he was playing trumpet or flugelhorn on that. He had kind of a flugelhorn sound on trumpet anyway. What a beautiful player he was.

That was really the problem; I just didn't wind up having enough material, and we never got back to it. I was always sorry that I didn't because I loved the sound of that band. My intention putting it together was to record a thing and then be able to take a big band out and do concerts with it. It was a great band, with Lee playing lead alto and Zoot was in the sax section and Charlie Rouse. I guess it was Gene Allen on baritone; I'm not really sure about the other chairs now, it's been too long, and the trumpet section was one of those oddities. I've always thought it was a little bit like the trombone section of Duke Ellington's band, where you had guys with totally different styles who worked together in a section really well. I brought in Phil Sunkel, who was a good soloist, but let him be the lead player because he was, like, kind of the cleanest player of the lot, the one I could depend on. I really couldn't be sure what was going to happen because these cats were all, you know, every man for himself, but they worked so well as a section.

It was really funny; Phil and Jerry Hurwitz, who didn't have the kind of sound that anybody would think would work in a section, Don Joseph, who was kind of a prima donna and sort of the reason for all this other thing going on, and Don Ferrara was the other trumpet. Idrees Sulieman was in some of the rehearsals, but I guess I wound up using four trumpets instead of five. But that section really got a great sound, four guys with totally different tones and four guys who seemed so unsuited to section playing you wouldn't think they'd even phrase things the same. They sounded wonderful. And the bone section had Brookmeyer, and I'm not sure of the other guys now.

Next came the album with Thelonious Monk. It came about by accident because Thelonious and I were pals. We visited each other back and forth; we only lived a few blocks from each other and spent a lot of time together. I'd be over at his place a lot and, oddly enough, we never played together. We were always hanging out at his house talking about writing, and we'd show each other things we were doing on piano and ideas that we had for orchestration and so on. And I spent a lot of time transcribing some of his tunes that he didn't have written down.

So he had a date with Riverside Records. I found out about this from Orrin Keepnews. He said that he went down to the office one time to talk about this date and it came up in conversation that Gerry Mulligan was waiting outside for him. They said, "Oh, you know Gerry?" He said, "Yeah, we're old friends." They said, "Do you want to make this?" Well, as it turned out, originally they had wanted to record the quartet that Thelonious was playing with down at the Five Spot. He had John Coltrane on tenor and Coltrane was tied up in a contract with somebody else. They couldn't get a release for him to play with Monk on the Riverside album so they were kind of stuck. I guess they were thinking Thelonious would make a trio album, and then when Keepnews found out that we were friends, he said, "Well, do you think Gerry would record something with you?" Monk said, "Sure, sure he would." So, that's how that came about.

I said, "Sure, I'll do it," and I felt like I was walking on a tightrope because, not having ever played together, I was feeling my way. You know, the way Monk accompanies you and the way he approaches chord progressions really demanded a whole different melodic approach from me. I could hear in places where I was getting it together, like getting into a groove with him that really fit, and in other places I was really stumbling because I couldn't find my way.

For all that, I kind of marvel at my guts to go record something like that, to put myself in the frying pan that way, especially since it turned out to be the only time we ever recorded anything together. And that in itself was kind of a happy accident. I'm glad we did it even if it's got big bruises on it.

Around this time I was on a panel discussion at the Newport Jazz Festival about jazz musicians and the music business. It was one of those afternoon symposium things. We were talking about the complications of this and that and managers and this and that and I said, "You know what, I understand all that stuff, but my ideal way of working—and I don't understand why this can't prevail—is to agree to something and shake hands and that's it. If I agree to something, I do it. I don't understand why other people don't do the same thing."

Norman Granz was also on the panel and he turned around and said, "Well, I feel the same way." So we started a conversation between us and here we are in front of all these people and he said, "You want to record for me?" I said, "Yes!"

That's how we did that. Most of the time there were lots of things we had to spell out on paper, but the main thing is that you agree to what you're going to do and that's the direction you take and this is why, and you shake hands and then you lay the things out. Norman made other things possible, too, because he really spent a lot of money putting together a tour in the States for the big band in 1960 and then taking us on tour in Europe.

It was a period after that, that I wanted to really be able to feel a little security instead of always living hand to mouth, because any time I made any money I always sank it back in the band. If I suddenly found myself with a few thousand dollars in the bank, I'd be out buying arrangements or paying for a recording project, you know. That's why Tommy Tucker said, "If you want to go into any business, I'll back you as long it's not music." He knew he was absolutely safe.

So Norman put me on a retainer for a while. It was, instead of paying me the royalties or paying whatever outright, he would give me like two thousand dollars a month or something, so I could spend some time studying or writing or doing whatever I wanted, without the pressure of having to be out working. And I think it was great of him to do that.

I think the first record that I made for Norman after our conversation and a shake of the hand was with Paul Desmond. Backstage I was talking with Desmond and he said he really wanted to record something with me where we would do the quartet thing, the pianoless quartet, only he would be the other horn. Instead of a trumpet he would do it with an alto sax.

This time Norman said, "Listen, I've been listening to you guys go through the same conversation for the last few years. Do you really want to make this record?" We both said, "Sure we do!" "Well, when are you going to do it?" I said, "I don't know." He said, "Do you want to do it?" I said, "Yes." He said, "Okay." So Norman set the thing up and we found ourselves with a contract and the whole thing and he said, "Okay, so now you're recording on such and such a date. Be there!" Norman was great that way, man: no procrastinating.

We were playing a lot during this period and I used to sit in with other groups whenever possible. It was kind of a joy being able to do that and it was my pleasure to go around and to hear different groups, and when they asked me to sit in, I would sit in. Sometimes for instance, I would go see the Dukes of Dixieland. I'd become friendly with them traveling around. They had a good little band and were good players, and I used to sit in with them and play clarinet. I'd be playing the Dixie stuff on top, but with my own approach it worked out differently. I really enjoy that kind of rolling ensemble too; it's fun to do and sometimes Red Nichols would invite me to sit in. Duke's band always invited me to sit in when they were playing at a location job somewhere.

Whenever anybody wanted to invite me, I'd love the challenge of trying to find a function in somebody else's band. It's a pleasure. I had some really good musical experiences that way. Only once I sat in on a location job that Dizzy was doing. It was a week in a club somewhere and it was that group he had with the guitar and bass, drums, and himself, and no piano. And I'll never forget, I guess he played the whole set on Harmon mute, and the music we played was so gentle and so beautiful between us. We really worked very, very well together as you might expect we would, because we were both arrangers, and at the time that Dizzy was writing, it was kind of a similar style so I would expect that stylistic compatibility. But it was only this once that we did it, and of course there was hardly anybody in this club. But it was kind of an eye-opening experience. I've always wished that we'd had the chance to do something like that in a studio. But the only thing we ever did was like one on one—the two of us in some kind of public setting.

The other times we played together, there were millions of people around and it was always sledgehammer time; playing all these things that were more like his big band with the hard, loud sound. But to do something gentle and easy and soft, small band thing, was something we never did.

Norman Granz produced several sessions during this period, including the album with Stan Getz. We had a good time with that. That's what I'm saying. I never knew what to expect. Stan wanted to do the thing on my tune "A Ballad." That was his idea. I wish we hadn't done the exchanging of horns thing. I'm not sure whether Stan wanted to do it or whether Norman Granz did. It doesn't sound like something Norman would want to do. I think that Stan wanted to do it because I didn't want to do it. You know, I would have done it with Zoot's horn. I would have done it with Al's horn or Brew's horn, because I could play their mouthpieces well and sound good on them. I could not play Stan's mouthpiece. His reed was too soft, man, and I just really sounded awful to myself on it. He controlled it and sounded fine, but it sounded awful to me.

I didn't like the way I sounded, and I didn't like the way I thought on his horn. I don't know why he used such a soft reed because he had strong chops. He made my reed sound soft, which it isn't. He had a lot of buzz in his sound. So I didn't think either one of us sounded particularly good, and I didn't think it was nearly as good as the stuff we played on our own instruments.

Anyway, the session went without any problems and wonderful players, those guys. I think that was with Lou Levy and probably Ray Brown and Stan Levey. Great guys to play with. So it was a good session. But the problem with Stan (Getz) was that he was unpredictable, and he had these attitudes that suddenly jumped up that I never understood. God knows I've experienced a lot of these put-down attitudes over the years from different guys, and for varying reasons, but I've never really understood what the root of it was with Stan.

Toward the end of 1957 I took part in a television program called *The Sound of Jazz*, where I played with a variety of stars. Oh boy, I was the kid in the candy store. I don't know how they got the idea to do that, but I was delighted that they did. I was out on the road someplace with my quartet and they recorded the music from the show—I think even a couple of days before the television show. They could have had Harry Carney for the show, but I couldn't play the record date, so they got Harry to play on the record and then I came in and did the TV show, and I found myself playing in the Count Basie band with as many of the old players as they could get. The saxophone section was Earle Warren on lead, Coleman Hawkins, Lester Young, and me. When it actually came time to do the show, Lester wasn't at all well. He didn't have the strength or the patience to wade through the section stuff. When we did the rehearsal, it was so nice because he could do it, but he just was too sick to sustain it, so Ben Webster played the other saxophone. The trumpets were Emmett Berry, Harry Edison, Buck Clayton, and then guys in the later band. Joe Newman, I think was there, and I think Roy—a dynamite trumpet section. The bones were Dickie Wells, Benny Morton, and I can't remember the other bone player, but two of them at least were from the 1930s band, and the third might have been too, I forget who it was; Jo Jones on drums and I'm not sure who was on bass.

But anyway, that was really a gas, even though the music we were playing wasn't from the early band. I mean, it was loud because you've got five trumpets going there and Jo really played loud for the thing, I mean much louder than he would have done in the old band, but for all that it was a gas, and Freddie Green was there. The saxophone section they had; to be playing in that section with those guys really floored me. By this time I felt like I could handle it because years before when I'd been playing with Gene's band and playing with his dynamite saxophone section, I was scared to death—I couldn't come close to them. In the meantime, I'd gotten on top of the horn so I felt comfortable, and musically I had a great time with them.

The other high point for me was playing behind Billie Holiday. And they gave me a solo to play as well, which I was really pleased about. That's one of the most touching moments of anything that I've ever been in on film. When they do the close-up of Billie's face, I start playing a solo and the camera is on me, and then while I'm playing it goes to her face and her reaction. Man, it always brings tears trickling down my face on that one because she has such a sweet, serene look and, you know, that kind of Mona Lisa smile just puts me away. It's a lovely moment. So that was an incredibly fulfilling experience on television. Not the sort of words that you usually use for a television experience. The whole thing was live, and it was organized in a way that even with all of the long periods waiting around the place, it wasn't tedious to do. The way they had it set up, it was in this big studio down on 11th Avenue in New York. I think that PBS has it now. A big, big room, and they had the Basie band setup over on one side of the room and then a small band setup for the Thelonious trio over in this corner. And halfway down this wall was a setup for Pee Wee Russell and Jimmy Giuffre. On the opposite corner was a setup for all the horns that were kind of in a semicircle behind Billie. And the whole thing was that as everybody was playing, the rest of the people in the place were absorbed in what was going on. There was none of this thing that usually happens; the music is kind of just there. You're always conscious of all of the mechanical things going on: the cameras and the sound man and the makeup people running around. There was none of that there. The whole focus was the music and everybody else stayed as much out of the way as they could, so there was this focus from all of the musicians on each other. And there were some of the warmest moments and some funny moments. I mean, at one point in Monk's set, it's charming because they'd do a close-up, and Monk is playing some real angular kind of squawky thing that he would do, and the camera goes to Count Basie's face and a close-up of Count, and he's sitting there smiling and kind of nodding his head and it goes back to Monk again for a minute. Then it goes to Jimmy Rushing sitting across from the end of the piano and he's sitting there, frowning and scowling like, "What is all of this?"

It was the kind of thing that everybody who was involved with, and most people who love the music, would say, "Boy, why didn't they use that as a model and do it again?" But nobody ever wanted to do it again. They didn't know what they had done. Usually things with jazz are done like these big variety shows, fanning an audience into instant excitement and all of that nonsense.

Oddly enough, the man who produced the show became very bitter because people would come up to him who had remembered him and compliment him on that show. He would point out to them that he never produced another show. As far as CBS was concerned, he was a failure. It was the damnedest thing to try to figure out. When things like that happen, I realize how far removed, not only from my taste, but the taste of people who love music, I am from the people who put television shows on. So that poor man who produced far and away the best television show on jazz, maybe ever to be done on jazz, could never get another gig in television and certainly never produced another thing on music. I think he died of a broken heart over the whole thing. It's the kind of story that can make you really angry and the sort of thing we're up against with corporate thinking when we're dealing with the arts.

I did one of the Timex Jazz shows and they were bad enough for being overproduced and kind of a Las Vegas vaudeville presentation. They at least had the beauty of having some great people on them. They ham-boned it up. They always used Louis Armstrong in some kind of way, instead of using him in a musical way. It was always Louis the showman, you know; a very conventional kind of presentation. In one of those shows, Jack Teagarden and I went to the guy who was supposed to be producing the show, who'd been the office boy at Joe Glaser's office and got a promotion. His promotion was to be the producer of this show. Great, that's really good thinking!

I guess they figured there was a lot of creative common ground there, between being an office boy and a TV producer. But Jack and I went to him and said, "Look, there's a little thing that we'd like to do together and if you need to take the time from something, we can take a minute or two here from my set and a couple of minutes from this other set so we could do something together." He said, "No, the show's all laid out."

Well, the show wasn't all laid out at that point. This was early on in the rehearsals. Jack and I shrugged our shoulders and said, you know, you can't fight those attitudes, and the opportunity to do some musical thing that was a little different, a little out of the ordinary or a little special, they didn't care about that. It was all show biz. Get out and do your tap dance and get off. It's very unrewarding. Some that they did later were even worse on CBS; just dreadful things. One they had us all dressed up like gamblers. There was no reason for it other than we're jazz musicians and well, what do you do? I said, "Okay, riverboat gamblers!" They got us all dressed in these gray cut-away outfits and then they wanted me to do some number from the *Birth of the Cool* and we did one of my pieces, "Jeru" or something. They got all these dancers, and the choreographer of *The Wiz*, who was like the hot item on the dance scene at that point, and he's got all of these dancers posing and sitting around and they're all snapping their fingers and doing this whole exaggerated thing. I tried to get to the director to say please, don't have them snapping their fingers like that and finally, because nobody paid any attention to me, I went to the choreographer and said, "Listen, man! Please, that's just not the way people listen to music." So he then announced to his dancers in a very sarcastic way, he said, "Mr. Mulligan says this is not the way people listen to his music, so no snapping your fingers." As a consequence, my name was mud around CBS for years after that. But the guy who put that show on, man, I'm not going to mention his name, but I got conned into doing another show with him and it was even worse. So my name has not fared well in the halls of CBS, mainly because of this guy, who is just a thoroughgoing jack-ass. Why these thoroughgoing jackasses get the opportunity to do these shows, I guess, is because they really talk well at lunch.

That's always been one of the big problems. Radio was a great medium for music, made to order. Television is a killer. Television has no use for music except in the background, because what is interesting to hold a camera on somebody playing a horn? If you're an audience in a club, there's an atmosphere, there's a reason that you're doing it. But when you're watching television, there's no reason for doing it; they don't need to be watching that. And this has always been the problem; what do you do visually while you're presenting the music? It's not just jazz, all music suffers from this, especially more formal music. Maybe you're dealing with country and western and they're doing a show and there's more action. They're dressed for action, whether it's cowboy and cowgirl outfits or dungarees or whatever it is, man, they're putting on a show. But jazz players, we don't put on a show, we don't do all that.

The symphony suffers from the same thing. I find it so distracting. You'll be looking at the thing and you're kind of drifting off or you're fol-lowing the music and they'll be doing a long shot from the back of the hall and they'll say okay, it's just there and it doesn't matter, it creates an atmosphere. Then the music is going along and you're with the music, and all of a sudden you've got this jolt in front of your eyes when the camera comes in for a close-up of the hands of the French horn player. Now you're involved with the French horn player's life, because you see the poor man needs a manicure and he chews his thumbnails. So then the camera starts pulling back and you say, my God, he also needs a shave and he's got a pimple, and as you pull back you see the guy next to him, who has some other set of problems. Of course this has totally distracted you from the music. This is their idea of making a variety of shots. They don't realize what they are doing is an intrusion on your concentration. I don't want to know that the man chews his nails.

The 1958 Newport Jazz Festival was a high point. Duke and Billy Strayhorn wrote a piece for Harry Carney and me and I loved doing it with him. I was around Duke a lot. We traveled together on those

Gerry and Duke Ellington. COURTESY GERRY MULLIGAN COLLECTION, LIBRARY OF CONGRESS, MUSIC DIVISION

shows for three or four or five years in a row. So by that time we were old friends. I had such great feeling for him and respect, and loved his approach to music. That was really something because he always introduced me as the world's second-best baritone player.

Of course Harry and I became great friends. Some of the things we did . . . we wound up in Japan at the same time they were there, and Harry and I hung out together in Tokyo for days. It was just a wonderful experience, gentle, smart man he was.

They wrote this piece and decided to play it up there. I can't remember what the preamble to it was. I think that they just wrote it and presented Harry and me with the parts and said, "Here, go!" It's a nice piece. I'd like to do it some more.

They wrote another piece a year or so later that we were supposed to play. We played it at a concert in Boston, and ultimately it was one of those things that we played it the once, and God knows what happened to the parts and the score. They just disappeared, as a lot of Duke's music did. You can recreate, or nearly recreate some of it by transcribing it if it was recorded, but the piece Harry and I did the second time wasn't recorded, so it's in the ether somewhere. And with all of the people who have gone through the various stacks of music, they still haven't come across it. So I don't suppose they will.

I loved playing with that band. The countryside, man, five raccoons and a cat. That story means nothing to anybody except that it's one of those things. You know, there are things in your life that you remember that are like photographs. So many things that you experience or do with other people or places that you've been, no matter how interesting or how involved you were, you simply don't remember anything. And then for some reason, something that has nothing to do with anything important will stand in your memory like it's a photographic album. And there are a number of things like that. So because of those things, I'm often tempted, in terms of doing a memoir or an autobiography, to include those because it always seems like there must be some reason your memory grabs on to these things.

I guess during that period, I must have put together the quartet, which, in a way, was one of my favorite quartets. I really liked that group, because Art Farmer brought a totally different kind of approach to it and the arrangements that we evolved. Whether they had arrangements or written out, they were altogether different. It was kind of a different departure. So I liked that group a lot.

It pretty much evolved. I would have an idea in mind of who I would like and who I could work with. Someone who would be complimentary to the others and that we'd be able to adapt to this whole thing of a small ensemble concept, which is a very particular thing and not always easy for the guy. As I've said many times since then, it was hard for him to adjust to the approach of the pianoless quartet. Working without the piano for one thing and working in these tight arrangements where I'm constantly playing harmony to him. I'm taking over the role of the piano in that group. It was a big adjustment for other players to come into that setup. Then when they had the feeling for it, and they established rapport, then it was great.

We did a lot of things, and each one of the groups was different. What Chet and I did was one thing and what Bob and I did was something totally different. There were things coming out of each group that were something special, and it would be maybe something totally different from this group to that group. As a consequence, each of the groups has, still, a different kind of interest. It's very difficult for me to have a favorite of those groups because they're each so different to my way of hearing. But the thing with the quartet with Art, in its way, is probably the most sophisticated of all of the groups. I probably wrote more for that group too. I wrote a lot of arrangements for it, and the kind of thing that I was always trying to achieve with that group was that the written things shouldn't sound written. With the other groups, a great deal of the time it was the other way around. When we were gathering around, we would play things and heard things that sounded arranged. I was arranging things and they sounded like they were real arrangements.

20

ALEC WILDER AND THE ALGONQUIN HOTEL

FOR A LONG PERIOD, instead of having a place in New York or keeping a place, I lived at the Algonquin Hotel. I guess it was sort of my feelings about history. I was always fascinated with the place and the people around the *New Yorker* who had made it their headquarters: Robert Benchley and Dorothy Parker, all those people.

Alec Wilder and I became good friends. Alec always lived there; he was kind of a transient in life. He wasn't really interested in having a house or a home, particularly. He liked living in a hotel and then, when he was tired of that, he liked nothing better than to get on a train and ride wherever the train was going and get on another train. He would spend weeks traveling around on trains not really getting anywhere. He would just go around the country.

So we had a lot of things in common and I was fascinated by him. I thought he was wonderful. Such a great guy. You know, you can tell from the pictures of him that he was a lot older than I was. I don't really know how old he was then because his face was so kind of ravaged with life. I think Alec had also gone through years of heavy drinking and had stopped that. So we used to spend a lot of time together. Eventually, he wanted to write a piece for the woodwind quintet. One of his favorite people was John Barrows, the French horn player. He wanted to do it with the two solo horns, the French horn and me. As it turns out, John got sick or injured or something and wasn't able to play, so we never did the thing together. But I think the times we did it, we probably did it with Jim Buffington.

There were two pieces. One was the woodwind quintet with the French horn and baritone, and the other was a woodwind quintet just for solo baritone. Two pieces. And yes, that's the kind of thing that really feels good too; also, a sense of community, a sense of belonging if you will, that somebody I'm friends with, we should be friends with, would write a piece of music for me. I love that. I wish there were more of that possible on the scene. There were so many writers that wrote for bands, and I loved the way they wrote and learned a great deal from them. Of course, after the bands were gone, there's been so little connection and to do anything is so expensive.

We performed them a few times but we never recorded them. In fact, I always meant to bring that up with Gunther Schuller, because he has a lot of Alec's music in his publishing company, and eventually I'd like to record the two pieces. I think about it once in a while, and I'd love to play it again.

My home life was sort of semi-existent until it disappeared altogether, and so I was just kind of either a bachelor or a loose cannon, depending on how you look at it. I must say, it was kind of enjoyable being a bachelor. I met a lot of very nice ladies during that period, some I spent more time with than others, but it was nice.

One time I was invited to a party for the guys who put on *Beyond the Fringe*. *Beyond the Fringe* was a British four-man show with Dudley Moore, Peter Cook, Jonathan Miller, and Alan Bennett. Anyway, I had become friendly with them in some kind of way. It's hard to connect all these things because I was on the scene a lot. A good deal of the time I was living at the Algonquin Hotel. I went to the theater a lot and I met a lot of theater people. Several people became good friends during that period, and some guys I've seen since then and it's like, "Remember when" . . . like Kenneth Haight, who was in *Look Back in Anger*, and his girlfriend, Fay Weldon, who wrote *Upstairs Downstairs*.

Anyway, I used to hang out with them, and also Walter Chiari, an Italian singer/actor who was in some show on Broadway. The kind of people I met at the Algonquin were people who became friends, and we used to hang out and have dinner together. Like Sebastian Cabot; lovely man, you know the kind of happy roly-poly type with a great face and a beard. So I used to have a good time in that kind of milieu, which felt like an old-fashioned theater world that I always kind of admired. I used to love to stay at the Algonquin. I figured someday I'd run into Benchley's ghost in the hall or something.

During that period, Brendan Behan turned up in New York and it got to be kind of difficult to get through the lobby of the hotel coming in late at night, because Brendan would be holding down the fort in the bar and he'd grab me and the next thing I'd know I'd be keeping up with him drinking. So it was not too healthy a time in some respects, especially when Brendan was about. So that was kind of the theater connection, and the fact that I was always attracted to the theater.

I was around a lot and it was in this period also that the *Beyond the Fringe* guys started a club in New York, and they brought over a troupe that they had organized in England called The Establishment. They started this club and called it—what was it that John Lennon said? They said, "Well, what do you guys call your haircut?" He said, "Arthur." No, not Arthur.

It was a name. It was really funny because it was just like a non sequitur. Well, that's what they called the club. The group was called The Establishment. It was an interesting club. There was a bar here and a room behind that, a good-sized room where most of the time Teddy Wilson was playing with a trio, and in this big room next door they had the show a couple of times a night: The Establishment. Some of the people in the show became great friends who I still see when I go to England: Eleanor Bron, a very, very great comedienne. She was doing comedy then, but she's also probably better known as a dramatic actress because she turns up in great things like D. H. Lawrence's *Women in Love*, which they made a film of.

I got invited to a party at Bobby Lewis's house. Now, Bobby Lewis was a director, and I met him because one of the shows playing on Broadway was *Jamaica*. Lena Horne was in it. I used to go by frequently because Lennie Hayton was always there and I used to go over and hang out with Lennie, who was a great guy. Lena, too, but I was a much better friend of Lennie than Lena, who I was always kind of in awe of. She was one of those women that you kind of go, "er, um, er," around. I did a thing one time—her dressing room was right in the back of the theater and the back of the theater was on the next cross street, so I used to go in the back way. I was in their dressing room one time, in the outer room, and she was taking off her makeup after the show in the other room, and Lennie and I are sitting talking. She calls Lennie and he goes in the other room, and so I'm sitting there and I unconsciously started whistling some tune. I don't know whether it was from the show, or something I was thinking—whatever.

I hear this voice yell from the other room, "Who's that whistling? Is there somebody whistling in this dressing room?" And about this time Lennie comes out and says, "My God, what have you done? You were whistling." And I said, "Oh God, what have I done?" He said, "Man, that's an old theater tradition, whistling in the dressing room, and she's so superstitious. It's like anything that goes wrong for the next two months is going to be your fault."

After that we left the theater in Lennie's car and, man, Lena wouldn't even talk to me. She just wasn't having anything to do with me, this idiot whistling in her dressing room. I said, "Oh, God! What have I done?"

Anyway, Bobby Lewis thought I had something to do with the *Beyond the Fringe* guys, because I guess maybe he saw me around with Lennie. I guess he got me mixed up, because otherwise I can't imagine why he invited me. I mean, often backstage you talk to people and maybe people feel friendly and you don't even think about it. Anyway, I found myself invited to this party that Bobby was having for *Beyond the Fringe*. I go to this party and Peter Cook and Dudley Moore and those guys turn up and then a whole bunch of other people; a whole lot of theater people that I recognized. And Marlene Dietrich showed up. Well, the funny thing was that I saw Judy Holliday had shown up. I recognized her because I had seen the show and I knew what she looked like.

I noticed that all the women in the place were gathered around Marlene Dietrich, not the men. The men would probably be too intimidated, but the women—it was like Marlene was holding court with all the women, and they're all enthralled with her and hanging on her every word as gospel.

Well, at some point in the evening, Judy and I started talking and she knew who I was and she loved music. She was very involved with music and so we got along really great and had a lot of interests in common, and she invited me to the theater.

So a couple of nights later I went down to the theater and went backstage to see her, and we just started meeting after the show. I'd take her out to eat or something like that, and that's how that evolved. We became good friends, and more than good friends, for quite a while, and then I took an apartment that was close by her place up on 72nd Street. She had an apartment at the Dakota. She also had a place in upstate New York that she and her husband, her ex-husband, had rebuilt. So in the summertime, I had leased a car and we spent a lot of time going up there. That started us writing and it was fun to do. We enjoyed working together and, actually, she's the only lyricist that I've ever worked with closely. So a lot of the things that we wrote together, she would contribute to the music and I would contribute to the words. It really was a collaboration.

I had wanted to write songs before that but I had never had any luck establishing rapport with a lyricist. It reminds me, back when I was writing for Krupa's band, Buddy Stewart had an idea for a song that he wanted to do. It was Buddy and maybe Dave Lambert, too, because they were working together then and it was after Buddy left the band. But Buddy had an idea, "See if you can make a song out of this, *I'm Hob-Nobbin' with a Robin*." He liked the sound of that phrase and so did I. I made a whole tune around it and gave it to Don George, who was a lyricist who had written a lot of stuff with Duke—"Beginning to See the Light" and a lot of Duke's pop tunes from around that time. Don immediately took the thing and put the *I'm Hob-Nobbin' with a Robin* phrase in another place in the tune than I had conceived, and that seemed wrong to me. So I kind of lost interest in it.

Then, after that, I realized I'd been kind of hard-nosed about it and that Don had solved a lyric problem and he was right in the way he had done it. But by the time I realized that it was too late. But the experience, I think, had a good effect on me in later collaborations because, in working with Judy, we'd come up with something, and she'd have an idea and I would put a musical phrase to the idea and work on that. She'd say, "Why don't you try so and so?" And I'd say, "You can't do that. That won't work; that's impossible." And I'd go away for fifteen minutes and think it over and come back and say, "Okay, it works." In other words, I learned how to collaborate. Some things seem simple on the surface but take some learning. When I thought about it in later years, I wish I'd been a little more flexible where that little tune was concerned, because it was a cute idea and they were all enthusiastic about it and Don had done a nice job on it. But here I was, the hard-nosed pain in the ass. I think I spent a lot of my youth being that. God knows what I was so angry about. I never really found that out, even in analysis.

21

SUBTERRANEAN BLUES
BACK TO HOLLYWOOD

I WAS PLAYING AT A CLUB in New York with the quartet and Arthur Freed and Vincente Minnelli came in to see me one night. Arthur was a film producer from MGM. Minnelli, of course, was a director who worked with him on a lot of projects. Arthur spoke about a project that he was doing. He wanted to make a film of *The Subterraneans* and was very enthusiastic about the idea. He wanted a musician to play one of the characters in the film, and he and Minnelli were both curious to meet me because Arthur said that they may have used my name inadvertently as the character Gene Kelly played in *An American in Paris*. That was Jerry Mulligan. He said he wasn't sure how that came about but he wanted to meet me. He wanted to know if I was interested to be in the film and I said, "Sure, fine." At the time, I hadn't done any acting roles, but give me plenty of help and tell me what you want, and I'll try. So I agreed to do the film.

I liked Arthur a lot. He was the producer at MGM who did all the big musicals and he was an old songwriter, so we got along great, and Minnelli was very nice as well. For *The Subterraneans* he wanted to do Kerouac the way Kerouac was. Sort of the statement of the 1950s that reflected the disaffected of the 1920s. To him, in his mind, it was related, the expatriates who went to France and all that.

So Arthur hired me to play a role in *The Subterraneans* and I went to California in 1959. André Previn wrote the music. They usually record the source music beforehand. That's the music that's going to be played by instrumentalists in the film. They do that so that the performance can be synched and they usually do the underscore afterward. I think that I was probably on the source music but I can't recall if I played on the underscore or not. Might have, might not, but anyway there was some very nice stuff.

Arthur had taken a tremendous amount of flak from the front office on *The Subterraneans*, and they had forced changes on the thing that had totally destroyed what he wanted to do. I mean, he never really figured *The Subterraneans* was going to be a moneymaking film. It should have been able to break even, but he wanted to do it in black and white. He wanted to do it as the book was done, including all of the values involved in the thing. They were the kind of values going on in the real world, but the front office didn't want to know about that. They didn't want to know about existentialists and beatniks and all of this kind of stuff. They kept forcing changes on Arthur to make it much more nicey nicey. They changed the character and they felt they should get a well-known actress to play it. They didn't want to have a female star because, in the book, I think the girl was mixed race and, of course, forget that at the front office. These were all the things that Arthur wanted to do. He wanted to make a picture that really portrayed what was going on.

You would think with the kind of track record of success and the money that Arthur had made for them with his various pictures, they would let him have his way because in the end it would have paid for itself. But they don't think like that, you see. They're all control freaks. Arthur actually did only a couple more pictures and then the battles over ownership of that company went back and forth. There were a couple of projects that they'd get almost to the point of shooting, and then the front office would drop it without telling him. There was just this wall of silence from the money people, and I think all of that hurt Arthur a lot too. So it was kind of the end of his career out there, and I think all of those pressures together were just too much for him. He was a wonderful man.

At that point Judy Holliday was still doing *The Bells Are Ringing* on Broadway, and they were scheduling the filming of *Bells*. It was supposed to start in February the following year, but they kept postponing it and, as it turned out, the shooting time for *Bells Are Ringing* was the same time as *The Subterraneans*. I wound up doing *Subterraneans* at the same time she was doing *Bells*, so I was around there for a lot of the filming.

That turned out to be a very difficult period for Judy. Things would happen one after another that really threw her off balance. It wound up being a very tough time for me because I was trying to help her keep some kind of balance, and I don't know if you know much about singers or actors, or actresses, but a lot of times performers can be very insecure people. And Judy felt she wasn't prepared for the whole thing. She really looked forward to doing it, but I think she was aware that this would be the only musical she would ever film, so it was very important for her.

She was overweight, and when she would get nervous, she was a compulsive eater. It was always a problem with her, being so insecure and having a means of propping herself up by eating. It's a disaster, especially for an actor; it's terrible and she felt she was too old for the part. It was like you can do things on stage and people will suspend disbelief, but the camera is not nearly so kind. She was aware of all these things and very nervous about it.

For a change, I was in the position of trying to help somebody instead of somebody helping me. She had done the show on Broadway for two years and then did it on the road for a couple of engagements, I think in San Francisco and maybe Los Angeles. So by the time they finally got around to starting the thing, she was having doubts about doing it, because there was a kind of a basic problem to the show. At that point she, and also I think probably Minnelli and Freed too, felt that the writers hadn't solved the problem, the problem being that *Bells* was a little show. It was all based around a character that Judy played, and it was charming because of what Judy brought to it. She brought the character and the whole show to life. But really, it was a very slim show. There wasn't much of a show there, and it was problematic to try to open this up into a film. I don't think that they ever intended to just film the stage play, so you had the possibility of opening up a picture in all kinds of directions. Well, when you open the thing up you realize that there's not much of a story there, and it kind of diffuses the focus on Judy. So that was a problem they had to face in the writing. And, of course, Judy had stuck up for her friends Betty Comden and Adolph Green, who had written it for her originally. She thought they should do the film writing, although Arthur told me that he really wanted somebody else to write it because he felt maybe they were too close to it and they hadn't solved the problems. But anyway, she stuck up for them and wanted them to do the writing.

Well, by the time they were ready to go into the filming, Comden and Green were busy on Broadway doing something else and it kept getting postponed as to when they were to show up in Hollywood. They ultimately didn't get there at all, at least not while the picture was in its starting stages.

So they wound up with the problem of trying to make an extravaganza out of a little show, and the movie that they had done just before that was *Gigi*. It was a big, big, big, colorful extravaganza spread all over Paris. Well, this was absolutely the opposite. The main action in this picture and everything on stage took place more or less in one set, a room in a New York brownstone. And there weren't many people involved and there wasn't any way of opening it up. They had really a basic problem and here they're going to do the thing in CinemaScope and Technicolor and the whole thing.

Well, I think that Judy certainly had qualms about it, and she finally got to the point of terror about doing it. She just really wanted to get out of it. In fact, I was reading Hugh Fordin's book on Arthur Freed at MGM the other day and he pointed out that at one point, I didn't know about this, that Judy went to Arthur and tried to buy her way out. She said, "I'll pay you whatever you've spent up until now and see if you can recast it and get somebody else to play it," because she just felt awful about doing it.

Once the wheels of a machine that size get turning, it's inexorable and it goes, and it moves anyway. Arthur was very helpful, and before the film started shooting, Minnelli was also very helpful. I remember Minnelli invited us over to lunch, I guess on a Sunday afternoon. It was a great house he had, right diagonally across the street from the Beverly

Hills Hotel. He had a great place. It was like a little oasis in the middle of all this. Here you are on this busy corner in Beverly Hills and you go through these gates and it was like being in another world. You know, just absolutely isolated in a kind of a private New Orleans–feeling jungle. It was great. For some reason I always felt I was in New Orleans. A lot of hanging things, but that may have been just an impression. I met Liza at that point, who must have been about twelve or thirteen, a great kid with lots of vitality. And Vincente was as charming as all get out.

Well, that week they started to shoot. First they did the pre-recording, which meant all of Judy's songs and all of everybody's songs that had to be synched. You have to record the performance, then you have to do the performance to the playback. Tough to do, especially in comedy, you know. Judy had been playing this thing for about three years. She got to the recording sessions and they had rewritten arrangements. It wasn't just a question of sweetening the arrangement, which was a Hollywood term for adding strings and making it sound more grand. There actually were different arrangements on some of the things. Well, for a performer, this was a killer. So much of her performance in *Bells* was based on what she had done every night, and she was used to those arrangements. And all of a sudden it was like taking the cellar away from the building. Well, that was the first time I interfered. My relationship to the thing became one of interference on top of interference, but there was nothing else I could do. Judy asked me to do it and I probably would have done it anyway.

I went to André Previn, whom I knew, and I considered we were good friends. I respected him a lot; he was a wonderful writer. The arrangements were great; that wasn't the point. What they had done with them sounded gorgeous, but the trouble was that they didn't necessarily incorporate Judy's performance. And she wasn't going to have the chance to go get a performance together to the new arrangements. If she could have gone out and played with the new arrangements, even for a week somewhere, it would have been fine but forget it, that's not the way it works. So I finally asked André, I said, "Listen, at least for these big numbers at the end of the show, couldn't you use the original arrangements? You can always add some sweetening to the string parts because you've got a bigger orchestra than they had sitting in the pit."

Well, I think that André was pretty pissed off at me for getting into it, and they were very impatient with Judy. I said, "But you must understand something. Judy is a performer, a singer, she's not a musician. She has a good feeling for music, but she doesn't know anything about music, and you get her on a sound stage and she says this doesn't feel good and you start explaining to her technically why it's correct, it doesn't mean anything. It may be technically correct as hell, but the point is that it's something that she can't do a performance to. It's two different things." And he kind of swamped her with musical analysis of what was going on, and I thought he was being kind of condescending to her. It was like being able to see the different sides of the story. I was sympathetic, but of course felt that their responsibility was to make Judy as comfortable as they could. It was her performance that the whole thing was based on. Without her performance you had nothing; it was really a nothing play.

When it came down to shooting, Arthur had been assuring her all along that they would rehearse before they started shooting. I don't know if Minnelli ever did. She must have brought it up with him because she wanted the assurance. After all, there were about four people in main roles that she had to work with that she had never done the play with. Comedy, in its way, is much more difficult than anything else that an actor has to do in front of an audience. It is so tenuous that the difference between what's funny and what isn't, or what an audience laughs at, what an audience perceives to be funny, what catches an audience, is one of the mysteries. It'll always be a mystery. Really good comedy is not something that's easy.

So Judy comes to the first day of shooting and they're all set to start; no rehearsal. And this really threw her a curve. Now the funny thing in Hollywood—the star, God help you if the star is in any kind of trouble with the thing because if the star is having difficulty and says, "Wait a minute," you know immediately they're temperamental. You've got a jacket saying she's temperamental. So she was very conscious of that and was a very easy person to work with, but she needed the support and the cooperation of the people she was working with. Betty Comden and Adolph Green, who had written the show, never showed up. As a consequence, Arthur was pissed. He was furious. And she was very hurt because she felt that there were things that she needed, and she needed the writers there to do it. As it stood, she found herself in an artistic battle with Minnelli. She was well aware that you couldn't blow this up into a big show like *Gigi*.

I think her trepidation started when she realized what they were using for the opening. At that time one of the blocks in midtown Manhattan was all brownstones. It was in the fifties someplace on the East Side, and they had torn down the whole block except one building was standing. So here you have an area that's like a bombed-out area. It looked like a block in Berlin in 1945. Well, this had been a photograph in *Life* magazine and everybody said, "Oh ain't that cute, man, that one building is standing out of this whole block." Well, Minnelli decided to set the show there. It had nothing to do with the action, it just confused it. It was just an extra thing but, you know, it was some kind of a big gesture.

So that was the opening of the thing. They did the opening number behind the credits, you know, the telephone answering, "*Sue's Answer Phone*" service, and then it shows this bombed-out block with the one building sitting on it. Well, things like that were just gratuitous, they didn't mean anything, and so it seemed to Judy and it seemed to me, too, that he was much more interested in visual effects and trying to get humor, comedy, out of visual effects rather than getting it out of the actors and out of the characters. In this particular thing, that's the only place that it was. It was in the characters. If it's going to be funny, it's the relationships of the people, mainly it's what Judy did, man; she gave the whole thing life, or if she didn't, there was nothing left.

They get in the first day, and boy, they're ready to start shooting. Well, Judy put her foot down and said she wanted at least to read with the principals in these first couple of days of scenes so she could get some kind of feel for what was going on, get some kind of a rapport.

So, reluctantly, they wound up in a big room somewhere in the soundstage and proceeded to try to read through these first scenes. Well, they'd been reading for a little while and there's a knock on the door and somebody comes up and says, "Mr. Vogel wants to see you." Judy said, "Who's Mr. Vogel?" Whoever knocked on the door said, "Mr. Vogel owns the studios, he's from New York." Judy said, "Well, if Mr. Vogel owns the studio, of course he can come in."

Well, then these six cigars come in the room and five of the cigars look to the main cigar and he proceeds to make a speech. And the speech is something along the lines, "We've had a great success with *Gigi* and we put all of our facilities and concentration on *Gigi* to make it a big success. We want you to know that we're going to do everything for you that we did for *Gigi* and anything you want so that we can have a success like *Gigi*." It seemed like *Gigi* was every fifth word he said.

Finally he wound down. The cigars are now all standing there looking at Judy, and she realized that she was now supposed to say something. So with her kind of off-beat humor, she said, "Well Mr. Vogel, I want you to know I've danced my way into the hearts of millions." And the actors all broke up and fell over laughing and quickly stifled their laughing because they realized the cigars were not laughing at all. They were not amused. So Judy realized she'd started out with kind of a gigantic faux pas with the powers that be.

So it was a strange thing to see this wall grow between Judy and Vincente. He had been so nice beforehand, but once they got shooting, he was really mean to her. She couldn't understand it, and, of course, Judy was a very gentle person, and as I said, very insecure. So to suddenly really feel like Vincente was attacking her was hard for her to bear. I mean, it was obvious to everyone. It got to a point where Dean Martin was embarrassed because Judy would say something, or try to lighten the mood and say something amusing, and Minnelli would never laugh. Dean would say anything and Minnelli would just fall over laughing until Dean was embarrassed.

Now, she had done this thing as a musical on stage for some two and a half years, and there were lots of things that they did on stage that are not written in the script. So she would try to tell him, "You know at this place here, something that used to really work in this situation and get a laugh, would be such and such a bit of business," and Minnelli would always look unconvinced. He would say, "Well, show me." So she would try to show him, but to do little bits out of context when you don't have any feeling for the whole thing was an awkward thing for any comedian to have to do. But she tried to do it, and Vincente would stand there with kind of a pained look on his face and say, "Well, tell me, why is that funny?" And, of course, Judy would just kind of get a little more pale. If somebody sees a physical bit of business and they don't see it's funny, how do you explain to them why it's funny? And this happened a lot until finally she wouldn't make any suggestions; she just tried to do whatever he told her, and it was very difficult shooting the thing because it seemed to the actors that Vincente spent much more time rehearsing the camera than he did the actors.

I mean, they did camera moves. You know, the camera mounted on a dolly like a little truck that they wheeled around, and to do those moves is like choreography. You've really got to work it out because it's a kind of teamwork thing. There's the guy who's pulling the thing over the actual patterns that they work out and there's the man who's working the lens so that it's close or near, plus they're having to coordinate the lighting. All of this stuff. They'd sometimes take a whole morning just setting up the camera shots and sometimes a whole day.

At one point they had kind of a record. I think they had some fifty-four camera moves in one master shot, and the time spent just doing the cameras was frustrating to everybody else. Then when you got into doing it, it's like whether the camera always made it was as much of a factor as whether the actors did.

With some of the scenes, for instance, poor Eddie Foy was very miscast for the role. For the original show on Broadway, they had a guy who did a great Hungarian accent and did this whole hustler kind of Broadway record company guy. He was really great doing it because you felt like this was a really underhanded guy. But Eddie Foy didn't really look the part, nor did he feel it, and he was very nervous. There was something about the atmosphere for the actors. They all were very nervous because the way they were working was so uncomfortable for them.

I remember one master shot they set up; there were some forty-five or fifty camera moves and it was the introduction of Eddie's character. This master shot must have gone for about seven or eight minutes. However long the film was in the camera, that's how long they ran the shot. Eddie had some five or six props to handle. He had a hat and an umbrella, plus he had a big bundle of posters in one hand, a briefcase and a bundle of records in the other, and he had this dialogue that was very difficult for him because it was supposed to be with an accent. Well, they must have done the shot fifteen or sixteen times. The other actors were starting to get worried because poor Eddie would get halfway through and blow up and he'd drop the props and whatever. Man, it must have been a horrendous experience for him and they started to worry for him that he was going to faint or have a heart attack, because it was just a killer. He finally got through it, but it just was a painful, painful experience.

As far as Judy making suggestions, obviously anything that she said, Minnelli said no. So she stopped making suggestions, and then at one point the script girl pulled her aside with an idea. Now the script girl is a very, very important person, with a very, very responsible job. She's got to keep track of everything that goes on in the scenes. She makes sure that people are making their entrances from the right side and they're positioned in the right place and facing the right direction. She also makes sure the costumes are matching. If somebody's hair was sticking up in one scene then it's got to be sticking up in the other and the whole thing had to match. So in other words, the script girl was the director's right hand and he'd better have a good one, because without one, he'd be in a lot of trouble. That's happened a lot, but it has also happened that the script girl has bailed out sloppy directors.

In this case she took Judy aside after a couple of weeks and said, "It's obvious that Mr. Minnelli is not going to take any of your suggestions. So maybe we could try something. You tell me your suggestions and then I'll go and say it like it's my idea and see if we can get some of the things you want into what we're doing."

Judy said sure, she appreciated it and she was willing to try it, and it worked. She would tell the script girl that she thought they should try such-and-such in this place, and the script girl would say it as if it were her idea and Minnelli would say okay. So it took a subterfuge to get to that.

As shooting went on, I think that it became more and more obvious to Judy that the show had lost its connection with the original show, and she really didn't know where she was going with her performance because it just didn't feel like it fit anything. It was like having two movies going at once—like trying to superimpose some kind of an extravaganza on top of this little show. And she started to get more and more upset.

Well, I think poor Arthur Freed was really in the middle. During all of this time, I was around the studio a lot but I wasn't necessarily on the set. I used to spend a lot of time wandering around the studio with Arthur, and we had a grand time. Arthur was an old songwriter first, before he became a producer. He and his partner, Nacio Herb Brown, wrote a bunch of hits during the 1920s and early 1930s. His productions at MGM were some of the greatest musicals they ever did there. So it was really a great opportunity to wander around with him and hear what he had to say. He'd tell me about this film: this happened, that happened, all of these anecdotes of the old days doing musicals in the 1930s. I think the first one he did was something like *Broadway Melody of 1936* or something like that, and on through to the days of *Gigi* and *Singing in the Rain* and stuff like that. So he was really one of the most accomplished producers, and he knew how to get good people together and get the best out of them.

So I think this was really a hard time for him because it really wasn't working. I don't think he could figure out what to do about the pressures, because he was getting it from all sides. He was getting it from the front office, who were angry at any kind of delays and they were angry at any kind of dissension that was getting in the way, and obviously there was dissension. Since Adolph Green hadn't shown up, they were operating without the script that they wanted. Minnelli was upset about it and Judy was terrified.

So Arthur was in the middle, no matter what happened. I think as time went on it finally wore him down and he just got mad at everybody.

It got to the point that Judy was very dissatisfied with the rough cut of the film that they started to assemble from the dailies. She got it into her head to re-edit the picture; re-cut it. And of course when she started to talk about re-cutting the picture, I said to her, "Judy, you're about to do something that you can't win. You're here for this picture, you've got maybe six months or whatever on this lot and they're doing one picture, that's it. Minnelli has been here, has made how many pictures? He's the biggest moneymaker they've got and he works with Arthur Freed as a team. He's got all of this accumulated power and it's up to MGM to keep him happy because they need him. You, they don't need. So any battle of the kind that you're figuring on doing here, you've got to lose, you cannot win."

She said aside from anything else, even if she can't have the picture cut the way that she would like to see it cut, at least she'd have the satisfaction of knowing it could be done and maybe it would influence Vincente. Well, I had my doubts about all that, but she wanted to do it and I felt I had to back her up, otherwise she really felt alone on this whole thing. It was like suddenly the whole thing had turned against her. She had a feeling it was her last picture so I felt obliged to help.

We had the list of all the scenes and had seen the rough cuts, so once we started putting it together it really was fun to do. We got caught up in the thing and when we got it done, I was convinced, and she was too, that the picture we made was quite different from the finished film. It had an altogether different feeling about it. It had a totally different focus.

Well, ultimately, we never got to see it because Arthur said that before we could see it, he felt he was obliged to show it to Vincente. We had worked on the layout of the scenes ourselves, and Adrienne Fazan, the editor, had put it together. So it turns out that Adrienne, Arthur, and ultimately Vincente, were the only ones who ever saw the assembly the way that Judy and I had put it together. When Arthur showed it to Vincente, he was furious and he demanded that it be disassembled immediately and wouldn't let Judy see it. So that was that. That was the end of it. But that was kind of the last straw with the relationship between Judy and Arthur. And Arthur started to get mad at Judy because she was being so much trouble. It didn't matter that it wasn't easy for her and, of course, what I was saying was true. Judy is the transient there and Vincente is the regular fixture, so I think Arthur just wanted the thing over with.

So no, we never got to see it. We only had, really, the word of the film editor herself that it was as good as we thought it was. But we both had a feeling that it was good. Well, it was bad enough for Judy to have done that. Judy was already labeled as temperamental. She was in big trouble because, after all, she's the New York interloper and everybody in that field takes such pleasure in the downfall of a star. It's peculiar that way; it's probably the least empathetic business that I've ever encountered.

One time I took Judy around to see various musicians, and we went down to Birdland and Cannonball Adderley was there. Cannonball played some stuff and it was great. Right away she liked the idea that one musician listens to another. When something really worked out well that Cannonball was playing, I was as elated as he was. I wasn't angry. Then after that, he finished his set and joined us. The three of us were wandering around and heard various people. And Cannonball was the same way, man. Whenever we heard something great, he really made us feel great. And she thought this was an enviable quality and it was something that she really reacted well to, because she felt it was so different in the theater where, if somebody does something good, the other people are all impressed. And this is one of the things about the jazz scene that really struck her. So she really felt a tremendous kinship with the music, with the players, and with the scene, and as a consequence, the guys loved her too. She was just there, she used to come down to Jim and Andy's with me. She'd hang out with the musicians and we'd have a great time. But people in the theater couldn't get her to move for that.

Well, that fixed my reputation in Hollywood and ever after, even with people I'd known in the business who were friendly to me and had used me for things in the past. I was a trouble-maker and I should never have interfered with all this stuff and, you know, they had a point. There was nothing I could say about it, although they never approached me to find out what I had to say. As I said, I felt obliged to help her do it because I was dealing with somebody who was in an extremely precarious position and if this is the thing that would help her, I felt obliged to do it. I had to suffer the consequences of the reputation as Gerry Svengali, which I thought was pretty funny.

By that time, God knows my name was mud in California. In fact, there was somebody, a man that was one of the producers of *I Want to Live*, that I liked very much. He was very hip about music, Max Youngstein. A few months after we had finished that thing up, we were back in New York and were doing whatever it was that we were doing. I think Judy was probably hibernating or trying to recover from her collection of bruises that Hollywood had laid on her.

I heard from somebody that Max was really pissed off at me for interfering in this thing, that I shouldn't have done it. I tried to get a hold of Max to talk to him about it. I never could reach him so I gave it up. I said, you know, if people want to believe things or they feel justified, you can't always do anything about it anyway. There were few people, really, that I wanted to defend myself to, but there were a few people that I respected that I would like to have been able to. Because I felt, you see, that there was nothing else I could do—that it was a question of whether I was going to have loyalty to my friend, who was in trouble and asked me to, or whether I was going to ignore the whole thing. I said, "No, I won't do it."

So when the finished picture came out, Judy didn't like it all because it was kind of rambling and she felt that she didn't look good, so it was a bad experience for her. After that I think that Arthur didn't really want to have anything to do with me because I represented to him this whole painful period. This always kind of hurt because I liked Arthur a lot.

Oddly enough, *Bells Are Ringing* did very well. Profits were like a million and a half or two million, something like that. I don't know if it was on the scale of *Gigi*'s success, but it didn't lose money. I think it was fairly obvious that Judy still had some drawing power and was still able to pull people in on her name, because it wasn't much of a show.

It's kind of fascinating to be around filmmaking, and in this instance, I hadn't started the big band yet, so I was out there most of the time. I only took off a couple of times and played stuff with the quartet, plus I did a lot of playing around Los Angeles.

Ben Webster was out there then, so I managed to keep working and stay out there while Judy was shooting, and I realized that she needed the support because she was really alone there. There was something about that I never understood. I still am a little confused by it because she made a lot of friends there over the years, but there were very, very few people that she would contact, call up to visit. Some of them I was dying to meet, so I would kind of nudge her to see some of them, like Ira Gershwin and his wife. I would love to have met Ira Gershwin. She always talked about Ira Gershwin and Gene Kelly, people that she admired, respected, and had a great time with. I said, boy, these are people I want to get discovered by, so I'd like nothing better than to meet them. I'll write tunes with Ira Gershwin for Gene Kelly. Well, forget it, man. I couldn't get her to be in touch with anybody and I never understood what any of that was about; all of the old friends that she had out there. When she would introduce me to people, I would get this cold shoulder from them and they were automatically down on me because I was with her. That was with people as diverse as Aaron Copland to Frank Sinatra. I truly never really quite understood it. Judy explained, at different times, what she felt the problem was. With Copland, I guess she had had a little affair with Copland's assistant. They had gone out and they liked each other, so she always felt that Copland was a bit jealous about this. So when she introduced me to Copland and this assistant was still there, she felt that it related to all of that somehow. Copland just cut me dead. Some of these things were kind of a shock because some of the people that I met from the symphonic field knew who I was, and in a musical way it was great because they didn't have their noses up in the air about jazz. Some of them had respect for me and appreciation and had heard of me. But some of these people who I admired so much were really cold, and that threw me a curve. Same thing with Bernstein. Judy had apparently gone with him a bit in the early days, when they had The Reviewers and he was their accompanist. I won't go into the story that she told me because I'm not trying to do a "kiss and tell" biography here. I don't know why I should be so reluctant to do that since discretion was never one of Lenny's considerations, but it always makes me feel a little peculiar to talk about people's personal problems. They're not my problems, and the fact that it wound up reflecting on me in some kind of way was kind of a shame, because he was another man whom I respected a great deal. Boy, would I have loved to have studied with him. And I've learned a lot watching him rehearse an orchestra, for he was a brilliant musician but a man loaded with problems. So his problems, and the relationship with Judy, again reflected on me.

Anyway, in Hollywood or Beverly Hills, it was impossible to get her to do any socializing. In a funny way Judy was naive enough to be optimistic about a lot of things. Now, for some of the people who knew her knew she had a basic streak of sadness. I guess it's the traditional Pagliacci, the clown who is really sad at heart. Very common. It's a cliché, but a cliché based on some kind of reality. And Judy was no exception. Judy was just such an outcast all the way around.

22

THE CONCERT
JAZZ BAND

I ALWAYS WANTED TO HAVE a big band, and the Concert Jazz Band kind of evolved out of the various smaller groups. But I think if it hadn't been for the pressure from some of my friends, I probably wouldn't have put the band together.

Nick Travis was a trumpet player who was a friend of mine for a long time, and I had met him when we were still in high school because he was from Philadelphia. I went to that boy's school that had no music, but there was a public vocational school on the other side of Philadelphia and they had a band and music courses. There were guys there that transcribed arrangements of the bands so that they could play them.

Concert Jazz Band, Carnegie Hall, 1978.
© FRANCA R. MULLIGAN

When I heard about that I used to go over to the school and hang out a lot. I would listen to the band and hang out with the musicians, and one of the people there was Nick.

So at this point Nick started to pressure me. He said, "Come on, man, you always said you wanted to have a big band, now's the time, let's put this band together." Kind of trying to light a fire under me.

Brookmeyer liked the idea and so I said, "What the hell." The money that I had made was burning a hole in my pocket, so I started to organize this band. That started me thinking about what the instrumentation should be. Instead of having this big, big, big band, with this powerhouse sound and feeling and to be locked into that kind of approach, which was what all the bands sounded like at that point, I decided that it would be better for my purpose to have a smaller band. Six brass and four saxes was a whole lot different in the approach that it demands, as opposed to seven brass and five saxes. To people who are not arrangers that may not seem like a big difference, but when you're an arranger, it's a tremendous difference. And it's the kind of thing where you can be aware that the impact of the two instrumentations is totally, totally different.

In a way, adding all those instruments backed the bands into a corner in the 1940s because, as they added to it, they kind of negated their own flexibility, and more and more they tended to sound alike. When you have so many instruments and you use them all the time, you wind up having a sameness to the textures, and the textures lose their transparency and become thicker and heavier. The bands of the 1930s were much more fly and fleet, and they could move with more agility because they didn't have all of that weight. Compare the weight—Benny's band swung and moved in the middle 1930s when it was still five brass and four saxes. With four saxes they could do things that were a part of the rhythm section, and they popped these things out, man, and the whole thing just hopped. It had really great time feel and then, later on, bands started to trudge and plod because they were so overloaded.

Well, I became more and more conscious of that and decided to take a smaller band and try to go back to the fleetness that I liked in an ensemble, and in some ways, I thought, well, I could do a thing that would combine a little bit of the *Birth of the Cool* instrumentation. So my original intention was to have three trumpets, two bones, and a tuba and then the four saxes, besides myself. I didn't really think of it as four saxes; mainly, it was four reeds. The first chair was clarinet and the early book is all written with clarinet, lead alto, tenor, baritone, one of each, and then I was available on baritone for another voice. I could work with any section, but it was not that often that I had written with the saxophone section so it was really the four, and bass and drums. In retrospect I wish that I had thought of having a piano in it. It would have taken a lot of the pressure off the rhythm section. There were certain things that I wanted to do, combining the approach to arranging that we were able to do with the pianoless quartets. And in this band, the idea was to be able to do that, either with me and Brookmeyer or me and one of the trumpets.

Well, in the end I never really had a trumpet player who really worked in a quartet manner with me. Later on, when I had some guys who could have done it, the book was too well set and I was limited in being able to afford more material and certainly the time to do it. In fact, all the time I had that band I wrote only two or three charts. My whole idea for having a band was because I wanted a band to write for. I've never really been good at being a split personality in that way. I'm not schizoid in that I can take care of business and then just turn around and go write music. I just couldn't do it. So having such a limited time to write and being able to get myself in the frame of mind to write, I wound up doing only a few charts. I had already done a couple of charts on "Walking Shoes." So very little new thought went into it, even though it takes me time to make a new arrangement; I mean, it's not just a copy of the other ones. Let's see, the next chart that I wrote was number 35, "Come Rain or Come Shine." "Walking Shoes" was number 2, and the only thing of mine in between was a reduced arrangement of "Young Blood," which was number 13. Toward the end of the life of that band, I wrote the chart on "Getting Sentimental over You," which was number 65. It was the last number in the book, and I never got around to using it.

It was a full-time job putting that band together and getting it working and taking care of business, and you know, when you start a band, you're a small business, like it or not. If you don't take care of business, you find yourself really out on a limb, and I had a big investment in that band, spent a lot of money on it.

The instrumentation ended up being three trumpets, two trombones plus Brookmeyer on valve trombone, and then four woodwinds, bass, and drums. This was an altogether different instrumentation, sound, and impact from the band that I had recorded in 1957. So we had to start from the ground up putting a book together. I brought in Bill Holman from California. He was in New York for a couple of months working on arrangements. I got an apartment for him, outfitted it with a piano, and put him to work. Bill did the bulk of the original book. He was concentrating on that and nothing else. Brookmeyer did quite a bit of it. Al Cohn did a few things. I was always after Al to do more, but he had so many commitments in various places. Wonderful arranger, he was. God, he wrote great things for us. I got Johnny Carisi to write a couple of things that he had done, like "Israel." We had a very, very nice arrangement that he had done. Actually, it was the same arrangement but it had more to it because we had the big band. Another piece he called "Lestorian Mode."

So that's how we got started. We didn't ever have road managers or band boys or anything; we did it ourselves. It was after we actually had made some of the first records that Brookmeyer decided, and I agreed, that we needed Mel Lewis for the band. We felt he was the only one. I mean, the other guys had played very nice, but he said, "You've got to have Mel."

Mel was still on staff at ABC in Hollywood, and I used to fly him back and forth to rehearsals and to play gigs around here until his staff job was over. He was finishing up there, and then he came east and joined the band full-time. But as you might surmise, I went through a whole lot of money doing that, bringing in Bill to arrange and having him on salary, and flying Mel back and forth. And, you know, all the other expenses: rehearsal halls, copying, you name it.

Gerry and Bob Brookmeyer, late 1970s.
© FRANCA R. MULLIGAN

But we finally got it together and took the band out, and the way we ran it was that Mel, Brookmeyer, and Nick helped me take care of business. Each one took kind of a job on themselves on the road. Brookmeyer was always kind of the captain in charge of the music, and Nick helped me with the business, and Mel too. A lot was handling the equipment on the road because I didn't want to carry just those cardboard-front bandstands that the bands all used.

When I was in school as a kid in seventh, eighth, and ninth grade, I was always designing bandstand fronts. So then when it came time to put my band together, I thought that was kind of corny, so I had those regular black Hamilton studio stands that weigh a ton. I had a whole set of those for the band. God, they were bulky. I had two gigantic cases of those, plus I didn't want the guys sitting down and I didn't want to make them stand up all the time, so I had stools like drummers' stools, so that they were higher than they would be sitting because I never liked to play just sitting down on a chair. If you're elevated a little bit, it's like your body is more into it.

So I was carrying all this equipment plus the regular stuff like the lights, and then the big box for the book—the library. So it was really something on the road, because we never had a band boy and we used to travel in Europe a great deal of the time by train. One of the wonderful things about it was that the spirit of the band was great, even though we were invariably tired because the band always drank too much. But to see the band pull into a station on the train, man, the windows in the car would come down and we'd have our stuff unloaded. All this heavy equipment plus the bass and the drums, and we'd have the whole thing unloaded in about three minutes flat. All the guys jumped in and it was like the gang on the fire brigade passing the water down the line. That's what we did with the luggage and the equipment, and that's how we traveled as a band. So it was a great time for everybody.

We wound up having our first tour thanks to Norman Granz. We only played four or five dates in the States, which he put together because he wanted us to have some experience with the band in front of an audience before we went to Europe.

This first tour we played first in Stockton, California. In Stockton we had a strange experience with the band that we never really knew what was happening, but not necessarily being of a trusting nature, we figured that we were being infiltrated by the FBI or something.

We were setting up and rehearsing in the afternoon, and this guy came around and started bugging me. He was asking questions and acting like the rube fan. I fended him off as best I could, but he really got to bugging me. So Nick and Brookmeyer and Mel were always kind of watching out for me because it was kind of a tough role for me, especially because equanimity in the face of squares is not one of my great virtues. I was still cool with this guy, but he kept bugging us, and something happened and he kept asking questions about the guys in the band, implying did we want to buy some dope or something, and the whole thing started to smell a little fishy to us. We finally got rid of him in the afternoon. That evening we were playing in an auditorium that was connected to the hotel. We came down in the elevator and the four of us are walking along, and this guy comes up and starts in on us again. I can't remember what he said but whatever it was we were all getting really teed off at him. He was a pain in the neck and he obviously was trying to start something, and we thought this guy has got to be planted here by somebody's police or other. Why do they bother with this nonsense? And he said something that just was . . . that was it, man, and I hauled off and hit this guy with my fist and really knocked him out. Nick and Bobby and Mel are standing there looking at me, like, where did that come from? I never had a reputation as a fighter, man, and I just knocked this cat out flat. It tickled them so much. And that was the end of it. He never bothered us anymore. It's too bad you can't get out from the things that bother you in life that easily all the time.

So we went from there to, I can't remember if we played a date in San Francisco or not; I think not. I think we went right from Stockton. One of the things that Norman wanted to do was record the band live at our concerts, and he figured there were certain halls where we would have good recording equipment, so we would have a chance of doing it three or four times in controlled recording conditions and have a chance for some choices for an album. The first place we did was Santa Monica Auditorium, and we brought down all the equipment, so we were really set up for that. That came out all right.

While we were on the tour, Judy was now doing a play called *Laurette*, which was a stage version of the biography of Laurette Taylor, who was a woman she admired very much. In her later career, Taylor's probably most famous for *Outward Bound*. She was widely acclaimed for that role. Oddly enough, in the pictures of Laurette Taylor, Judy looked a lot like her. There was a physical resemblance, and Judy felt kind of a kinship with her.

The producer was Alan Pakula, who has since become very, very successful as a producer and director. He was a very talented man and a sweetheart. He really was a good-hearted man and he really loved Judy, and he had this play, and she wanted to do it because it was a dramatic play. He thought it was time to do something besides the dumb blonde. It was time to find something that was right for her age and for her point in her career and so on.

Well, the play was written in a kind of a surrealistic way that just really didn't work. They were kind of doing a flashback thing, starting at the end and kind of flashing back to episodes in her life. And, you know, it was kind of eerie and it was stagey in a way that was unrealistic, especially with Judy playing it because, unfortunately for this play, when Judy first makes an appearance, everything stops, applause, applause, applause. Well, her first appearance was on stage, but you don't know it, because she was lying down on a couch with her back to the audience and she's supposed to be drunk and sleeping. So for her first appearance they had to stop for applause—it totally threw Judy. I remember Patrick O'Neil and Joan Hackett played the young couple that were, I don't know, her niece and nephew or something. I can't even recall. They'd walk onto the front of the stage talking as if they're outside the house. Patrick is supposed to press an imaginary doorbell button. And of course, in a thing like that, it's inevitable. He goes to press this imaginary button and it doesn't go off. You know, it starts out with embarrassments like that. And the play was loaded with stuff like that, stagey bits that are the kind of tacky things that an audience kind of cringes when they see it. Even if it works, it was kind of distracting. So everything about it was just off-kilter and it didn't work, man, it was just like a dud.

When they started playing it on the road, it was the out-of-town run to try to get it together. I remember very well, as I was starting out with the Concert Jazz Band at that point. I was rehearsing a lot and by the time they got to Philadelphia, I was out in California with the band. I remember that Judy, as this thing progressed, was very depressed by it because she really wanted to do it, felt she could do it, and she just couldn't get it off the ground. She just couldn't make that first feeling that she's going to be able to find the hook, the way to play this role so that it's going to work, but she kept doggedly at it and tried to find it.

Well, I remember very well, I guess by this time they were in New Haven or Boston or someplace, and she was really enthusiastic because at some point she started to feel that parts of the play were going to work and the effort they had put into it was paying off. They had been seriously thinking of just dropping the whole thing because of the problems with the book and the fact that Judy couldn't get a feeling for it. But as soon as she felt that first glimmer and some connection with the part, and that it was going to work, Alan said that he would take the thing on the road as long as she wants, as long as they need, and he was going to get the book rewritten the way it should be. It was like a whole optimistic sunrise.

Of course, he was having a problem with the writer all this time. The writer wasn't doing what needed doing to make the thing work, and he was also going to stand in the way of getting another writer. Well, Alan was trying to get all of that ironed out—to get somebody in who would really do it, and do it chronologically. No more flashbacks and stagey stuff, and it was really starting to look good.

I forget where I was, it was probably when we were doing the thing with the band at Santa Monica Auditorium. After Santa Monica we got a day off and then the band was traveling by bus to Tucson or someplace. A long haul, Salt Lake City or something, I don't recall.

I called Judy, who by this time was in Philadelphia. On one hand she was really excited because the play was going well. The thing was really starting to feel good. On the other hand, she was upset because she was having problems with her voice. She was very hoarse and she was having problems with laryngitis. So the next morning I called up and I was trying to decide whether to fly in to see this performance, but I figured I'd get a chance to see it the following week when we got back to New York. I called up and I talked to one of her friends, Paul, who had worked on *Bells Are Ringing.* Paul was a very good friend of hers and was working as the stage manager of this thing. Judy was really quite frightened because they had a doctor in to examine her for her voice and he found a lump in her breast. She was going to have to go to New York and have it examined immediately.

Well, Judy begged me to come in to see what they were doing, because she figured if she leaves this thing to have to go into the hospital, they're going to close this down. But as soon as she's finished, they're going to take it out and put it together again. That's what Pakula thought to do as it came together.

So I got on a plane and flew to Philadelphia. Well, when I got there, on a red eye I guess, the following morning I got to the hotel and went into the suite where she and her friends were, and it was like walking into a wake. She had decided that she needed to go to New York immediately, and that she wanted to play the thing once more just in case, because if they're going to operate on her, then it's going to be a long time before she does anything. And if they don't operate on her, then it's still going to be a while and she wanted me to see the thing.

Well, they opted finally not to. The doctor I guess pressured her into it. It's one of those decisions that when the doctor decides, nobody dares go back on it. At that point, one more day wasn't going to make any difference, but there was no convincing anyone of that. So I never did see the damn thing in some kind of a form that she was pleased with.

I took her to New York for an examination. They did a mastectomy while she was there. He was the kind of surgeon who assured her that if he had to do any kind of operating, it would be a small operation and she would be able to wear regular dresses with regular necks, no problem. Well, he did what they call a radical mastectomy. It was impossible for her to wear anything except very close kind of neck things, dresses. The psychological effect on her was devastating. Well, that finished the Laurette project. There was no chance of ever getting that together again. And it was a long uphill battle just to be able to get her to face life at all, she was just so depressed.

During those three days, I went back to New York and was there with her through the operation. Then I got on a plane and went back West and did the rest of the dates we were supposed to do, then went to New York and played at Hunter College, then took off for Europe.

Our first dates in Europe were in Gothenburg and Stockholm. Gothenburg was another place that Norman wanted to have a recording take place, because he had the equipment over there and they were going to do it in conjunction, I think, with a radio broadcast or something. So that was to be one of the stops that was recorded. Then we went to Stockholm, Copenhagen, and on to Berlin.

Well, my band was having a little too much fun partying at that point. Berlin was kind of a disaster because a couple of the guys got themselves into the kinds of trouble they shouldn't have. I never really did find out but Willie Dennis, the trombone player, showed up at the concert that evening in Berlin with his right hand all bandaged and with a finger in a splint, the center finger. That's great, that's like right out of a comedy. It was taped up like he was giving the finger to the audience and playing his slide. He'd gotten into some kind of a scrape somewhere and most of the guys came in pretty torn up.

The next night we go to Paris, and wouldn't you know it, man, that wasn't one of the stops Norman wanted to use for recording but it was one of the stops that was broadcast on the radio. The band was really tired at this point. Recently these tapes from Radio France have turned up and they sent them to me. I held back on them as long as I could but finally said, "Well, what the hell?" Everybody else hears them and it sounds all right. It doesn't sound all right to me because in order to compensate for the fact that the band sounded so exhausted, I realized I was taking everything faster than normal, trying to substitute with fast tempos for the lack of energy that we had. It sounded like we were operating on sheer nervous energy. Zoot played a lot of choruses on this one piece as he usually did, but it was like ringing out a dry sponge, man. He just kept repeating himself. I listened to the thing and it brought it all back and I said, "Oh man, do we really want this record to come out?"

From Paris, I forget where we went, but we traveled around for a while and wound up in Italy. There was a friend of mine in Italy who wanted to record us. He wasn't a sound engineer at all, but he had access to a good machine. He had an Ampex over there, and we did a matinee and an evening performance. He recorded the matinee, and then in the evening he recorded over the tape that he had done in the afternoon. So a lot of the stuff that he did wasn't usable, but there were a couple of takes that we wound up using out of the things that he recorded.

I think one of the versions we did of Ben Webster's tune "Go Home" we used, because that would be so different from one night to the next. I wound up putting two versions of it on the album because it's like a totally different piece. And we ended up using some of the tape from radio. It was the army's radio station in Germany. They broadcast it so there were a couple of things out of that. It's amazing the album sounds as cohesive as it does because it was done in all different kinds of circumstances. The Gothenburg tape was lost altogether. We never could find it and had no idea what happened to it, but a few years ago it turned up again. We have no idea where it was, who had it, or who's been sitting on it all these years. I listened to the things and of course I wanted to edit them. Some of the things just went on and on and on, and I would have liked to have trimmed them down.

Anyway, we got an album out of the European tour with the Concert Jazz Band, and the album was called *On Tour.* We had quite a tour with the band. The band drank too much but we played all right. The guys forget that you're supposed to sleep when you're traveling.

I've always felt that in-person performances were totally different from a record, and I know a lot of fans like to have the record of a live performance so they accept it on those terms. But I can't. If you're sitting in a theater and a band does something and they stretch out and somebody takes another chorus, there's something physical that goes on. The audience is with you, they can see it and they understand why you're doing it. Whereas when you're listening, you don't necessarily have that same connection, and it musically may not make any sense at all. It's just like your playing is self-indulgent or whatever, and it can become a bore.

That's just one example. There are lots of things about the interaction between an audience and a band that take place when you're playing in front of them that is altogether different from the impact of music when this physical element is not involved. It's you, your ears, and music; it's a private coming together in your head, your senses. Totally different from the relationship between thirteen, fourteen, or fifteen musicians here and a couple of thousand people out there, and it's just not the same thing.

So I really would like to have seen the things edited down, but Norman is a great believer in doing things the way they are. He likes jam sessions for that reason—you know, let things happen—and he thinks that a record should be a realistic presentation of what happened. Norman and I always respected each other's opinions but have felt differently about the function of records. If I had a record company, I might be the way he is about it, but of course what I'm doing, man, I'm trying to protect my entity, which is my own band and my own music. So I want to put it in front of an audience in a way that's going to attract them to play it more than once. And that's a totally different thing, like a lot of these things that are long, long, long, long. I might play it once and say, "That's nice," and then never play it again.

To play a thing that has a form to it that you can get into, and usually, if people listen to the things that we've done—my studio dates that are geared for albums—if they listen to it twice then they're likely to play it over and over again. A lot of times you hear the thing the first time and it doesn't really hit you, it doesn't grab you, it builds slowly. So this is the thing you're up against with albums and with the competition for people's listening time: how to con them into listening twice. And part of the thing you have to be aware of is how you program the material, and the longer the records got, the harder it got to do. Today, man, you put over an hour of material in one album, and it's an altogether different ball game. When we were doing an LP, the maximum you could put on it was like thirty-five minutes and that was stretching it; usually it would be closer to thirty minutes, thirty-four tops. And it was a challenge then to sustain interest, so trying to sustain interest now for over an hour is something that I don't think is so easy to accomplish, and judging by the CDs that I've heard, I'm afraid it's true.

But people may be going through a conditioning process. They must be listening differently or something. Maybe this is another case of not being able to accommodate the new toys yet. People just go along with it because it's there.

I used to leave it up to the engineers, or my A&R man, whoever was supervising the date. It was important to have a kind of rapport so that we could trust each other, and I could trust his taste, and we'd be able to toss ideas back and forth, and I'd be able to count on him to supervise if I couldn't be there. In recent years I've been even more closely involved, because most of the albums I've done in the last ten years I've produced myself and then taken as a finished product to a company. That way we have the control from the beginning. Even the last couple of things that I've done for Telarc, they came in and recorded, but I had this stuff pretty well organized before we got to that point. I kind of keep a good control of what we're doing.

Well, that's really kind of wrong, because I seldom went in a studio with an overall idea of what the album was going to be. It has to evolve out of the material that we're doing, especially if I'm doing new material. I don't know where that's going to lead me. I have no real idea. So I'm dependent if I record for somebody else; I'm dependent on their ability to go along with me, to let me find my way, because it's like a tightrope walk to be able to do all of this in a minimum of time. I don't have open-ended time to do it. We don't have hundreds of thousands of dollars like they're spending on pop dates. I've got to bring these things in at some kind of a reasonable amount of money.

And so, taking that in conjunction with the idea that I'm finding my way as I go along is kind of an ongoing challenge, and Telarc has been very good with me about that, you know. The people that are recording and the main engineer is one of the partners in the company, and he just seems to appreciate my way of approaching things and doing it, and we come out of it with good material. So it's been a successful method so far.

I can't really plan all of that stuff ahead, especially with a small band. When you're dealing with big band material, it's got to be more thoroughly organized. I'd love to be able to let things evolve more easily with big bands, piece them together, take this and let's try that, but that's expensive. Even just doing it in rehearsal is expensive. Rehearsal time costs damn near as much as recording time. So I don't have the luxury to do those things. With the small band I have a little more leeway to let things happen, and I can wind up with an album that sounds fairly planned from beginning to end that wasn't at all, but that just kind of evolved out of the material and the approach to it.

One of my favorites for that was the one we did called *Lonesome Boulevard*, which was like a very well-thought-out album. It sounds not like a quartet of a horn with a rhythm section; it sounds like a band. The stuff felt like it had the advantage of arrangements that made a setting for each of the solos, and the thing evolved in a very natural way. When we were doing it, it didn't seem like that at all. It seemed like a very haphazard affair. I think people look at it and say, what's he doing? So, whatever, it worked.

Any kind of a musical project is expensive. These are things that people who are not connected with the business don't see; what a musician goes through putting together an album, they have no real conception of, especially the expense involved, and to realize that in jazz there is seldom going to be investing of any great amount of money. Jazz is a nice idiom for the record companies because we're cheap to record, the guys are professional, know what they're doing, and they can go inside of the required number of dates and walk out with a decent album. Depending on the players, you can walk out with a great album, but you'll seldom find anybody investing any great amount of money. Whereas the pop scene, they're very much in the habit of spending a hundred, two hundred, three hundred thousand dollars for an album. It's like put these guys in a studio for a month and hope for the best. So sometimes they hit and mostly they don't. But they're not doing that with jazz. So we're there as kind of a stopgap measure. We're easy to record and we're cheap.

23

THEME FOR JOBIM

I MET Antônio Carlos Jobim (Tom), João Gilberto, and Sergio Mendes when they first came to New York and did a concert at Carnegie Hall. When I went into the dressing room, it was Tom and João there, and they took one look at me and João started to sing. He sang the record of, I think it was "Bernie's Tune," beginning to end with the solos and everything in it. It was so funny, but they knew very well all of the stuff that I had done in the quartet and the tentet and the *Birth of the Cool.* Jobim and I became great friends. We always called each other "brother"—my Brazilian brother.

Jobim and João both asked me to record with them. They both wanted me to, and my response to that was that I needed time to become acclimated to the rhythm feel. I didn't want to go in and just try to play with it, with that rhythm section, because an American rhythmic sensibility superimposed on a Brazilian rhythm section sounds so angular that I wanted to be able to get something of the real flavor and be able to think in those terms that Brazilian music had, and it flows in a totally different way. My feeling has always been about that. Wherever a jazz player is from is reflected in his approach to playing, especially in his approach to rhythm and melody, because the languages that we speak all have different cadences to them.

It's not easy, for instance, for a European, or it's not easy for an Italian or French man, to be able to convincingly phrase in ways that are similar to an American player. They have to find their own way based on the cadences that they're used to.

Gerry with Antônio Carlos Jobim, Botanical Garden, Rio de Janeiro, Brazil, 1986.
COURTESY GERRY MULLIGAN COLLECTION, LIBRARY OF CONGRESS, MUSIC DIVISION

This reflects, in a way, the dictum of Lester Young. Which was in order to play tunes well, you should know the lyrics, you should know what the words are, because the melodies relate to the words. Well, the English language is a far more angular, and accented in a more direct way, than any of the Romance languages. That's why you'll hear, in Brazilian music, a kind of floating one. They'll play things that I can find very confusing, where in the playing, you're not sure where the one is, the one floats. It's someplace behind where you think it is or ahead of where you think it is, and they do it as second nature. It doesn't faze them at all; it's fine that it's floating.

Most of our music is dead on the head. Now there are players, and this of course is not talking about free jazz or any of that stuff, because people are superimposing, they're not dealing with melodies that relate to language. Secondly, they're not dealing with a kind of pulse that we're talking about in a rhythm that's expressive of a people. What they're doing is a totally different thing. It's like modern symphonic music that's its own idiom, a figment of somebody's imagination or fantasy. So I'm not thinking that.

But, you'll hear it a lot in players from the 1960s on, where they purposely try to disguise where one is and they can really turn you around. And you're thinking. And often you're wrong. I always felt uneasy when guys would do that, start shifting one. I would start tapping it in my head, or tapping it out with my foot and often, they came out in the wrong place. Everybody adjusts to where they now think one is. I started counting those things just because it made me uneasy, and whereas most of the time I don't have to count, I know where it is. I never liked the idea that I suddenly had to start counting something to feel naturally. So I was delighted to find that half the time the guys were shocking, they didn't know where they were either.

But this was not the case in Brazilian music. It's that thing of the vanishing one, or the invisible downbeat, that always fascinated me. Listen to a tune, like "The Waters of March" by Jobim, and I defy you to find where the hell one is on those phrases. The whole thing is put together and sounds natural, but boy, it's not natural to our rhythmic sensibilities, and he does this whole thing with shifting underneath. The Brazilians can do that as second nature. So I didn't wind up doing the thing. In the meantime, kind of a funny thing happened.

The record companies wanted to cash in on this new music sweeping the United States, the Bossa Nova, and they said somebody better get to making Bossa Nova records. They got Laurindo Almeida and he did some. Then somebody said, "You know, Stan Getz already recorded a bunch of stuff with João and Tom." They didn't even know it. They had it already in the can. Then of course they released the stuff. They had it and they were sitting on it. What an irony.

So one of the things that came up when João and Tom said they wanted me to record with them was that João started to sing one of the choruses that Stan had recorded, and he was making fun of him because the phrasing sounded so corny to João. I said, "That's precisely why I want to spend time becoming familiar with the whole time feel. You know, we're talking about something else altogether and I really don't feel like going out and making a fool of myself."

Well, in the meantime, they got Tom and João to make another record. I think it was with Stan and Astrud Gilberto. The record company wanted to do it so Tom and João didn't fight for it, so that was the end of that. I would have liked to have done it with them. I just wanted a little time to absorb it, but wanting a little time in this business to do a thing properly was just enough to keep me out altogether.

24

HOLLIDAY WITH MULLIGAN

I DECIDED to put together an album of mainly songs that Judy and I had written together, because that was our hobby. We started writing songs together, and we did a few things that were nice and that we got other people to do, like Dinah Shore did a couple of our songs, including our Christmas song on one of her shows. But we didn't have any capabilities as song pluggers, so we'd write these things and then they'd lie there. So we thought we'd record them. Judy was game, although the idea of making a record, like almost any kind of performing, made her so nervous. Her idea of a normal record date was the one she had done for Columbia called *Trouble Is a Man,* which was very nice, with good arrangements by Glenn Osser. It was well put together, but she'd go into the studio and go to the ladies' room and heave and then she'd come back and be ready to sing. And, you know, the kind of thing of saying, "Doesn't everybody?" But the whole idea made her so nervous, although there are other singers who are like that.

It kind of reminds me a little of Pee Wee Russell's story. Pee Wee was having trouble with his stomach. He didn't really feel well so he went to the doctor. The doctor said, "Well, maybe I can get an idea of what's the matter with you. Tell me what your daily routine is like."

Pee Wee said, "Well, you know, I get up in the morning and have a glass of rye or bourbon and then I go to the bathroom and heave. Then I have a little more bourbon and go and have some coffee." The doctor said, "You mean you get up every morning and you heave and you drink like that?" He said, "Yes, doesn't everybody?" Of course, poor Pee Wee did his stomach in pretty well with that kind of daily regime. But with Judy it was just nerves; it was absolute panic.

For *Holliday with Mulligan*, Ralph Burns and Bill Finegan both wrote arrangements. They wrote such beautiful things and I realized that the way that we all wrote for it, we were writing things that pleased us. We wrote really well in ways that made it really hard for Judy, because those things were really tough to sing.

What I should have been doing was providing that comfortable cushion underneath, because she was able to function a lot more comfortably on the *Trouble Is a Man* album. The arrangements by Glenn Osser featured strings and created just a lovely nice soft cushion for her. But these things that all of us wrote were a real challenge to sing. It was Ralph, Bill Finegan, Brookmeyer, Al Cohn, and me. There were some beautiful things they wrote. Gorgeous things, and textures that were altogether different from the rest of our stuff.

The attempt was to make a little more of a cushion out of the ensemble by having the three French horns. Ultimately, we didn't use them that way. Our intentions were sincere, but I think the execution was a little selfish.

At some point I got a telephone call from Anita Loos. Anita asked me if I'd be interested in writing a score for a comedy that she'd written. I said, "Yes, I would." As it happened, that's something I'd always wanted to do. I said, "Great." So she asked me to meet her and I did. I think I probably went down to her apartment in a building across from Carnegie Hall, and we talked about it. She said that she had been on a panel discussion and they were talking about musicals and where are the writers? The original writers for Broadway all decided that things were kind of petering out; it wasn't very interesting on Broadway.

So she was on this panel and Nat Hentoff was on the panel, and Nat suggested that maybe where the writers would be coming from was jazz. That would seem a logical thing to him, and he thought that there were people in jazz who would be ideally suited to write for the stage. So after the panel was over she asked Nat, "You suggested maybe a jazz musician might be good to write the show of the future; you must have somebody in mind?" and Nat suggested me. He said that he thought it might be something I probably would be interested to do and that he thought I could do it. So I went and talked to Anita and she gave me a copy of the book, and then she asked, "Is there anybody that you have written songs with, because you need a lyricist on this project?" I said, "Well, actually no, but I had written a number of songs with Judy Holliday, who was a friend of mine." She said, "That's great; not only could she do the songs, but maybe she would appear in it." I said, "I don't know about that. Yes, it would be great if we could do all of that, but let me see if she's interested to take on a project like that." So I went back to Judy's place and told her about it, and Judy was very excited. She said, "That's great!" She was dying to do it. So I called Anita and that was that.

About that time, Judy had decided she was going to take a house out in the Hamptons and have a vacation that was really away from the scene and recover from all of the Hollywood nonsense. I remember very well; I drove out with her to Bridgehampton, which is like the last one of the Hamptons toward Montauk. It's way out there, and it kind of worked out in a way that, with the beginning of this holiday, we had this place that she wanted to go look at, so we drove out to the Hamptons and the house was great. It belonged to a woman named Carrington, who was a famous writer of soap operas in the 1930s. It was a beautiful place. And the reason I bring that up about the soap operas and Elaine Carrington is because of the people who were connected with her son, who were friends who wound up becoming regulars at the house.

Anyway, I went through the book, reading through it and deciding the things that could be musicalized, the ideas, the jokes, the characters, and all that. So we started to work on it. Now, had we known a little more, we would have been in a little less of a hurry to start actual work on the thing, because what Anita said was that she felt that the book needed rewriting, and since Judy and I had agreed to write a score, that we should get somebody to do the rewrite on the thing to try to bring it up-to-date.

Happy Birthday is a comedy that she had written, and I guess it was performed in either 1945 or 1946 and ran for a whole season. She had written a comedy for Helen Hayes in which this kind of straightlaced librarian type with the glasses and the hair in a bun winds up going to a bar, getting loaded, taking off the glasses, and letting her hair down, and she turns out to be a beauty, of course, and her life is changed forever. Well, Anita pointed out that this was the reason the comedy had never been filmed, because the censors would never stand still for a film that advertised alcohol as the means of success in life. But, she gets loaded and becomes a beauty and everything, and her life is all changed for the better.

So we started to work on ideas that were contained in the existing book. I didn't feel that it was too big a risk to do that, because it seemed if they were going to make this book the basis of rewrites, that if I'm doing things that relate to the character or doing things that relate to comic situations, that they should stay the same in the rewrite. Little did I know that Anita brought in a bunch of different people and they always would wind up writing and come back with a different show. Not necessarily better, and not necessarily with anything to do with the *Happy Birthday* that she had written. But they would always say, "We saved some of your songs," and of course I knew right away which songs they saved, things that you could use anywhere—a love song. There were two or three things that showed up in most of the rewrites. And as with so many other things in life, timing was the crucial element.

There was one man who came in, a writer named Joe Stein, and just talking to him, I realized that with him we stood a chance to get the thing together. We played the songs for him; he liked the songs, and he was approaching the thing almost like I, as a musician, would call an arranging problem. How do you use these materials, in what sequence, to make the whole thing add up to a whole and to achieve some kind of dynamic sense along the way and have a climax and so on. And he approached it that way, and it was great to have somebody who really knew something about music because, with most of the writers, it was quite obvious they didn't even care about the music. It's just one of those curses that you have to put up with if you're going to write a musical. Well, Joe said he was really enthusiastic. We liked him and he liked us, and he liked the whole idea. He said there's one thing though, that he's in negotiations with some people about a new show and if that works out, then of course he won't be able to do it, but if it doesn't work out, he'd really like to do this with us.

Well, wouldn't you know it, the show was *Fiddler on the Roof*, and that was where he went. The one thing about this whole period, we ultimately never did get the show produced, but I met a lot of interesting people who I wouldn't have met otherwise, and I learned a lot from them. Of course, I learned a lot of things that'll never do me any practical good, but I sure enjoyed learning them anyway. You know, I met men like Joe Stein, and Max Gordon would have been involved in the thing. It was one of those things that really felt like it would have been great. It almost worked out. Max had been the one who produced *Born Yesterday* on Broadway in the first place.

At one point we talked with Moss Hart and that was great too. He had a lot of interesting comments to make about the project and about the play and what we had done with it. And had he lived, he might have been involved in some way. He kind of liked the project. I think sometimes, people who have done all of these big shows like the idea of doing a small one. And this would have been a small show. It was the kind of thing where the characters that are involved, mainly the women—the Helen Hayes role and her father—and all of these characters, were really basically clichés. This is why, I guess, in the end, people felt that it should be rewritten to try to put more meat on the characters. But an interesting thing became clear to me very early on, and it's the kind of lesson that is basic to musicals. You can do a farce and have one-dimensional characters and it can be funny as hell and people will laugh and accept it as farce. But if you put a song in the mouth of one of these characters, they cease being a one-dimensional person. It's like it stops the forward motion of the plot, and you're now concentrating on this person, and the person takes on dimensions that change the relationship to all the rest of the action that goes on. It was an interesting lesson to learn, because the sorts of things that were inevitable in the changes were not so much a thing of the action of the play, but a thing of what happens because you put songs in the mouth of the characters; a character takes on some kind of human dimensions that it wouldn't necessarily have otherwise. In the course of this play, our main character gets loaded and falls in love all in one night, and we're supposed to believe this.

So this play *Happy Birthday* being essentially a farce, you could get away with that kind of stuff, but when you stop the action and do a song, whether it's a character song or a comedy song or a plot song, it starts making demands on the characters. They have to behave in a more rational way in order for the whole thing to hang together. And that's why ultimately it needed rewriting, or some kind of re-conception.

The house that Judy had up there during this period after she was operated on was a big help, because she needed to try to find herself. She was really alienated from her friends. The whole episode with *The Bells Are Ringing* left a bad feeling, or at least a kind of tense feeling, between her and Betty and Adolph who, after all, had been the greatest friends since they were young together. I used to try to get her to go out but she just didn't want to do it, until finally, I don't know whether it was Betty or Adolph called her up and invited her to a party they were having after the theater for Peter Sellers.

Judy said she'd always wanted to meet Peter Sellers because she really admired him, so we're going to this party. So great, she tells Adolph we're going. We get over there at about eleven-thirty or something like that and ring the bell, and Adolph's wife, Phyllis, came to the door and she was very upset. She was almost crying at that point, she was so upset, and she said, kind of crying, "Peter Sellers didn't come."

And Judy, without missing a beat, says, "E-I-E-I-O. Peter Sellers didn't come, E-I-E-I-O." And I just fell down on the floor laughing, and then I realized that Phyllis didn't think it was funny at all, because she was truly upset and not able to see the humor in all of this.

So this was my social introduction to her buddies, and we went in. I knew Betty and Adolph and always got along real well with them, and I liked and admired them. Adolph's wife, Phyllis Newman, and Betty's husband, Steve, were there, and so was Leonard Bernstein. Judy introduced me to Lenny, and Lenny said hello and that was the last thing he said to me. He sat Judy down and started talking to her, and he kept his back to me the whole time. He proceeded to monopolize Judy's attention and sat her down on the couch and talked to her. I'm sitting back here; man, I didn't exist and they go through this whole thing talking about things that they were connected with and fine.

Every once in a while, I realized Judy's looking over at me kind of rolling her eyes, and it seemed, because of my relationship with Judy, they were jealous of me. Lenny was jealous of me because, in some way, he felt it was taking away from their relationship with her. She was theirs. Strange thing. And when he did direct anything to me, it was really quite cutting. He could be very sarcastic. I was disappointed at that because I really admired him, especially as a writer. I didn't know him as a conductor at that point. And the stuff that he had done was really impressive, so that was kind of hard to take. Afterward, as we left, the main conversation was kind of why Peter Sellers didn't show up.

He had had his chauffeur or whoever was driving him around call up and say that he couldn't make it because of something or other; I don't remember what it was and I don't know whether he said he was feeling ill or something. They said, "Well, do you suppose he really was ill or he just didn't come because he was going someplace else?" They were so worried about why he didn't show up, and Judy turns around to me while this was going on with kind of a smile on her face as if to say, "See, this is why I don't go out."

Lenny sat there and said, "Well, I could have gone to dinner over at so and so's and I didn't have to get dressed up for that." Man, that's all they were doing then was bitching about why Peter Sellers didn't show up. So it was kind of a disappointing social occasion and it became harder to get Judy to go out after that, because it was not as if there was any stimulation to make her want to. And she didn't care about parties and hanging out for its own sake. She liked to be around her friends if they were going to do something.

But that happens in a scene like the theater scene; people become more conscious of the social aspect of it: being seen, being included, belonging, and all that. When we left, Judy said, well, you see now why

I don't go to parties. I said, well I guess I can understand. On the other hand, you have to take your chances with people. You go to a party and maybe it's a pain in the neck, but you might go to another party and meet somebody who makes you think. You learn something that's worth taking the chance.

So Judy, because of her attitude, became more and more of an outcast, and it became impossible to get her to go out and do anything.

After her operation, they said if a woman survives five years, then they feel like they've gotten the whole thing and that she can look forward to a long life afterward. But the percentages were not so good. A great percentage of women didn't make it past five years.

So we didn't know how this was going to turn out, plus there's the psychological blow. Nobody was talking about it in those days. It was much more of a private thing. Man, these were things that had a tremendous psychological effect on the women that had them. There was very little help psychologically to overcome the damage it had done to their self-esteem as women. It took Judy about a year to get on her feet and get out and do things. I was always after her to be more active. We wrote some songs, but there was no real activity going on.

Then came the idea for a musical. Mary Rodgers, the daughter of Richard Rodgers, and lyricist Marty Charnin wrote a score for a musical. It was going to be called *Hot Spot*, in which they wanted Judy to play this character who was like another variation on the dumb blonde. But she was supposed to be a Peace Corp worker in Africa or the Far East or some kind of a nameless continent somewhere.

I was out on the road at the time. Afterward Judy always said, well, if I had been there when they'd played this stuff for her in the living room, I'd have told her not to do it. So she blamed me for it. As it was, I was glad to see her getting active and she got enthusiastic about it. And when I saw the songs she sang, they wrote some very, very nice songs.

By the time they had staged and blocked the show in New York, they were opening in Washington, out of town, for a few weeks. Morton DaCosta was the director. Tec was his nickname. He was a very successful, very well-known director, but he hadn't done anything for a while.

Joe Campanella was playing the lead and Arnie Freeman played a cut. He was called a nadir, which was like the king of this little place. Arnie was the brother of Bud Freeman. He looked a lot like Bud. We had a good time with him.

But the songs were nice, and what Judy meant when she said that if I had been there I would have said, "Don't do it," was because a good deal of the humor of the songs was the kind of thing that was funny to New Yorkers. They were like inside theater jokes or inside New Yorker jokes, and for the New York sophisticate it could be very funny, but for anybody else, a good deal of the time they didn't know where the joke was.

They got to Washington, and I don't think they had rehearsed more than a couple of days, and Tec dropped out because he had an attack of ulcers and he wound up in the hospital. Getting a replacement director turned out to be an impossible task, plus they're supposed to be working on this play. I mean, first they put it together, then they had problems with it, so they needed to get the writer down and they needed more songs.

Well, I've seen some screwy situations, but this was like right out of the Marx Brothers, and you see how painful the theater can be. It's a sort of experience that if you've never done it or never been close to it, you say, boy what fun to put together a musical; but phew! You can't imagine how wrong you are until you see something like this taking place. And it's like a juggernaut out of control.

So now they're stuck without a director. I don't remember if they had anybody come down and look at that point—they probably did—but they couldn't get a director. Then, one of the producers tried to take over as a director. He was a very nice man and he was very considerate of everybody, trying to smooth over all of these problems, but he wasn't a director. Well, he gave up. Then he asked Judy to direct and so she tried for a while, and it went on like that. Man, it was just insane and nobody was in control.

I got the onus of being the Svengali again, because when she started into this thing of directing and trying to help to get the thing on its feet, I'm busy keeping notes for her. I became her script girl sitting up in the balcony. I said, man, if you're on the outside of an organization and you're doing anything, as far as anybody's concerned, you're interfering, so it's a thankless job. And I gladly would have abdicated.

They brought in writers from Hollywood, two writers who wrote for the *I Love Lucy* show. As it turned out, they were turning up in Washington the same day as another pair of writers who were coming down from New York. Well, now they have these two writers from Hollywood in one hotel and the other writers in the other hotel, and they didn't want the one pair to know that other pair was in town. You can imagine the things that went on, and there's no director.

Then one of the partners of the producers starts getting in the middle of the thing, and he's all upset and he's putting up a lot of the money. You've got all these people calling the shots, nobody running the show, and I don't know how the hell they ever got it together as much as they did to open in New York. I just saw the whole thing as a Marx Brothers farce, and of course for the people who were in it—the composers, lyricists, and all these writers—it wasn't funny. Then when Betty and Adolph and Jule Styne came down, and other friends, everybody was down with their expert advice.

Here I'd been spending all this time trying to help Judy, but nobody ever said a word to me; they just cut me out altogether. At one point I really got so teed off at being a fly on the wall. Nobody ever asks a musician's advice, and I think the musicians know better than they do.

So they were talking about a number that they needed to do, and I said, "Yeah, I hope it won't have one of those double-time things like the number in *Gypsy*." And finally, man, all eyes turned on me and I kind of went, "Hee hee hee," and left. So the only way I could get anybody to notice me in the middle of all of that, or even to talk to me, was to say something derogatory about one of the tunes from *Gypsy*. The funniest thing being that I didn't feel that way at all about it, man, I was just pissed off.

At one point Steve Sondheim came down and wrote a tune, an opening song with Mary Rodgers, that was wonderful. It just was so great and the kind of thing that makes you realize what could have happened if Steve had been able to take the thing over. He wrote a song with Mary, and Steve said it was mainly Mary's song. He said he wasn't taking that much credit for it. I told him it was just really wonderful. It was a character song and you now had a setup for what went after, and it gave some kind of meaning because, the first crack out of the box, you establish a character for Judy; she's not just an object like answering things with the dumb blonde. There's some reason for her being the way she is.

This whole song was about, "I'm going to do things this way, but then on the other hand . . ." and it was always like that. "I'm going to . . . but on the other hand . . ." You know it was somebody who was indecisive in their life, and it was, like, a revealing song. Things like that, when they work—to see it work, man, is just like a masterful thing and melodically terrific. Mary was a very, very talented writer. And Marty Charnin too. His lyrics were interesting; it's just that I felt he was aiming for a level of humor that didn't help to establish Judy's character. Years later, actually not too long ago, I heard somebody say that Marty had been on a program or a symposium someplace and he was asked about the show, and he was very, very critical of Judy because he didn't feel that she had done her best effort. He felt like she was not enthusiastic enough and kind of pulled the thing down. When I heard this, I marveled at people's conception of what's gone wrong, because I never saw anybody work harder to try to help a thing come together, and not by being dictatorial or authoritarian, but trying to be cooperative and help them overcome their differences.

There were all kinds of people involved who created problems from their own field. They all felt justified. There was terrible tension between the choreographer and everybody else; the costume designer, the set designer, and all these people had their own ideas, and it's like none of them ever got together. They were all fighting, and this in a project that had no captain of the ship, nobody to steer the damn thing, no director.

They finally got the thing opened on Broadway, and I don't know how they did it. In the end it wasn't a very successful show and didn't really hang together very well. But that was her one theater experience after the operation, and I helped influence her to do it just to get her out and make her work, make her face an audience. In that respect it was good for her, because then what she was facing wasn't quite such a secret thing that she was going through, because a lot of women came to her at that time. They'd come backstage and some of them were in worse psychological shape than she was. So she found herself giving motherly advice to other young women who had gone through this sort of thing. I think that helped kind of jolt her out of this terrible sadness that she was in.

25

SONG FOR AN UNFINISHED WOMAN

ULTIMATELY THERE WAS not much more that Judy did, and then she became ill again, and there was about a year's decline involved while this developed. And it was one of those things in life to witness that you can't quite believe unless you live through it: the mechanism of denial that we humans are heir to. She never, to the end, believed that she had cancer and that it was terminal. She always believed that it was something that had been misdiagnosed and they'd come up with the right diagnosis and come up with something. This was partly based on the decision of her doctors not to tell her, which of course is up to the doctors and the surgeon, but this was even post-surgery; this was her regular doctor. To make the decision not to tell her, they need the cooperation of everybody concerned. The doctor contacted me and Judy's best friend, the lawyer named Arnold Krackauer. He was a great guy and really tried to take care of Judy as best he could, because her finances really got complicated. As the years and the illness progressed, it became more and more difficult. So he was always trying to take care of her.

So the doctor got Arnold and me in his office, and he said that he'd made the decision, especially given Judy's family situation. Her son was maybe ten years old and her mother was in her seventies. Her mother was always kind of a depressive. It was part of Judy's hang-ups, of her grasp of reality, and also the fact that she was kind of psychic, especially where her mother was concerned.

I remember the story of her when she was married to Dave Oppenheim. He was a marvelous clarinetist and was the TV producer for a lot of the stuff they did with the New York Philharmonic and the shows that Lenny did with the orchestra in Russia, and the shows for the kids and all of that. When they were married, the thing that happened a couple of times was that Judy would wake up in the middle of the night and say, "My God, my mother's in trouble." She would jump in a cab and go down and sure enough, she'd find her mother with her head in the gas oven trying to do herself in. So this was always another fear of Judy's, that she'd kind of inherited this terrible depressive streak that I wasn't really aware of—her relationship with all the other people that she knew, or the New York scene. Our relationship really was based more on our connections with music and personal connections not having to do with the theater. But still, I'm not of the theater, and not of that world, so I didn't know her effect on other people.

Not too long ago, I was talking with Steve Allen and his wife, Jayne Meadows, who was on the scene a lot in those days when Judy was. So she knew her very well, and she told me, "When Judy was young, she had the ability to walk into a room and bring a cloud of gloom with her. Within minutes the whole place was sad." And you know I hated to believe that, and hated to hear it. I could believe it was true because it was. I had never seen this myself. The few times that I went anywhere with her, she went and saw old friends and they were always so glad to see her that this never occurred, but Jayne knew her years and years ago when they were young actors on the scene. And I realized that Judy was very depressive in her personality. It was an odd . . . I shouldn't say odd; because of the way that Judy was, I wound up learning a lot about how to be with another person.

I'd always been so self-centered and totally focused on music, and because of my focus on music, I just felt that nothing else was important, and as a consequence I was kind of like a bull in a china shop in life. Because it was all focused on music, I felt that whatever it was, I was perfectly justified. You wind up . . . it's possible to hurt people without meaning to, without considering it.

So dealing with Judy, I started to become very conscious of somebody else's problems. Especially the way these problems grew. During these periods, the most important thing was being the crutch for her, to help her cope with these problems as they arose. And they were not small problems. They were all-encompassing problems to her. To everybody else concerned, they may have been small, but it was her life.

She was a very intuitive woman. I think there were a lot of things that she was kind of superstitiously aware of, whether or not she admitted it to herself. There was one time when Antônio Jobim and I were at her apartment together in the Dakota, and we were taking turns playing the piano. He'd play me something he wrote then I'd play him something I wrote, and then he'd play something and it went on like that. Judy sat there and as this went on, she started laughing and said, "You two guys are ridiculous. I'm the Russian Jew, I'm supposed to be sad, but you guys—Brazilian Portuguese fisherman and this Irishman, for God's sake—each piece that you play is a little sadder than the one before. You guys are the Russians."

So given the history of depression that already was a strong element in her family relationship, as I said, because of the relationship with her mother and her own insecurities, the doctor decided she shouldn't be told what was happening when the illness jumped up again. So that was a very tough time for Arnold and me because we knew what was going on and had to try to plan for it and to keep things going around Judy. And, of course, she had the son and the mother to take care of.

So during that period I wasn't out on the road very much. In fact, most of the work I was doing was with the big band. We worked a lot in the city. We worked maybe three or four weeks at a time at the Village Vanguard, and it was really too expensive to take the band out. We didn't work as a dance band, so that whole way of working was cut off from us, and there just wasn't enough going on. There weren't the people producing tours or promoting individual concerts to be able to do it. So most of all the work we did was around New York, and we played often at the Vanguard. In fact, that was the beginnings of having a big band in there. Nobody had ever had a big band in that little place before. Now it's a tradition. Of course, our band was considerably smaller than the Thad and Mel band from later years, which I thought was just a little too big for the place, but it's a tradition nonetheless. Then later on we were frequently at Birdland, and that kept us in the New York area.

I think Judy's illness hit first about 1960, and she died almost five years to the day that she was operated on the first time. That was a tough period that I at least was able to keep some kind of equanimity and some sanity when I was around Judy and her family. But it tended to make me a little crazy in the outside world, and it was something to adjust to and was probably the most severe learning experience that I went through: to be able to get a handle on what's important in life and that it's not necessary to display your feelings at all times. There comes a time in your life when you realize there's a lot of stuff that's best left to yourself. And there are things, in order to be considerate of other people, also that you've got to keep to yourself. But that was obviously a difficult time. It took her a year from the re-emergence of the illness before she died. Then, after that, there's kind of a touching thing that happened because, during that period, Nick Travis went to the hospital with what seemed like a minor ailment. It was one of those cases where there was quite a bit of talk afterward that somebody in the hospital had made a mistake and given him something that he shouldn't have had, and he died. I went to the hospital to see him one day and I said, "Okay, I'll be back the day after tomorrow to see you," and the next day one of the guys called me and said, "Nick died last night." We were all pretty well shaken up at that one. He was kind of estranged from his wife at that point so we had no contact with her. We tried to get in touch with her to find out if she was going to have a funeral or what's it going to be, because all the guys that loved Nick wanted to be there.

Because she and Nick were fighting, she did the thing as simply and as impersonally as possible, made whatever arrangements she had to make to have his body taken care of, and that was the end of it. So we got together and one of the guys, I don't remember who, knew Father John Gensel, who had a church up on Broadway. We talked to him and he said, "Why don't you have a memorial service for Nick here?"

We said, "Yes, we'd like that," because, whereas I've never been much on funerals, if you know the family of somebody, then you go to them to pay your respects. Usually though, I steered as clear as possible of funerals, especially if they showed signs of turning into three-ring circuses. I avoided Bird's funeral because I couldn't face all that was going on around that. Ultimately, since I wasn't invited to it, I didn't go to Duke's funeral. I would have if the family had invited me, but since nobody did, I wasn't about to go. I don't like big crowds anyway. I did go to Lester's funeral and a couple of other guys', but it was something I avoided.

So in this case it was kind of an oddity that we, a bunch of young guys, decided to have this memorial service. Then I realized that you have a service for yourself because, to lose a close friend so suddenly, it left us all kind of hanging emotionally. So we decided to have this service. Judy was always there, kind of on the fringe, as we were organizing and talking about it. So what we did is that a couple of us got a little group together and played and told stories about Nick. It turned out to be fun because the guys were telling funny stories, so it was satisfying for everybody, and it felt good to talk about Nick and kind of get this all out. Well, Judy didn't want to go up there; it was too sad an occasion for her. She just couldn't face going to the service for Nick. Judy had established friendships with all of the guys. They all loved her because she was just so down to earth and very, very savvy about music. They respected her and really loved her, and they all felt like her friends. So she felt as bad about Nick as the rest of us did, but she couldn't face going to the service at the church.

Then, after the service was over and we're starting to go out, I went around ahead of the guys and I see Judy has been watching this whole thing, holding the door and watching. She couldn't bring herself to come in and sit down, but there she was. At some point, I guess it was a couple of days after that, she said, "You know, the service you had for Nick, for some reason I kind of feel like that was my funeral." She said that she would like us to do a service like that for her.

So she was already thinking that way, and I guess as far as her awareness was concerned, she knew what was happening to her but the conscious mind wouldn't accept it. And we would have done it that way except, when she died, everybody turned up and took over, and they had it over at Frank Campbell's Funeral Home in New York. It was a circus with people in the streets and they had a string quartet or something, very lugubrious music, and a lot of people wearing their hearts on their sleeve. I made it through all that as best as I could, because it was very oppressive and I really wasn't pleased with it, and I wasn't pleased to be there.

The other reason for being there was because I felt that somebody should be watching out for Helen, her mother, and Jonathon, her son. So I kind of took them in tow and tried to steer them through it. But we never did do the service for her. We should have but at that point I wasn't totally *compos mentis*, I think, to deal with the real world.

So the two stories that run concurrently here—of the Concert Jazz Band in its first edition, the things that happened around Judy—came to kind of a close, mutually. I guess it was somewhere close to 1965 that we did the last job with the Concert Jazz Band, and after playing a few weeks in Birdland, we closed and the club closed, and that kind of put an end to a whole era.

26

IT'S SANDY
AT THE BEACH

I GUESS IT WAS not too long after, or sometime around that time, I began a relationship with Sandy Dennis. Sandy was a natural thing to kind of cling onto. The reverse happens, especially if that's your first big experience close to death; it brings home your own mortality. One starts looking for life, so we started going together. The one thing that always stood out was the difference in personalities between Sandy and Judy. Judy needed my support and wanted to discuss things and everything needed to be very out in the open with her. Sandy, on the other hand, was a very private person. It took me a long time to realize to what extent she never wanted to discuss the things that had to do with her work. She was always reluctant to have me read for her, and it was always peculiar to me because I was very open to what I'm doing, what I'm thinking, the projects that I'm working on, the plans that I've got or ideas that I have for the future. I'm even more forthcoming on that than people want me to be. You know, we all have our own way of approaching things, and Sandy was quite the opposite.

I started early on to feel kind of shut out because she didn't particularly care or need anybody. Early on we started to drift our own ways, and I started to spend a lot of time in Europe. It was a very kind of disorganized and unrewarding period for me. I think some periods may well be learning periods, but they sure feel rotten while they're going on. And a lot of things happened during that period that made me feel even more separate.

There was a world tour that we did with that group, and in some ways it was really a low point, actually it was. Because we wound up staying a long time in Australia because the Japanese passport department wouldn't get our work papers together. So it was one of those things that every morning at ten o'clock they'd say be downstairs, we'll be leaving for Tokyo if the papers are here. Well, we did this every morning and the papers never got there. When the papers finally showed up, it was the day before the concert. Well, we got out of there, flew to Hong Kong, stayed overnight and then flew into Osaka the next day. And that concert was, like, in the late afternoon. So it was one of those things. And we had a flight directly from Hong Kong to Osaka, getting out of the cab and getting your horn out, after waiting for a week in Australia, to barely make the thing. Man, it was really infuriating. And also, because of this business in Australia, we couldn't go anywhere. I wanted to go and see the Great Barrier Reef but, I mean, every day we were supposed to be ready to go, and that had a very bad effect on all of us. And Sandy went on tour with me, and I know I made her life miserable. I mean, I just was not good company.

Then from Japan we went to Europe, and it just was downhill all the way. Terrible tour, not for me, but for Sandy. So after that, we probably took off for Europe again. It wasn't easy. And, of course, the thing was the inability of Sandy and me to communicate with each other. I needed to talk about my problems, and she didn't really want to talk about things at all. And we just were very hard on each other.

Musically, that was a fairly unrewarding time for me. Philips Records started a new label, Limelight, and another label that they called by another name. I had been with Philips Mercury with the sextet, and I really didn't want to go back with them again. They came to me and wanted me to sign with the company again because they were going to have Quincy Jones be my A&R man. He had just joined the company and he was going to supervise my dates. Well, he kind of won me over on that because I liked the idea of having Quincy—having an arranger to help organize the things. I always need help in putting these things together. Left to my own devices, I'm great at starting things but I'm terrible at finishing. I get so involved in the details of it that I have a hell of a hard time getting it finished. So having somebody ride herd on me was very important.

Well, as it turned out, Quincy never did. From the first date that we had for the label, Quincy was supposed to be there and he sent in a sub. I never did see him. These are the kinds of things that record companies agree to but don't follow through on. Back then I didn't think to put it in writing. Of course, today I would be a lot smarter. It would be in writing and if I didn't have Quincy, I would have backed out again.

As it happened, there was another guy that they brought into the company named Jack Tracy. Jack had been an editor at *DownBeat* magazine, and I knew him real well and I liked him. Jack and I could kick ideas off of each other, and so we functioned in another way. We did a lot of things that I liked.

For the first album we kicked around ideas, and I had looked at a bunch of the tunes of the current songwriters, like the Beatles and Bob Dylan and Roger Miller. I found that some of them were quite good melodies. I didn't necessarily like the instrumentation they were using or whatever, because I don't really like guitar-heavy bands anyway, but there are some quite good melodies. So I started the idea of doing an album, getting some good guys together and just approaching these things like tunes, like standards. Forget where they came from, just do them like tunes.

Well, then one morning I got a call from Jack and he was laughing his head off. He said, "I've got an idea, man; it's so funny I fell over. We'll call the album *If You Can't Beat 'Em, Join 'Em*." I laughed too and said, "That's a funny idea." Well, in the end I don't know if it was a good idea or not, because it kind of covered up what I was really doing, and it may have sounded like sour grapes. I'm sure it was probably criticized somewhere for that. But it had no significance other than the fact that Jack thought it was funny as hell and was trying to figure out some way of dressing me like the Beatles or something, for laughs.

But the idea of the album was quite simple: to take the tunes and put them in our own setting. And some of the things came out very well. The version we do of "Engine Engine Number 9," Pete Jolly plays such great choruses on the thing that you realize the material has more possibilities than are necessarily evident in the versions that everybody knows. So that was the idea of the thing, just to treat these pop tunes in ways that related to the way we play and the way we thought, rather than where they came from.

For the next one we wanted to do a pretty album. I wanted to do something with a string section and we had somebody to do it: Julian Lee. Julian was a very talented guy who had done some things for Jack. Jack liked what he had done and played it for me, and I thought his writing for a small string section was terrific. So we just planned this album out, and *Feelin' Good* was the title because it was one of the tunes that we had done on the thing; very effective, simple arrangements. The material was dead simple. We did the tracks first and recorded the stuff, always in mind that Julian was going to add string parts to it. So I left open places and so on. We kind of plotted out what we were going to do, and then Julian took the finished tracks and went off and plotted the string parts.

I always loved the way it came out. There's some really beautiful stuff in there that I found moving then, and I still do. I felt his writing for the small string section was great. A very, very talented man.

So I made a number of albums for them and played around various festivals and spent a lot of time knocking around Europe. I was playing mostly with European rhythm sections, but I didn't enjoy it very much. I was used to having my own band and playing what I want. You never have enough rehearsal time to get things together. It was a pain in the neck.

Nothing had come of the *Happy Birthday* project, and I still had quite an urge to do a musical. I suppose it was maybe a couple of years after Judy died that Gene Lees had the idea. He thought that *Diamond Jim Brady* would be a good subject for a musical. He wanted to do the lyrics and I wanted to do the music. I started to do some research on it. I spent a lot of time at the library. I went through all the newspapers and various books about Brady, and I agreed. It was an interesting subject. So we started working on the thing and plotting it out, what we wanted to do. We thought it was stupid to get really into the thing until we had a better idea of whether there was going to be somebody interested in doing it, so we're not doing it on speculation, and to get a book to work with, which Gene may well have wound up writing. But I think we should have gotten an experienced book writer to do it and we should do the songs.

Well, as far as the first part, which was, was anybody interested in producing such a show? Would anybody foot the bill for the thing and help to defray our expenses to write it in the first place? We went to Hal Prince. I'd met Hal through my friend Herbie Gardner, who wrote *A Thousand Clowns*. And Herbie had introduced me to Hal. We'd been at Herbie's house one night and met Hal. I liked him very much. He's one of those people who makes things happen. He's got imagination and he's enthusiastic.

So Gene and I went up to Hal's office and he told us this idea. He said he'd recently had a call from Jackie Gleason, who wanted to do a musical on *Diamond Jim Brady* that he and Lucille Ball would do. He said maybe he could work it out to do it in conjunction because they're only in the talking stage. We said, "Sure, we'd be interested but if they've started the thing going; they've probably got their own people." We never heard again about it, and of course we let it drop, because even though we both had a hunch that it would never happen, you never can tell in that business. There's no way of knowing if it's worth pursuing or not. They never did and that was the end of it. I was always kind of sorry about that because I think that it would have made a good show, because everything about it offered great theatric possibilities. Brady was a bigger-than-life character, and the kind of stuff that we had learned about him in doing the research suggested an interesting story. And the period, the whole thing with the staging and the costumes and things like that, it could have been good. But, you know, the best of intentions wind up in the garbage if the timing is wrong. And that's where that wound up.

Around that time I did my first film score, which was a movie called *Luv*. *Luv* was kind of a study of how not to go about it. The man who was the director of the film liked my music, and I suppose by that he liked the quartet and stuff that I did. I wasn't really sure precisely why he chose me to do it, because I hadn't done any film scores before then. But I got out to Hollywood and my situation was totally unlike other composers. Most of the guys composing for movies would like nothing better than to have the director hand them the picture and leave them alone. Usually it's the other way around, the director is on his neck all the time: "Why don't you do this, why don't you do that, why don't you do the other?"

Because of my lack of experience but also because, it seemed to me, that in order to try to do a score for a comedy, that I would really like to work with the director. What's going on is not always obvious to me as a viewer of the thing. Clive Donner was the director, and I realized when I got there that he was not really happy with the film. He felt that there were real problems involved, and when I watched the picture over and over again in the screening room, I realized that one of the problems was there were three totally different styles of comedic acting. Each one of them terrific by themselves, but they affected each other in ways that didn't always produce the desired effect. It's like it became something else. I found the picture very funny, but the three styles were represented by Jack Lemmon, Elaine May, and Peter Falk: three totally different styles of comedy.

I had seen *Luv* on Broadway, where it was a two-character comedy that all took place in one set. So we wound up having this problem again of opening up a two-character, one-set play into a movie, where you really can't stay in one place. Part of the thing that was so outrageous about *Luv* was that the whole thing takes place in the middle of the Brooklyn Bridge; these two characters talking, three characters, talking ridiculous things. Well, by opening it up you open kettles of troubles, and I think Clive was hoping to kind of pull the thing back together with some kind of musical cohesiveness.

When he was there, I had the idea that we should approach this thing with a style of music like a Dixieland band: rough-swinging, loose-jointed kind of thing. He said, "Terrific; that should do it." Well, he went away and I sat and watched this damn movie day after day after day. And watching a movie doesn't do a thing for me. It just doesn't kick off any inspiration at all. Doesn't work.

So I became swamped with the thing and frustrated and kind of helpless. I got Bill Holman to help me to try to pin myself down, and Bill, of course, didn't have much experience with film writing either. So I think the pair of us were kind of in the dark, and instead of doing this kind of simple thing that I had in mind, we wound up orchestrating all kinds of stuff in a very conventional way. It was terrific writing. Bill arranged some of these things so that, taken away from the movie, they knocked me over. They were great, but for the movie they didn't really do anything. So I realized much too late that my original idea would have been the best way to go.

As I said, Clive was there only a couple of days and then took off and had another project to go to. So when he came back, we were getting ready to go to the sound stage and record, and he was kind of stunned to find out that I hadn't done what I said I was going to do. Instead, I had all these arrangements. I could see that he was not pleased, and I wasn't pleased because, you know, in the beginning he said, "You've got to help me." Which was a director telling the composer, "I'm depending on you to tie this together."

Well, I failed and failing is not easy. It's a very difficult, bitter pill to swallow, and I didn't take kindly to failure. What was I going to say? But it was the kind of thing that for months after that, even years after that, I would wake up in the middle of the night dreaming about this project and thinking about what I should have done, what I wanted to do at this place and, oh man, I would give anything if I could do that score over again. I'd pay them if they let me do the score over again.

There was one thing that we did, a Dixieland kind of band, and it was the high point of the score. It was great! We had some great players come in too. That night Clive came in with a bunch of other people while we were recording and everybody loved it. Zeke Zarchy was on trumpet and I can't even remember who all, but this one thing was really nice.

27

SOCIAL AND POLITICAL CHANGES IN THE 1960s

DURING MY EARLY YEARS in New York was the one period when I didn't feel like an outsider. I was very much accepted by the other musicians, many of whom were my own age and many of whom were older. So the early years, through the band period, through the 1940s, then when I had my own group in the 1950s, this was my life and my world and I belonged to it.

The social and political things that were going on in the 1960s were kind of peripheral to my life. I had a feeling that it was to jazz in general and to a great extent, because I think we chose not to really feel much kinship with all of that, and I was very skeptical of what was going on. I'm always suspicious of movements, and suspicious of much advertised renaissances as we suffered through in the 1960s. And I always was holding my breath waiting for the other shoe to drop because the whole thing that happened, that kind of new attitude toward freedom and some of the little mottos of the time, and "let it all hang out," there were some that really offended me. If you're not part of the solution, then you're part of the problem.

There was never any of the distance created by the racial attitudes in those years that I experienced. This is not to say that they didn't exist. That's what was going on in the real world outside, but the thing that was going on in jazz was quite different. It was like jazz was in the forefront of trying to get people together. Jazz was in the forefront of having blacks and whites work together in bands. Even before they were working together in bands in the 1920s and 1930s, black arrangers were arranging for white bands and the white arrangers were arranging for black bands. So these were things that created a different atmosphere.

When I came into that I thought it was completely natural because my experience with black people related to Lily, her husband, her daughter, and the house she lived in, and the neighborhood she lived in, where I was at home. So I didn't know about any of that stuff, and I didn't know what a lot of the stuff meant. It was one thing to tell me that the black musicians stayed with people in the community when they traveled through town because there weren't hotels. But it never occurred to me why there weren't hotels, and it seemed a wonderful thing to me that the community absorbed them. It's great; I loved that.

Well, there wasn't any real distinguishable thing for me because the black guys were in midtown every day. I used to see the well-known players and the band players. We used to go to Charlie's Tavern on 52nd Street and then Beefsteak Charlie's, around to the place next to the Metropole.

There were always things going on; there were the guys who played on 52nd Street and the guys who played in the traveling bands. There was always this natural mix going on, and I still wasn't really aware of any tensions between white and black. And, of course, with my background, it never occurred to me because I didn't grow up with that. My family never discussed things like that, and Lily was my touchstone with reality and my contact with her lasted until I was eight or nine years old, when Lily died. I remember going to the hospital and spending time with her there. I must have been already nine or ten, just about the time we left the town.

So I didn't really know about it. I was naive enough that I could accept life the way it was. Later on, I know that Curly Russell, the bass player, and Brew Moore would go uptown together. And when they'd go uptown they'd be together and hanging out. When they got off the train at 125th Street or someplace, Curly would always walk some steps ahead and leave Brew lagging behind him. Finally, Brew complained to him and said, "What the hell is that, man?" and Curly said, "Listen, up here I don't want to be seen walking around with you," and he followed three steps behind.

So you learn about these attitudes and tensions. But in that situation, Curly made it kind of amusing the way he put it and it didn't stop us from going uptown. The black guys were friends with the white guys and we worked together.

When I was a kid in Philadelphia and going down to the Earle Theater when the bands were in town (I must have cut school a lot because I would go down there on weekdays to the daytime shows), I'd hang around backstage and some of the guys with the various bands would befriend me. One of the guys who did, I think he was playing in Bob Chester's band, was Trummy Young. So I ended up hanging out with Trummy every day. I spent as much time with him as I could. I loved him. He was a great guy. I guess they liked having a kid around who was enthusiastic about music. There was Trummy and another guy, Leon Cox, the trombone player. He was with Krupa's band just before I got in. He was a dynamite player, wild man.

So, a lot of things that came about because of adversity and because of racial politics at the time were things that created a sense of community that was beneficial to the people themselves. In some ways, I think that this is the thing that's going on now, where great portions of the black population feel a sense of community, whether it's based on their similar economic conditions or whatever. But the whole thing, talk about brothers and sisters, this is symbolic of the kind of family relationship that exists, and sense of community that exists with black people.

I was really unaware of the problems outside of jazz. And they didn't start to come into jazz until the 1960s, when all kinds of new political fronts were heard from. The politicization of the jazz musicians who were now well into Black Power came on the scene with a chip on their shoulder, saying, "Whitey stole our music." Come on, man, what do you mean, "Whitey stole your music"? As far as I can see, music is there for anyone who can do it. If you can do it, great. If you can't, put the horn away. But this was a very prevalent attitude at the time, and it spread even to musicians who were older. The guys that would come along in the 1940s, well, maybe some of them had been the ones to establish some of the attitudes. I remember very well walking into the band room one time at the Roost when we were there with the *Birth of the Cool,* and Art Blakey was sitting back there with a bunch of young black guys, and he was preaching a religious/political line about whites and blacks and it was necessary to be tolerant of the white people no matter what they did. Those were my first brushes with how the competitive spirit got translated into some kind of racial connections. And I was very sorry to see it happen because the fun started to go out of the scene altogether. And what had formerly been a sense of community in the music scene altogether, sort of ceased to exist. It became fragmented, and this whole generation of black guys came along who were angry with the white guys.

I had black guys, new on the scene, who were enjoying a great deal of success. I think in their way they were enjoying a great deal more commercial success than I was, because they were selling a lot more records, and they were in demand. These guys with chips on their shoulders would do really rotten things to me and they didn't even know me. And it would surprise me.

Dizzy once tried to explain to me that he thought the cause of a lot of that in my case was because I had been accepted by the leaders and important people of previous generations like Duke Ellington, Count Basie, and the men in their bands. All these people were friends of mine, they accepted me, and they liked me. So here I was a couple of years older than these guys, and they were resentful. Well, this was Dizzy's explanation and I always thought there was probably truth to it, although it always sounded so feeble to me as a reason to hate somebody.

I guess my orientation was different. I was so glad to have the opportunity to be with the musicians who had been with other musicians that I admired, to play with guys who had played with guys back in the teens. The connection to me was important.

Well, it wasn't important to them and it became more and more of an attitude that jazz really started with Charlie Parker, and then later on, the next generation said that jazz started with Coltrane and that Parker was old hat. They had silly attitudes and missed the point of what was the importance of music and the attraction of it and the functions of music. And to cut themselves off from all that enjoyment, because, after all, music is meant to be enjoyed; it's not to be suffered through.

I did all of my suffering outside. When I got to play, that's when I came to life. Music wasn't the hard part; it was the rest of it. It was getting to the gig. That was the hard part. So that made the 1960s kind of an unattractive period for me. I saw the total fragmentation of the scene, and I saw the kind of cutting off of communication between important elements: the people who should have been in communication with each other and were now suffering from a kind of resentment and negativism that was destructive. And that went on through the 1960s and I guess was even worse in the 1970s.

It certainly hasn't abated to this day, because what's happening now is jazz is becoming much more institutionalized. It's not always too comfortable to be a white jazz musician, because very few of the benefits are coming the way of the white musicians. We've sort of been written out of the history by white critics and white writers, as well as by black writers. It's like the Jim Crowism we thought was invented by French writers in the 1930s is thriving in this country. To me that's shameful, because the attraction for me, when I became aware of these things and became aware beyond the pleasure and joy of the music itself and the joy of playing it and learning it, was the social significance, the cultural significance of jazz, which was that we're seeing for the first time an art form evolve out of the relationship between two diverse peoples.

The African attitude toward music is unique. There are many varieties within Africa itself toward music, but there are certain things about it that are universal in the African approach to music, the African approach being totally different rhythmically from the European approach. The thing that has always fascinated me about the music of different places and what I look for, for myself, are similarities rather than differences. The differences are easy to see. The similarities are not always as evident.

And so, early on, when I was first able to get records that were the first records made in Africa from the Denis-Roosevelt expedition, the thing that fascinated me was that the music evolved from totally different kinds of instruments. The music had a totally different social relationship to the people and the communities of people, and the rites and celebrations of the people, and evolving with a different kind of rhythmic approach, but it still had kinds of melodic and structural similarities to European music. That floored me when I learned that. That there are certain common elements to music from different parts of the world. To be able to see those similarities helped me to understand how they came together in this country, what it meant, and the beauty of it. The western hemisphere was the recipient of all these crossbred art forms.

It's fascinating to see the difference between what evolved in South America, as opposed to what evolved in North America. In South America, the European influence was Spanish or Portuguese, and their music was quite different from Northern Europe. It was different from British folk music, which is a very dominant force in American folk music, and consequently in American music generally, melodically, or from the music of Italy or Germany. So the Spanish or Portuguese influence, meeting up with the African influence in South America, plus another element that was excluded from North America was the Indian influence, the Indigenous people. So these three elements wound up with a music that came to be the samba.

Peculiarly enough, there was, especially in the seaport towns of South America, there was a music that evolved that was similar to the jazz of New Orleans: similar instrumentation, similar feel. I was amazed to find that out. But on one of the trips that I did for the USIS (United States Information Service) in South America, I met a man who started to tell me about this. He said, "Wait a minute," and he took me to a record store and picked up some records of bands that were recorded, I guess, in the 1920s or early 1930s. He said these were an example of another thing that was going on that still exists but never became an overpowering influence as it did in the North, but it existed. And he played these things and, man, these bands could have been playing anywhere in the States in the 1920s. The music was that similar.

It was these other elements that came into it that produced the samba and the kind of rhythmic approach that distinguishes Brazilian music.

Notice also, it was primarily Brazilian music that was the Portuguese influence, not Spanish. In the countries of Spanish influence, the music is unique in each one of the places, but in no place does it have the vitality of Brazilian music. And you have another place of seaport music, the music of Buenos Aires, which was the tango, and that was primarily a music that was brought to Buenos Aires by German seamen. The bandoneon is a German instrument, and that's the primary instrument of the tango. That, with a kind of Spanish dramatic dance, and you can get kind of a hint of where the tango evolved from.

The only period that I felt real antagonism from black musicians was in the 1960s, and in that period I became "whitey the enemy" and had some really hostile attitudes laid on me. I had black musicians in my band, but if you're hiring a black musician, it just means that you're exploiting them. You can't win. You're either playing too black and stealing their music or you're not playing black enough so it ain't jazz. Whatever you do, it's cause for criticism.

But in the earlier days, when I finally had success with the quartet out on the road, I often traveled with those big shows that featured my quartet with maybe Brubeck and Duke Ellington's band. I had become friends with Harry Carney even long before that because I admired him so much and he was such a warmhearted, friendly man. He was really great. So as it turned out, when we would travel on these things, I'd wind up traveling with Duke. He loved trains, so if we could get there by train, we often did the tours by train, just he and I. And if we couldn't do it by train, we'd travel with Harry in his car. I had a wonderful time traveling with them, and the guys in the band all befriended me. I felt like part of an extended family. They were great to me. Whether it was Paul Gonsalves and Jimmy Hamilton, Johnny Hodges and Russell Procope, Harry, Lawrence Brown, Ray Nance, Cat Anderson, Sam Woodyard; the guys were all friends of mine and we used to have a great time because of that.

I always had a good relationship with Count and with a lot of the guys in the band; of course, I knew Harry Edison and Buck Clayton from New York. Count was always asking me to write for the band and

I did a couple of times, but you know it's one thing to ask me to write, but he never played anything I wrote. I'm not sure of the reason for that.

But between the guys in those bands and the times that I worked at the Apollo, I felt it was my natural world and didn't really know about the things with the black cats first playing with the white bands in the 1930s.

I'm telling you I was naive enough to think that what I had walked into was the real world. I didn't know how it had gotten there and didn't know why it was dying around me. So I had to try to figure out the whole damn thing.

The 1960s were kind of an abrupt change because a whole group of musicians came in who were angry as hell, man, and I just was a symbol to them as part of the thing they were angry at. I never really understood, and I never really was able to get through Dizzy's memoir, *To Be or Not to Bop*, but I've skimmed through it a couple of times and find the damnedest references to myself, and I don't recognize what they saw with what I was and where I was. It finally dawned on me that people around Dizzy had a tremendous resentment of what was going on around Miles, and it was like we had chosen sides: Dizzy himself and then probably Ray Brown and some of the other guys, maybe Milt Jackson. The fact that we were doing this and we were like the intellectuals, and what they were doing was the real music.

Well, it was amazing to me to find out they had made this division in their heads and we were the enemy, because no matter how many nights Gil and whoever was around—Gil and I and maybe Johnny Carisi or Miles or whoever—there'd be anywhere from two to eight of us who would wind up in the Three Deuces listening to the Things to Come band; we loved the band. The fact that it was a different kind of band and a different approach stylistically, who cares. We're not all trying to do the same thing. You wind up at different goals even from the same motivations. What was the famous comment of Louis Armstrong when he heard Bix Beiderbecke? Something like, "This little white boy plays just like me." Well, he didn't mean he was playing just like him in terms of the technique, because it wasn't like Louis. But he was playing like him because of the thing that made him play and the fact that he was concerned about making something of his own; it was the thing of motivation and ideals.

So it was a shock to me that they had made this division and that we were the enemy. During those years, too, I was very good friends with Dizzy. He'd invite me out to the house and we had a grand time together. I liked Lorraine very much, so it was always a pleasure to hang out with him. As the years went by, a funny thing evolved with Dizzy. When Dizzy and I were alone together we were great friends, like on equal footing, like two guys. It wasn't even an older guy and a younger guy, we were just two musicians. As soon as anybody was around, his attitude toward me changed. It took me a long time to recognize this, but the way it finally hit home was that sometimes my wife, Franca, would get really angry with me because I took such shit from people and let it go because I didn't want to offend people who I thought were my friends. I wanted to be liked. It reminds me of the story of Lenny Bernstein and Ned Rorem having a conversation. I guess Rorem says, or maybe Lenny says, "The trouble with us, Ned, is that we want everybody in the world to love us," and the other one says, "Yes, and there's just not time enough to meet everyone in the world!" I think a lot of us suffered from that; we want everybody to love us and there's not enough time, and we're stunned when they don't.

One time, maybe ten years ago in Nice, I was there with a big band, and Dizzy came in late because they had flown in and were supposed to play that night and had a very rough day of traveling from Istanbul. So they showed up and as it happened there was a little encampment with trailers around it. There wasn't a soul standing out there, which was very unusual in itself because usually there are people milling about, but there was just Franca and me standing in the middle of this place. Dizzy comes up by himself, comes through the gate, and sees me and puts his hands out like he's walking toward me and we're going to hug and he really was genuinely glad to see me. About this time a door to one of the trailers opened and Art Blakey sticks his head out and immediately launches into the play on the dozens thing (playfully insulting each other). Dizzy, instead of taking my hand and putting his arm around my shoulder, gives me a shove and then goes over and hugs Franca. The shove was hard enough that I went over on my butt and it knocked me down. I sat there on my ass with my eyes wide open and my jaw hanging open, saying, "What the hell was that?" Then he goes into this whole number with Art like I didn't exist and this was just all very funny. I said that was it. That absolutely was it. I didn't speak to Dizzy for the rest of the time. He got on the plane the next day and walked right by me. Man, I just was not having it anymore. I finally got fed up with the attitudes of Dizzy, who was so changeable. He was a friend when we were together but if there was anybody else around, he put me down and did embarrassing things to me on a couple of occasions.

Between him and the kind of ill feeling that Getz created onstage and the negative vibes that some of the other guys had, I realized that things were very, very uncomfortable. I'd look and it would always be the same guys—the gossips—and I didn't want to get onstage with them anymore. I refused and said, "To hell with them," and Franca said, "Finally!"

It was odd because not too long after that the French were doing something. I don't know what, the big celebration, but they wanted an American bunch of jazz musicians and were going to give us all the order of the Legion of Honor, pay a good price, and treat us in a grand manner as dignitaries. I thought about it and told Franca, "I don't want to go onstage with Dizzy and Stan. They make such a bad atmosphere; they're always so mean and competitive with each other and their attitude toward me. Man, those cats all act miserable when I come around. I don't feel like putting myself through that anymore." She said okay. So that's why I didn't get the Legion of Honor.

I started to get like that. The things I put up with for years; I didn't see any reason for putting myself through the kinds of things that were constantly putting me into negative ways of feeling and negative ways of thinking. I think I became very self-protective of my own enthusiasm, and I couldn't see exposing myself to destructive attitudes.

Now I kind of wish I had put up with it and had my Legion of Honor and all that, because it's nice to have awards and prizes and recognition and everything. But on the other hand, I stuck to my guns on that one and just wanted nothing to do with it.

Dizzy's problem was he wanted everybody to like him and so he went along . . . he was the comic personality they wanted him to be. The Dizzy that I knew really wasn't quite like that.

But as time went on, Dizzy became more and more this kind of characterization of himself; he wasn't so much a real person, it was the public Dizzy, and I finally came to the conclusion that that was the problem; he really was split that way. When we were together it was the real Dizzy, and the public Dizzy, who wanted everybody to love him, was something else.

28

COMPADRES

THE SAXOPHONIST
WHO CAME TO DINNER

I GUESS IT WAS in 1968 that I was without a quartet and Dave Brubeck was without a quartet, and George Wein had a festival in New Orleans that he wanted us to play. Dave had some things coming up, and he was getting a rhythm section together with Jack Six on bass and Alan Dawson on drums. So I went down to New Orleans and played that thing with him. It was very nice; I enjoyed doing it with him.

Then some other dates came up because we had done that together. People started asking for us. We played in Mexico City. Really a nice date. We played at the beautiful Bellas Artes Theatre in Mexico City and recorded an album there called *Compadres*. Well, that started a period of working with Dave. It gave me a rest from being a bandleader. I had gotten to a point where I was really tired of being a leader. I was tired of the responsibilities. I was tired of the details. I was tired of having to go through the thing of hiring musicians. I'd had enough.

We just kind of fell into it because it was fun to do and I always enjoyed playing with Dave. So we had a good show of material to do, and I kept writing for it. So I became the saxophone player that came to dinner! I just never left. Aim me in the right direction and press the button and I'll play. You know, about seven years later I realized it was longer than I had ever been with a band, for heaven's sake!

I did a tour for some weeks with Hampton Hawes and the two guys who were playing with him. I enjoyed playing with Hamp. I liked him and he was off in his own little world with no problem. Well, after the

Gerry with Dave Brubeck. COURTESY GERRY MULLIGAN COLLECTION, LIBRARY OF CONGRESS, MUSIC DIVISION

tour was over, we played the last night, I think it was probably Largo di Garda, a town on the lake up above Verona.

It was late after the concert and the other guys, Hampton and the bassist and the drummer, were leaving the next morning. I guess they were going to bed, so I told the guy that was running the show, Alberto Alberti, I said, "Hey, they've got to leave in the morning. Will you get me up in the morning so I don't miss the car?" I left the call at the desk so I'd be up when the guys left. I wanted to give them some extra money for playing for me. So the next morning I get my call and I go downstairs and they've gone; they'd already left. So I said to Alberto, "Why didn't you tell me they were going early?"

Alberto always played the scatterbrain. He was always loaded. So I said, "Don't worry about it, it will be all right. But listen, I wanted to give the guys some money for playing for me; it's not right they played for me every night. I wanted them to know that I appreciated it." So I gave him like eight hundred or a thousand dollars, or something like that, to give to the guys, and he never gave it to them. I could have killed the guy for that, because I got a very nasty letter from the bass player that I was a white square and this and that and the other thing. Whereas I was fairly incensed in the way that he chose to put me down, the fact that he was expecting to get some money at the end of the thing and didn't get it, you know, he had some right to be angry. And I was furious with Alberto because he just put the money in his pocket. He was supposed to see the guys that night. Oh well, there are some things you just have to accept and that's that. There's nothing you can do about it.

I suppose I could have, back then, after getting a snotty letter from the bass player I could have sent him something, but somehow, I just lost my incentive for it.

29

THE AGE OF STEAM AND MEETING FRANCA

THE NEXT THING that I really did on my own was *The Age of Steam*. A friend of Roger Kellaway's wanted me to do an album for A&M. He was producing things for Herb Alpert there and asked me if I was interested. I said, "Sure!" So I went over to A&M with him and Herb and it was great. He said the whole idea is to do an album where there's one guy responsible and it's his music and he lays it down. I was very pleased with that. So I started as soon as we had decided on a recording date. I holed myself up at the Beverly Wilshire Hotel and had a piano brought in. When I had this stuff written I came out. Up until then, it was me and room service. And out of that came *The Age of Steam*, which was kind of an interesting instrumentation.

The idea was that the material I wrote for that could be done and performed in different ways. I wasn't just writing it for the album, I was writing to perform it. It had a five-piece rhythm section and a four-horn front line. It could be done without the front line, or it could be me and the five-piece rhythm section, or five-piece rhythm section and me and these other horns. Then there was an ensemble to back it up with a couple more trumpets and a couple more trombones, so it added up to a good-size band. It was flexible.

In its way a simple idea it might be; it was more complex than it needed to be. But, ultimately, I worked with it like that. I did a couple of concerts with it with a full band. I did some things with it with just the four horns. Then I started this new sextet that was based on the rhythm section and just one horn. Ultimately, the idea did work, and it was practical. I always liked the album very much, the stuff that we did on the thing. I had some interesting guys on it, too: Harry Edison, Tom Scott, Roger Kellaway, and Howard Roberts on guitar, Bud Shank, and Brookmeyer. All in all, it was nice. There were other guys that were in the ensemble who didn't even play solos—Jimmy Cleveland, Ernie Watts—if I'd known I was going to have those guys I probably would have written solos for them. They were brought in by Steve Goldman. Steve got the ensemble guys together. It was a nice little band.

I did most of the writing in about a week or ten days. I did a lot of the stuff where I didn't write out the whole score. I wrote a lot of fragments. I would plot out what the thing was going to be and then I would write what I needed. You know, I was trying to avoid overwriting the thing, not writing it like an arrangement where they're playing all the time, but where the functions become the replacements for an arrangement. In other words, there'll be stuff that the rhythm section is accompanying. And that's one whole sound, because a five-piece rhythm section is like an ensemble. You know, it's feeling like three different ensemble groups. So I'd write a chorus here that I would add the ensemble to, and chorus over here, and it was all bits and pieces. When I got done with the thing, I didn't have any scores. I had all this stuff. This can be the hardest thing to keep track of, and I had all these parts and no scores. That's why I wound up with this, let's say this person, as a copyist. The transcribing job I had her doing was to make scores out of these things because I didn't have any good scores and I needed them. But we wound up with more than enough material.

I wrote a piece on it called "K-4 Pacific" that was based on the sound of a locomotive. Back at the old motif. And "K-4 Pacific" being a loco-motive, I called the piece, the whole thing, *The Age of Steam*. Well, to me, that's an ambiguous statement, an ambiguity in itself, *The Age of Steam*, because immediately everybody thinks the 1920s and 1930s, what are steam locomotives? Which, of course, is ridiculous because most power, in order to function as power, has to be turned into steam to work. You know, at least up until periods now. But as far as I can see, the same thing pretty much is true of the rockets that go to the moon. So to me, this is *The Age of Steam*. But I kind of like to play games with myself.

The oddity that came out of that was, I knew there had to be locomotives somewhere in the Los Angeles area. The photographer, really I don't know how interested he was, he couldn't find a place. So we wound up taking a whole bunch of pictures in a Model T Ford. I said, "You know, this is really not what I had in mind with *The Age of Steam*!" I usually wind up going along with things like that because I don't know what to do to fix it.

Well, as it was getting into the afternoon, it was getting quite late, and we're driving around in the hills in Burbank and, lo and behold, there's a big sign, one of the city signs, of a locomotive museum. I said, "You guys have got to be kidding!" I mean, here this place was just over the hill. You know they really researched the location and come out with this damn Model T!

So we went and he shot a whole series in the cab of that locomotive and another series with another locomotive on the other side of me and at different stops, hoping to get something. That's why it's such a dark picture; because it was late in the afternoon and there was no light left. So much for ambiguity.

It felt like *The Age of Steam* was a turning point altogether. I'm not really sure why it had that effect, but it really kind of recharged my batteries to do that. Because I had been in a doldrums stage, really depressed and down. The aftereffects of Judy's death and just the general depressed position that I felt I was in, nothing felt right. I didn't know what to do with myself, and *The Age of Steam* kind of got me enthusiastic again. You could tell, even from the structure of the instrumentation, I was starting to think again in terms of performing my own stuff. I had given up worrying about doing my own stuff because I just didn't feel like going through having a band and I couldn't deal with it. As the years went on, for some reason it became harder for me to deal with the band, rather than easier. It's not as if all of my experience added up to any real benefit. It just became hard to deal with people, and so I guess I spent more time retreating than anything. So *The Age of Steam* kind of got me moving again.

Then after that, I started another group based on the rhythm section of *The Age of Steam*. And we had some very nice tours with that group, which included Bob Rosengarden on drums and George Duvivier on bass. George was such a wonderful player and a funny man. And Dave Samuels was a young guy that was my vibes/percussionist. I guess it was his first band. He liked to play the vibes more than he liked to play the percussion, so before too long the percussion kind of got lost by the wayside, which was all right, because he always added something nice to the arrangements with the vibes. The guitar player, Mike Santiago, played very, very nicely indeed, and I don't know whatever became of him. I asked around about him, and nobody knows where he went. And Tom Fay on piano, who had done some arranging for me as well. He was trying to help me get some of my material together for playing with orchestras, especially with pops things.

So that was a nice band and we had it together for a couple of years. I kept essentially that instrumentation for a while and whatever changes we went through.

That brings up a particularly enjoyable event for me, which was recording an album with Astor Piazzolla, who was the most important composer in tango in this century in Buenos Aires. He made a brand-new idiom out of it as a serious vehicle for composition. It turned out he had a kind of fantasy of doing an album with me dating from twenty years earlier, when he first heard the *Pianoless Quartet*, the *Birth of the Cool*, my tentet and all that.

So there were these Italian guys, some of whom I knew, that gave him the opportunity. They commissioned him to do this album, and so he started to work on it. He wrote all of this music, and I wrote one piece. Actually, I wrote three but two of the pieces were lost in the mail.

Ordinarily that wouldn't be so terrible, but they were having a postal strike in Rome at the time, and I remember seeing photographs in the paper. Out of sheer frustration the postal workers were just burning mail because there was just more mail than they could deal with. I looked at the paper and I said, "There go my pieces, up in smoke. Now I know why Astor never got the things in time." But one of my pieces got through and Astor wrote an arrangement out of it for this group, the group being kind of a tango instrumentation that he had devised. He played an instrument called the bandoneon. The bandoneon was like the grandfather of the accordion. It had no keyboard, all buttons. Watching him play, when I finally saw him play, was incredible because he would do these very modern voicings on the thing and in order to reach these buttons, man, his fingers looked like snakes. There was just a really uncanny sense to it. He was triple-jointed in his fingers, and he could do things with his fingers that I never saw anybody else do. Truly triple-jointed, man, unbelievable. But he had a piano, a bass guitar, percussion, and a bunch of strings.

So he was in Rome and I found out all of this story later on. Franca (who later became my wife, but I hadn't met her yet) had a little apartment in Rome, and it was kind of a gathering place for South American poets and musicians. There were people there like a painter from Venezuela, a poet, Vinicius de Moraes used to go there a lot, and Astor went there. Astor was all enthused about doing this project, and he's crying on Franca's shoulder and he said, "You know, I'm going to do this thing and I need someplace to write." She said, "Listen, I've got this house over on the Marche, which is on the Adriatic Coast. You can work as much as you want, socialize when you feel like it, be by yourself when you want." So, sure enough, that summer he goes to the Marche to the house and worked there.

Ultimately, we recorded the thing in Italy and it was such a pleasure to do. He wrote beautiful, beautiful melodies for me to play, and the whole thing had that kind of Spanish, Argentinean seriousness to it, personified by the flamenco dance, and I really loved it.

I was recording with him and one day when Franca came into the studio. Because it was, I guess, the last day of recording. She was in Milan and Astor was after her, saying, "Come on, you haven't been by the record dates." She said, "Okay." So she comes by. I look up in the control room at one point and I'm busy in the middle of recording. I look up and I said, "Astor, who's that?" He said, "Who's what?" I said, "That beautiful girl in there. Who is she?" He said, "Oh, that's just a girl." He wouldn't say anything. So we go in and we're listening back to the thing that we just recorded, and he introduced me to her, and of course we were tied up listening to this thing. By the time I get done, I walk back in the studio. I figured she was going to stay there awhile and I'd get to find out what's going on here. I looked and she'd left. I was really kind of teed off at Astor and said, "Man, who was that?" He said, "You don't really want to know."

So it was the last night of recording and we went out. Astor was busy doing something. His wife, Emilita, had come, so they were off someplace. I went off with the guys that were involved in the thing, and the engineer, Mario Fatore, a guy I knew a long time. He was in the movie business. He made a lot of television commercials and so on. There were only one or two restaurants open late in Milan, so we went to this place called Santa Lucia.

We get to the entrance to the place and we start to go in and I sank low, and I'm going through the whole number. I see Franca sitting there with another woman. So I aim our whole party, push them in the direction, like a sheepdog, over toward the table and sat down next to Franca. Well, what I didn't know was the woman she was sitting with was her sister-in-law, the wife of her brother, and they were in the midst of a project. Her sister-in-law, Yolaine, had designed a line of clothes for children and they were photographing the clothes for the *Harper's Bazaar*, or what they call the Baby Bazaar, and Franca was the photographer. So during the course of the dinner, Yolaine said to Franca, "Why don't you ask him to come out and pose with the children?" Franca didn't know who I was, other than I had played saxophone on this thing with Astor, and so she didn't know anything about that. But her sister-in-law did. Franca said, "Well, I can't do that." Yolaine says, "No, go ahead, ask him." So Franca turns around and asks if I would like to come out tomorrow morning, Sunday morning, and have my picture taken with some children for the baby fashions. I said, "Of course!" Ten o'clock Sunday morning; just what I was dying to do. But I said, "Okay."

Countess Franca Rota, 1974. COURTESY GERRY MULLIGAN COLLECTION, LIBRARY OF CONGRESS, MUSIC DIVISION

She gave me their address, and I was going to come by and pick them up at her sister-in-law's apartment. So the next morning I get there and I guess it was nine or whatever time they said to be there. Of course, neither of them were up yet. I knock on the door and I hear all of this turmoil inside like they're racing to get up and get dressed. So they let me in and I get my horn out, and I'm kind of noodling around.

The reason I bring this up is because Franca took time out from getting dressed to take a picture that turned out really well. It wound up that we used it on a couple of albums after that. Then we go out and we have the pictures taken. We spend the morning and the afternoon doing stuff with the children. Well, the following day, the Monday, she got the stuff developed and she took it into the art director of the magazine. He said, "Well, you've got Gerry Mulligan in here." She said, "Yes." He said, "Listen, instead of him being in this thing, why don't you do a feature article on him? Where is he? Do you know where he is?" She said, "Yes, he just left for Rome." He said, "Well, okay, you go to Rome and you do an interview." She said, "Well, I never did an interview." He said, "Well, okay, you learn."

Photo shoot for Harper's Bazaar, *Milano, October 1976. Gerry with children.*
© FRANCA R. MULLIGAN

One of the pictures that she had taken in was one of the pictures we had done in the apartment. So she did indeed. She called up a couple of friends of hers, who have since become my best friends, and best friends with her as well; Lula and Luigi Pezzini. She was asking them about me, and they were very enthusiastic because they both thought I was terrific. You know, they thought that Franca was weird that she didn't know who I was.

One thing that Franca said to Luigi, "They want me to run down and do an interview. What do I do?" Luigi said, "Well listen, I think if you tell Gerry that you're doing this interview but that you're not really experienced, I'm sure he'll help you because he's a very nice man."

So sure enough, that's what she did. She came down and we met at my hotel, and we sat there and had dinner together and had this interview on tape. And it's so funny, because we're drinking vodka or something and during the course of this tape, our tempo gets slower and slower and our voices get lower and lower until we just practically put ourselves to sleep. So I saw her home to her apartment, which wasn't far away from the hotel that I was staying at.

The next day I had to take off for the States and so I went and got her for breakfast the next morning. It was like a picture out of an Audrey Hepburn movie. She's like running across the piazza with her hair flying and waving, with the French embassy over here.

We played that music with Astor a number of times in theaters in Europe, in Paris at the Olympia Music Hall, at the big meeting or conference they have in the Balearic Islands, Majorca, and we played it in Venice and a lot of places. At the theater in Paris, some of the guys were from my group and the rest of them were Astor's musicians. Tom Fay was playing piano and we were on stage. It was quite cold and we didn't have the heat on in the theaters. We were rehearsing with coats on. Of course, everything was written out; it wasn't improvised music. So Tom's got these piano parts that were really heavy, I mean, fifteen-page parts. We'd be playing along and it was so cold in the place, and Tom would feel a draft and he'd turn around and say, "Would somebody close that stage door? It's cold in here." It would quiet down for a while and then

Gerry and Astor Piazzolla.
© FRANCA R. MULLIGAN

pretty soon the music, this big, heavy piece of music would go flying up and off of the piano and he'd have to retrieve it and he'd say, "Come on, will somebody close the door?"

Well, this happened two or three times and then finally it dawned on me what was happening. It wasn't that somebody was opening the door and there was a draft. It was that Astor was standing next to him and the air coming out of his bandoneon came out with such force that it lifted this heavy piece of music and just tossed it off the piano onto the floor. And then it hit me, the power of the wind going through this instrument was incredible, just remarkable. I had no idea that it was creating such an incredible windstorm. Man, it was something. It was always a joy to do. I'd love to do that stuff again.

30

HAPPY BIRTHDAY 1974

AFTER SEVERAL YEARS of trying, *Happy Birthday* was finally staged in 1974. Anita Loos was always enthusiastic about doing it, and long after Judy died Anita would call and say, "I've got a producer, you've got to come right over and play the stuff for him." Well, what I would have liked to have done was to put it on, you know, spend the money and get a good tape made of the thing, but we ultimately never did it. I wasn't really organized enough to do it, and Anita liked the idea, for some reason, of my coming over and doing the song plugger routine. Sitting at

Anita Loos (left), Birmingham, Alabama, Happy Birthday *musical.*
© FRANCA R. MULLIGAN

the piano and saying, "And then I wrote . . ." And so I wound up playing this thing over and over again for potential producers and directors and stars; there have been so many I've forgotten.

I remember once playing it for Julie Harris. How she got Julie Harris to even listen to it, I don't know. Had Julie Harris wanted to do it, it would have been terrific, and I'm sure she could have done the comedy it called for. Because this was the thing that Anita had always said about it as a play—as a comedy—she said it had been done by so many actresses and the material always worked, from Helen Hayes to Joan Blondell, to you name it; lots and lots of different women had played it over the years.

I played it at one session. She'd gotten Tommy Smothers interested in doing one of the characters and ultimately I guess he wasn't interested. All Tommy Smothers could talk about was that he was looking for an apartment, and he wound up going to look at something that my ex-wife was going to rent to him. And he kept putting me on about this ridiculous scene he'd had with her about it. I wasn't particularly interested to hear any of it and thought it was fairly insensitive of him to be confronting me with it. But I played the music eventually for different producers, and it was kind of an ongoing thing. I'd get these calls periodically.

Well, later on (and this was based more than anything on some things that Anita had said along the way), she got it into her head that she had asked Judy to write the score and that Judy had brought me in, which was backward. It was that she asked me to write the score and I brought Judy in, but I guess it sounded better when she was telling the story to her friends.

The fact was that it never worked out with any of these producers. Then once, of all things, she decided that it would be a good idea to get a producer interested in doing a black cast version of it. Well, that seemed like an idea that could have worked, but she went, for some reason, to Cicely Tyson, who told her, "Yes; it's a nice idea but you should get some black songwriters to do the songs." No matter what I do, man, the songs get thrown out. So then another producer had the idea, take the lyrics and we'll get new melodies written. I said forget it. Judy wrote those things with me and also, the way the contract was written up by her attorney, and the reason he had done it, was to try to protect us because Judy had a big tax debt. He didn't want these to become part of a football that the tax department could play with, so she became a "Lyricist for Hire." That's another category, a "Lyricist for Hire," and so we were protected, but legally they were my lyrics.

In the biographies, a couple of them of Anita, they castigate me all over the place, saying that I was uncooperative with the producers; I wouldn't allow them to take the lyrics and put new songs to it, and I objected to the people they wanted. At one point this one producer said he wanted to have Imogene Coca do it. I said, "Imogene Coca is very funny but it was written for a much younger woman," and he said, "Well, but she's very funny and she's interested to do it." I said, "Fine, do it with Imogene Coca." Well, in the book about Anita, it says that I put my foot down, I absolutely wouldn't do it with Imogene Coca. It was a load of crap. I realized again I had been elected the villain of the piece. And I could hear Anita telling these friends of hers, "Well, you know, Gerry was dragging his heels on this one," and he wouldn't cooperate on this one, and she told people that Judy had been the one she had gone to first. She got all her information a little bit mixed up and so again I found myself in a kind of beleaguered position. I resent some of the things that I've read in the books about Anita, the mentions about me, and since they're not important, you forget about it. There's no point in fighting battles like that.

The one really interesting thing that happened out of all that, though, was Anita had a friend named Jim Hatcher in what they call the "Town and Gown" theater down in Birmingham, Alabama. It was associated with the University of Alabama, and Jim wanted to do the show. It was a big anniversary for the theater, I don't know, twentieth or twenty-fifth anniversary or something, of his being there. She asked me if I was interested in putting the play on there and I said, "Sure."

So, I had to get ready for this *Happy Birthday* thing in Alabama, but I wanted to see Franca again. I called her and invited her to breakfast the next morning. She said how can I be calling her now and taking her to breakfast the next morning; he's calling from the States. What she didn't know was that I was already at the airport when I made the call. So I got back into Milan the next morning and took her to breakfast, and I found out she was going to Venezuela to visit some friends. I decided to go to Birmingham by way of Venezuela, so I joined Franca on that trip. Then I had to leave to go back to Birmingham, and she came to Birmingham a few days later when she left Venezuela.

I was going to get a hotel for Franca so she didn't have to live in the house with all of the gang, but it really was fun. We were living in a very primitive way in some ways, you know, nobody running the kitchen and living out of cans. Franca said she'll do the cooking if she doesn't have to do any cleaning up. That sounded like a good deal to us, man, and we all volunteered to do the kitchen work and she wound up cooking for us. So now we had a cook, and the reed section, and the arrangers all living at the house. It was really hard work, and I found myself in all kinds of screwy situations.

I brought a couple of musicians down with me: Tom Fay, who was playing piano with me then and helping me with a lot of the writing. He was helping down there, too, arranging the stuff and organizing the parts and all that. And I brought the young lady from New York who had transcribed or reorganized some of the parts for my *Age of Steam* album and had taken some of the stuff from records that wasn't written out. I thought she would be helpful to do some of the kinds of physical things that needed doing, especially copying and organizing parts and all that.

Well, the nameless copyist transcriber, in the meantime, had ingratiated herself, I guess, with Fanny Flagg and the people around her and started carrying tales back and forth. God knows what she said to Fanny because the next thing I knew there was this whole animosity feeling growing up, as if we were armed camps. When I realized what was happening, it was like I had brought this girl along to work and she was gossiping in a way that was creating a whole unhealthy atmosphere. So I fired her and sent her back to New York, except she didn't go back to New York. She went over and hung out with what turned out to be the enemy camp. Damnedest thing I ever saw, man, it's like she just manufactured this problem, and it made for an atmosphere that was totally misleading.

I had seen Fanny Flagg in some movies. I thought she was terrific and what little I had seen of her work on this musical, I thought that she was going to be great. She started to have throat problems, which made me sweat because I've seen that happen so many times when actors, especially when they get into a singing role, start having these problems with the voice. So she was apparently going through agony with that, with all kinds of medication to try to keep it at bay. But Fanny was always kind of standoffish with me and I always figured it was just because of what this dumb girl had done. God, I really resented her for that because I had seen that a couple times with plays that Judy had done, where these animosities grow up—maybe out of some ego thing, sometimes out of nothing—and then people would kind of nurse their bruised feelings until you got people not talking to each other and all that. I just think it's not only useless, it misses the point altogether.

The whole thing about Birmingham was that it should have been fun to do, and I was determined to go ahead and have fun anyway. I was really sorry to see this grow up, because I know Fanny was having a hard time with problems with her voice, and to have this kind of hostility going on just was not helping her vocal problems. She wasn't really too kind about the songs, either. The song that was the best song that Judy and I had written for the character that Fanny was playing, she didn't like at all. I didn't realize it, but especially I think for a non-musician, it was hard to sing, and I realized then that it was giving her a hard time. But with all that, I thought Fanny did really a terrific job. I admired the fact that she was doing it under such painful circumstances because I know it was hard for her. But aside from that she was very, very funny, and she really did the hell out of the thing.

So for me, it was a great experience and a great experience also because of the way this thing was going, like the house with Franca cooking and Tom and me working on the arrangements. Franca brought a kind of spirit that was great because the musicians really liked her. The girl who was playing the tenor flute was kind of shy, and Franca made an atmosphere that got everybody warmed up and it felt great.

We ran the show for about a week, I think, and I realized the job they did with it was very nice. With a really hip director and some work on the jokes to bring it more up-to-date, it probably could have been improved for Broadway purposes. But even so, the way it was, it's too bad that there was nobody connected with it who could push it. I mean, even to do it in regional theater or dinner theater, it was a good project for that sort of thing. But that turned out to be the only time that we ever did it. And I'm really glad to have had that opportunity. Anita was there for the whole thing; she kept trying to rewrite it and did whatever necessary to make transitions in scenes and such, and try to adapt some of the stuff more for Fanny. I've always felt when you work with somebody you feel sort of a proprietary attitude toward what they do, so I was very pleased when I read her book and then saw the movie she made of Fanny's *Fried Green Tomatoes*. She really is great.

But that was the one experience of putting that together, and in its way all the more fascinating for having been the kind of thing it was. It felt like we were playing some roles that had been turned out by Judy Garland and Mickey Rooney. Listen, we've got a barn, let's put on a show: my mom can make the costumes and your mom can make the cookies. Jim Hatcher was a nice guy, and it's great to meet people like that who are enthusiasts. He just loved what he was doing so much, and he made it happen.

I wish Judy could have seen the thing, and, of course, if we could have worked on it together, we could have written some more songs for it and solved some of the problems. I mean, if your leading lady doesn't feel comfortable singing a song, I can understand that, so maybe we can come up with something else, use the melody in a different way. I'm not that flexible, it's not so easy for me, and I don't always know what's hard for a singer to sing. Then, when a singer points out that this gives them some difficulty I say, "Oh well, I understand that," but it's not a problem that I would have anticipated because I don't find those intervals difficult to hit. So it was something that was lucky for me to be able to finally bring to some kind of conclusion.

31

REUNION WITH CHET, *LA MENACE*, AND GOODBYE CHARLIE

In November of 1974 there was a reunion concert with Chet Baker at Carnegie Hall. It turned out to be such a complicated affair. There were too many people involved and too many strangers involved, and it was like a big show. It wasn't like we were able to get away from the whole thing and establish something. And Chet was operating under particular difficulties, and of course his particular way of dealing with that was to be surly and demanding, and he was just really mean to everybody. So it wasn't possible to really explore anything. We just had to try to get the material together that we needed for the show.

Gerry and Chet Baker, rehersal for reunion concert, Carnegie Hall, 1974.
© FRANCA R. MULLIGAN

As it happened, some things that we played Chet had never played before, so he had to learn them. But it wasn't really the kind of situation where we could stretch out or just feel natural with, partly because of the kind of attitude that Chet had. I mean, he had everybody in the place absolutely cowed, because everybody was looking forward to playing with Chet because they didn't know him. By the time he got there, the guys were all geared to try to be cooperative, but he came in and just laid such a pall over the place and all the guys were walking on eggshells. They didn't want to upset him, and he could really be mean if somebody played wrong chords. Man, he would lash out at them. So there was a pretty rough atmosphere in the place.

The other thing was that I had finally knuckled under to Creed Taylor's demands. I wanted to use my own guys who knew my music to save the time that it takes in rehearsal to get used to different music, and the guys who played on it were great, you know. It was Ron Carter, Bob James, and Harvey Mason in the rhythm section, but there were lots of mistakes in the rhythm parts because there wasn't really enough time to go through that much material. But I argued and kept holding out with Creed. I said, "Let me use my own guys. It will be much easier to establish rapport and it'll be much more compatible and save me a lot of aggravation." Well, he held out. He wanted to use the guys who were recording for him all the time. That added an extra element because Bob James and Ron didn't know the music, so they were starting from scratch.

Now, no matter how good musicians are, when they're playing strange music, it takes time. All of these things added to the strain of doing it, and the one thing that's inevitable in a case like that, there's never enough rehearsal time. You're trying to do this all in one afternoon and then go play a concert that night. It's an absolute killer. So I never really was very pleased with that whole episode, with those concerts, and what came out of them.

In 1977 I worked on another film project called *La Menace*. With *La Menace* I was able to put into practice some of the things that I'd learned not to do on the *Luv* score. For instance, the director, Alain

Corneau, came to me with the project. He came up here to Connecticut and sat down and told me the story of the thing. They had sent me an English translation of a kind of a treatment. So I was armed with that, and then he came and talked about what he wanted, flesh out the outline that he had made, and while he was doing that we'd talk about this character and kind of get an idea. So I was scribbling out melody themes for the various things that he was talking about, and he talked the movie through and then after that, he invited me to go to France to the place that they had picked out for the locations. So Franca and I took off and went over to Bordeaux and went around with him and he showed us the place he was going to use, and this is going to happen here and we're going to do this, and so on and so on. So it was like building up a kind of catalog of information about what to expect, and he also gave me six bottles of incredibly good wine. We really had a great time with him there.

When it came time to start shooting, we came back to Connecticut and then pretty soon after that they started shooting. But whatever, the timing worked out very well and he kept in touch with me by phone. He'd call and say the shooting is going well, and this and this and this has happened and this is nice and this has worked.

Then when he started to get a rough cut together, he began to give me timings on scenes, and, given that, I was able to start sketching out the ideas into some kind of pieces that would fit underneath these scenes. They filmed part of it up in Vancouver, the big part of it. I won't go into the story of the thing, it's too complicated, but the main story is that the guy, the hero, played by Yves Montand, is accused of a murder that he didn't commit. And then, because the person who was murdered was some bad guy or other who had bad friends, they took out after Yves Montand. They were going to kill him because they thought he did indeed do the murder and killed their friend, or their boss, or whoever he was.

So when they go off to Vancouver, this is part of a whole scheme that he had laid on to try to make these people think that he had died. He staged his own death over here. He was going to meet his girlfriend in

Rio. They did a thing—crashing a truck and it burned—so it looked like he was dead. Well, then, *deus ex machina* comes into the thing and these other truck drivers out there think that he's the one who's doing some other bad things to them. So they set up this trap for him and wind up killing him, so he is indeed dead.

Well, as they get into a rough cut and then into a final cut, I already had stuff fairly well laid out; I did all the timings by stopwatch on the phone as they were in this one scene and he wants me to catch some action. I said, "Okay, time it by the stopwatch; at what second does he put his hand on the doorknob to open the door?" And I'd say, "Okay, got that. At what point in the chase does he realize that these guys are after him?" Because he's just driving along and he thinks that everything is great and all of a sudden it dawns on him that he's in jeopardy. We did all of the timings by stopwatch.

I recorded the stuff at Don Elliott's studio in Weston with all my friends. Dave Grusin was there and did piano and keyboard stuff, and I think I went through all of my drummer friends and bass players, and we had a good time. We worked very hard to do it, but we got it all together.

I took the reels and Franca and I went to Paris and brought the tapes there in time for them to transfer them to film for French speed, and then we had, what do they call that when they lay all of the three elements together: the dialogue, the sound effects, and the music.

Alain and I were ecstatic, because all my things worked. Not only were the timings perfect for what they needed to be, but the mood of the things that I had written were exactly right for what was happening on the screen. We had made some choices that Alain and I were very pleased with. For instance, when Yves Montand's character gets involved with this truck chase, he's in a little Volkswagen Beetle, I guess, and he's speeding along a highway and three big trucks come up. One overtakes him and gets in front of him, another one comes up and pins him behind, and a third one is on the side of him. Well, the normal way to do this would be with the sound effects, like they're hitting and you hear the smashing and crunching of metal and so on of the trucks hitting this poor little Volkswagen Beetle.

What we decided to do, and it made really an eerie effect, and we thought it was effective as hell and really liked it, was to have all of that done with no sound effects, only the underscoring. And the underscoring, as I say he's driving along with the truck and the music is all terrific, like triumphal because he had accomplished what he tried to accomplish, and he thinks he's on his way to the airport to get on the plane to go to Rio. Then these trucks come up, and at the moment when he realizes that he's in trouble, the mood of the music changes but it's going on a long thing; it's like gallop-chase music. The final thing of it was, it really swung hard, and it really came out great. There was a helicopter shot where the helicopter was running along with the car and three trucks and then starts pulling back and up and up and up so you see the car down here, and then we see over the hill in the distance and there's Vancouver and the airport off in the distance, and it was really effective. Then they trapped the car in a place where a whole bunch of trucks had gathered, and Yves Montand was trying to get out and he thinks he sees a way, only we see that there are two trucks coming and they squash the Beetle like a bug. And that's the end of the poor bastard. The end of the film is the girl at the airport in Rio to meet the plane. It's a heartbreaking ending. Well, we were really pleased with ourselves that the whole thing had worked out the way it had.

Then what happened, they started playing it for distributors, and when they started playing it for the Canadian and American distributors, everybody's a film critic and I suppose it's even harder for a distributor not to be a film critic. They all started offering criticisms and, of course, the producer, Denise Petitdidier, was a terrific woman but she was trying to sell the picture. They suggested cuts and this and that. Well, they made a mishmash of the cutting of it. Like this whole long piece that was done without the sound effects. The sound effects were in, the piece of music was chopped into pieces, and there was a suicide scene where this woman walks across this big stone parapet and dives off down the side of the hill, with the river below. That also was done without sound effects and it was ethereal. It was like she just floated and this music picked her up when she floated off; man, it was so final. When they put the sound effects in, she was like clomp, clomp, clomp, and then they had that terrible sound of a pumpkin squashing when it lands, so Christ, man, it just was one of those things. I relive this moment as one of the most embarrassing of my life.

Not too long after that, when the picture was playing at a theater on the Champs Elysees, we had a concert to play in Paris at a theater and Franca was going to join me. She was in Milan. Well, I got a call from Franca in the morning that she wasn't well, she was feeling sick and had pain, but she was going to try to make it anyway. Well, it turned into a terrible day, because she didn't wind up getting on the plane that she was supposed to take. All I could find out was that she had been very sick in the airport waiting for the plane to leave, floored with this pain, and nobody knew where she was. Nobody knew if she got on the plane or whether she went home. By this time I'm tearing my hair out. I had a sound check in the afternoon and two of the guys didn't show up, which was unusual. Rosengarden and Duvivier decided not to come, and I really needed it that day. So by that night I was beside myself worrying about her and furious. And I say, again, I turned to anger to survive.

Then finally, like an hour or so before the concert, Franca showed up. The pain had subsided and she got on the plane once the fog had cleared. They didn't want to let her on the plane because she was in pain, but she had gotten on the plane and was much better. She went to the hotel. I said phew and heaved a big sigh of relief.

I played the concert, but I was still upset. Sometimes I'm able to take the anger out in playing. Usually it's fairly obvious, but in those days, I was able to control it so that I'd make music out of it anyway. We'd played a good concert and when it was over, Alain, who had come to the thing with his family, came backstage and there were a whole bunch of people around. Alain comes up to me and tells me how much he enjoyed the concert.

I turned on him and said, "How could you let them do that to our movie?" And I gave him hell because they chopped up the movie. Afterward I said, "Oh, what have I done?" Well, to this day, every time I think of it, man, I just cringe at having done that. If I hadn't liked him, if I hadn't had such a good time doing the project, if it hadn't come out so well, any of those things, I would say, well, all right. But all that wasn't true, man. I liked him a lot. I liked his family. It was the only time I've worked on a movie where I did the music that I enjoyed, and to have done that was just, it was a very hard thing to face.

Around this time I got a call from somebody connected with Joni Mitchell, and they wanted me to play on an album that she was doing of Charlie Mingus tunes. She had put lyrics to them, apparently.

Well, not long after that I got a call from Charlie, and he was saying that he hoped that I could steer the thing in the right direction because he really didn't trust her to do what he wanted with the thing. He said she's a strong lady and he was depending on me to get the thing together. I said, "Charlie, I hope your confidence is not misplaced."

So anyway, we got there. I got there about the time I was supposed to record, and I guess I was kind of thrown a curve to start with, because Joni had done a track of a piece that she had done a cappella, and she apparently had not gotten herself into a definite key to start with and then she kind of shifted the key along the way. So she wanted to know if I could improvise an accompaniment to it. I tried and I just couldn't find a center of the tonality. It wasn't one thing or the other. So that kind of got me off on a bad foot.

After that there was this one piece, and I did a harmony line to her singing, and Charlie was really pleased with what I had played and I was too. I thought it was really great the way the whole thing worked out and my line really worked. He took me aside and said, "Now, the thing that's going to happen on this, we're going to have Dizzy come in and he's going to track another line based on your line and what I'm hoping that you'll do is make sure that Joni Mitchell just uses those lines; what you did is perfect. Leave it alone and don't be overdubbing anything else or adding anything, just that."

I said, "Charlie, I'll try, man, but I think that you stand a better chance of getting what you want than I do because I have no connection here." So I don't know whether it was that night or another night that I called up Joni, and her manager I guess was there, and I told them what Charlie had said. Well, they really reacted kind of strangely to what I was saying, as if I were a voice from outer space.

I realized it was not going over at all well, that I was interfering, and I pointed out, "Listen, I'm doing this because Charlie had very definite ideas after he heard what I did and that you would leave it at that, and this is really what he wanted on the thing and he wanted me to tell you that." Well, I think they were quite insulted that Charlie and I were interfering, or at least that I was interfering, and later on I heard stories that they told, that Gerry Mulligan called up; it was really peculiar, he was talking about overdubbing a lot of saxophone parts. It was the exact opposite of what I had said!

I said, "I think maybe we've got a communication problem here and in some kind of way I didn't make myself clear." In the end, she did pretty much chop up what I had done and she had sent me a tape of my line and Dizzy's line together, and it was one of those things where I think somebody had taken that cassette and used it for something else. It was like a one-shot thing—you've got no other chance to get it. I'd love to have the thing as it was originally done, because she changed it around a lot in the finished take and chopped my line up and changed Dizzy's line and probably overdubbed other stuff anyway.

But the thing that I was getting to, aside from all of that, there are things that happen that you have no control over and sometimes, with the best of intentions, you try to do something, especially if you're trying to do it for a friend, and make a mess of it. So I always felt badly about that, not for myself, but because I wasn't able to get what Charlie wanted and kind of got myself in the soup in the process.

It's so strange to hear people interpret what you do and say, and some of those experiences had a big effect on me. I have really gotten much better at communicating with people. I do not assume that people understand what I am talking about, so I make myself very, very clear. Don't assume they know things that I think they know because I know it. I was always making that mistake.

Anyway, the last time I saw Charlie . . . Franca and I had been in Mexico at a Club Med. We'd gone to Club Med a number of times because there was a man who was what they called the Chief of the Village working for Club Med. He was Chief of the Village in different places, and he was a musician and he was a great guy. In fact, I first met him when I was putting the big band together. I said, "You know I'm starting to put this band together but what I really need is someplace to take them. I'd like to be able to take them out of New York and get them away from everybody for a week and just rehearse." He said, "Yeah, you'd really like that, bring them to Club Med." I said, "You're kidding?" He said, "No, bring them down," and we did. He took us down to the Club Med in Guadeloupe for two weeks and was able to get the airline tickets using the line of credit that they had. He took us down there and he said, "You don't have to play any shows or anything else; do whatever you want."

So it was the kind of thing where we had the brass rehearsing in this room, with the saxes over here. Years later I would run into people who'd come up to me and say, "You know, I just had the best time of my life at Club Med in Guadeloupe when you guys were rehearsing. We loved to go in and listen to the brass and we loved to listen to the saxophone section."

People loved to be involved in the band, in the formation of the thing. It was a whole different kind of involvement and a different kind of excitement, and the people who were there never forgot it. Still, people come up to me and remark about that.

Well, anyway, one of the places where Bernie (Bernard Pollack) was Chief of the Village was in Puerto Vallarta, Mexico, the one on the West Coast. It was a great place, great beaches, and I always had fun with Bernie because they had this thing where the band would go out and meet the bus with the incoming passengers two or three times a week, and they'd play the people off when they were leaving. Every time they had it, they would ring a bell or blow a whistle or something for the band to assemble and play. And I would always go down and play. I'd never ask anybody. When I had the band, sometimes the guys would do it and they enjoyed it, but at the one in Mexico I was just there with a quartet. We brought the other guys along just in case we wanted to play. So every time they were welcoming people in, I'd go down with my soprano, and played soprano, like a rollicking kind of street band. I used to have a ball down there.

Well, while we were there, there was a woman that Bernie had known. She'd hurt her back skiing and was confined to a wheelchair. She came to Mexico and Bernie took her to a healer whose name was Pachita, who was a well-known healer.

Bernie said she did an operation on this woman that just scared the hell out of him because she used an ordinary kitchen knife and made incisions in her back, and it was like she was tying up nerves. It just was really peculiar and if he hadn't seen it, he wouldn't have believed it. The healer told this woman, "Now you stay off your feet for a week, you don't get up at all, not to go to the bathroom, nothing."

So she did indeed stay in the bed for a week, and somebody took care of her. After that she got up, and she was walking. She was able to walk again. And when she was down there, I saw her in her bathing suit, and there was a little tiny pair of scars on her back. You know, things like that are kind of mind-boggling. It's like you don't know whether to believe this or not, because it's so out of the realm of the believable. But when Charlie (Mingus) was dying of lateral sclerosis, Lou Gehrig's disease, and there's no cure for it, we told him about this healer in Mexico. So he and his wife, Susan, decided to go to Mexico, and I was kind of glad to see him go because even if Pachita couldn't heal him with her herbal treatments, she could certainly alleviate a lot of the pain and make him more comfortable. Susan said afterward, after Charlie had died, that it really was one of the best times that they had down there. Pachita really helped ease the whole thing, because what a difficult way to go.

So the last time I saw him, he was leaving the studio then, because he and Susan were going to get packed and go off to Mexico. Charlie and I, you know, had that awkward thing because we knew it would be the last time we would see each other. So we were together, and there was an elevator because the studio was in the basement in the Village someplace, on Eighth Street I think. Charlie's sitting there in the wheelchair and I was standing next to him, and the car came down and the door opens and it was a caged affair, it wasn't a closed car, and he backed himself into it and closed the door. And here we are looking at each other and the elevator starts going up, and it struck us both at the same time and we started laughing. It was like something right out of a movie, man, like the elevator was taking him up to heaven. We just roared; it was so outrageous. Again, right out of a movie. We're waving at each other and there he is being whisked off to heaven. I said, shit, this is not happening, and that was the last time I saw Charlie. We left each other laughing. He was a good man. I liked him very much. But that was our Joni Mitchell episode, and goodbye Charlie.

32

ÉTUDE FOR FRANCA

MEETING FRANCA in the early 1970s really opened up a new era for me. Not the least of it was that Franca had a different kind of attitude. She was very much a realist and an optimist, and pragmatic in the way, if you want to do something, then go ahead and do it. Before too long she realized that I was becoming frustrated with not having my own band. And she realized I didn't want to have to face it. I had gotten to the point where I couldn't face dealing with agents and promoters. The whole scene had become something I couldn't handle. And too many times I turned out to be the patsy in some kind of a scam that would just drive me nuts. For instance, an agent would call me up on the phone and ask me to do something that I really didn't want to do. I'd tell him, "Well, I don't want to do that." He'd say, "Well, you think about it." I'd say, "Well, I'm saying I don't have to think. I'm telling you what I think," and he'd hang up. Then a couple of weeks later he'd call back and he'd say, "Have you thought about it?" I'd say, "Yeah, I thought about it. I don't want to do it." He'd say, "Well, think about it some more, man." And I would go through this, and I would say, "What do I have to do for you to take no for an answer? I don't want to do it." And this didn't just happen just once, this happened a lot of times that it would get down to the line.

I wouldn't hear anything from them for a while, and then they would call and say, "Well, you know, listen. You've got to help me out, man, because these people went ahead and advertised and now they're expecting you to come. And if you don't come, it like, you know, reflects on you." I'd say, "You bastard," and it would happen a lot. And it used to really, really tick me off that they would do all that. They would con me into doing things that I really didn't want to do. Franca said, "You're a fool; don't do it. You told them. It's no skin off your nose." I'd say, "Yes, but you know, it's like they've got this whole thing that jazz musicians are irresponsible," and then say, "Well, I'm not there to protect myself, defend myself, they're going to say what they want." She'd say, "So what?" I'd say, "Well, you're right," so she really started dealing with the agents at that point and just took no crap from them.

So I started another group, and I started to feel different because where these guys were used to taking advantage of me, and because in a lot of ways, even though people don't think of me that way, I have really an easy nature, I'm not really hard to get along with, and I'm not difficult to get to do things. If I don't want to do something I say no and I figure that should be it, you know. Why do you have to explain yourself? If I say I'm going to do something, that's it; I do it. If I say I'm not going to do something, I don't want to do it. I mean, that's obvious, but with a lot of agents, it only works one way and they want what they want. Musicians are all kind of babies anyway. They don't know what they want so you have to handle them. It used to drive me nuts. I don't like being handled and manipulated.

So Franca and I got into this thing, and it kind of felt like we were running the family business and she was taking care of the business part and dealing with the agents. You know, you start to get an organization together of people to do the things that we weren't equipped to do. You need a bookkeeper to do a bookkeeper's job and you need a secretary to do the secretary's job, and you can't expect to do it all. It's all true. All of that seems obvious, but trying to put the logical into practice is not always easy. Well, ultimately, we've done that, and it changed everything. The whole attitude toward working is different. She also made the attitude toward me different because agents now have to approach me in a businesslike way and we're not going to take any crap, and if we say we're going to do something we do it. We're reliable because now it's a business in the way that it's supposed to be, and you contract to do

Gerry and Franca.
© HANK O'NEAL

something and you do it. You try to get the best contract beforehand. You have to get everything written out and say, "Oh, no, no, we never promised you that." It must all be done in front.

I used to be able to drink all night with the guys and get loaded and wake up the next day and feel all right. Then you get to be thirty or so, and you don't feel quite so good. By the time you get to be forty, you feel really rotten and the hangovers get worse and you finally get to a point where the hangover comes first. It defeats its own purpose. That eventually led me first to cool it with drinking, because luckily I was never an alcoholic in the way some people are. I could drink, then not have to keep at it. I know a lot of people who are alcoholic who can't even smell alcohol, man; it just sets them off. So, in a way, I was at least saved that torture. But I spent a lot of years being drunk too much of the time, and it puts you in a negative relationship with the world around you. But as far as the anger is concerned, just feeling rotten made me very touchy.

Once I got rid of the curse of the demon rum and the same thing with the drugs, finally when I met Franca, who had a totally different outlook on life than I'd ever encountered, all of these things had an influence. The whole idea of anger just seemed inappropriate, unnecessary. To put meanings on things that weren't there, it's like substituting. You can be mad at this thing over here because you're really mad at something over there that you can't face. So it's a whole thing of displaced attitude and, eventually, all of those things became less and less important. Also, I understand much better now when things happen that in some ways I feel are against me, or put me in a bad position, or somebody is unfair, or the scene is unfair in some way, or I'm not given the recognition I feel I deserve, it's not very important. And I'm not sure it ever was important. I think it was just an excuse to get mad. And getting mad, I think that what I finally did realize with analysis, was that anger is kind of a cover-up for despair. And despair is a terrible thing. So, if you're angry you jolt yourself out of it.

It was the one teaching of the Catholic Church that I always understood. To the Catholic Church there's one unforgivable sin and that's the sin of despair; a very interesting concept. It's also a contradiction in terms of the whole cycle of sinning and forgiveness and that. But on a philosophical level, it's understandable what they mean because, if a person is in despair, they're totally out of reach of the church. Nothing the church can say, or nothing that God can say, is going to have anything to do with it. They're absolutely unreachable.

This puts me in my mind of something else, because what I learned in analysis, and this started me on an ability to enjoy my relationships with people in a way that I hadn't done before, was that any kind of emotional disturbance or any kind of neurosis or, even worse, any kind of psychosis, is extremely selfish. The self-centeredness of the emotionally disabled is a fascinating thing to watch and is especially fascinating to me now, because I've been through all that and I see it all so clearly and I can recognize it. It's incredible to watch it when it's at work, and to see somebody who's trapped in an emotional cycle they can't break. And they're so totally focused in on themselves and demand that everybody else be focused in on them at the same time. It's the most totally selfish thing.

Mental illness is entirely selfish. It makes an entirely selfish relationship with other people. It's why you can't get to them. That's why anything that happens with an emotionally disturbed person has to come from inside. You can't touch them from the outside, no way. I was always amazed that more of the musicians who were hooked on drugs didn't go into analysis. But almost all of them eventually turned to . . . if they quit using the drugs, they would eventually drink too much. So all of my friends drank themselves to death at an early age, and I'm very angry at them all for doing it because it's lonely without my friends.

After a while I really wanted to have my own big band again. And I guess, not only did I feel ready to face the agents and the business part of it, but now, really the prime mover became Franca. She realized that's what I wanted to do and that I was hesitant to take this on again. She realized how hard it was for me to sell myself to the agents and the promoters and all that, and as a consequence, I was usually taken advantage of. I wasn't getting the kind of prices that I should have been able to get, and I wasn't ever able to find a manager to do it. A lot of that was my own fault, too, because managers want to tell you what to do and a manager wants you to work all the time and I didn't want to. I don't like being out there week after week after week, which is what a manager will have you do, because you've got to make money.

So with one thing or another, I wasn't able to afford a manager and as a consequence, I had to do it myself. Well, when Franca started dealing with these people, the whole climate of my relationship with agents changed. They didn't have me, the easy pushover, to do what they wanted me to do, and we discussed what kinds of things I wanted to do and how best to go about it. I really wanted to have another big band even though it was very, very tough work to put things together—tours and dates—because carrying a big band is very expensive. Today it's even more prohibitive because the transportation has gotten so expensive; it was expensive enough in the 1970s.

Then Willard Alexander liked the idea that I was going to have a big band again, so he wanted to represent me, and I liked Willard a lot. He was kind of the last of the classy big band bookers. He was at MCA in the 1930s in the heyday of the bands with Benny Goodman, when things really first started popping. So Willard took a personal interest in booking the band and things went well. We did a lot of enjoyable things with the band. We toured a lot more in the States than I had done before or after. They were able to get tours together—concert tours, where we'd play one-nighters and travel by bus. A lot of things at schools, a lot of things done concert style in clubs in various towns, concert halls in towns that could support it, and we kept the band working quite well for years in the 1970s.

We made tours to Europe and a couple of tours to Japan. One of the tours we did was documented on the *CBS Sunday Morning* show. So every place we showed up there was a camera crew waiting for us, and it made us all feel like royalty.

I started out using the original Concert Jazz Band instrumentation and started adding to it because the guys kept pressing me. They wanted the fourth trumpet and also, we were going out now and doing festivals. So I started to add the other horns—the fourth trumpet and the fifth

Gerry and Franca at Gerry's birthday party on Alitalia flight with the Concert Jazz Band.
COURTESY GERRY MULLIGAN COLLECTION, LIBRARY OF CONGRESS, MUSIC DIVISION

saxophone—just for added power, because in a big band in a festival setting, you feel like you have to get out the sledgehammer. It's like no time for subtlety. Maybe I'm wrong about that, maybe I'm exaggerating, but that was at least the reason for the choices and why I added to the instrumentation, even though it wasn't musically what I wanted.

The sound of the band with those couple of extra horns was that much stronger, playing in big places and big auditoriums, especially outdoor venues. The band had more impact. I don't know what it is, there's a geometric equation on trumpets; three trumpets is a certain loudness, a fourth trumpet adds a great deal to the power of the three, but after the fourth, it's like you've got to add another four instruments for it to then again really change the volume of it. It doesn't just go arithmetically. Five trumpets is not louder really than four. It's like from four, you've got to jump up to seven or eight trumpets to really change the volume. So adding the fourth trumpet gave us the possibility of a much more loud ensemble, especially in outdoor things and particularly if you're playing a show where there's somebody playing before you and somebody playing after you. It's a little more of a sledgehammer.

The Concert Jazz Band was a much more subtle instrumentation geared really to the concert hall, not geared to the festival atmosphere at all. It's also the kind of band that I liked because the band that I had in 1957 was more like the band I had in 1972. The band in 1957 wasn't anything like the Concert Jazz Band. The timbre and the texture of the orchestra were just altogether different. But I went back to this other thing because it was intended as a concert festival vehicle. That's where we were going to work with the band, so that's what I was trying to adapt it for. We only made one album with that band. I would have liked to have done more.

One of the outdoor festivals we played was Newport. We went up there with the big band and they had this schedule worked out. We did the setup and were playing in the late afternoon, so we had to have lights on our stands because, by the time we got onstage the sun would be gone, and with the stage lights we couldn't see the music. Well, we were all set to go on at seven or seven-thirty, eight o'clock—whatever the scheduled time was—and we had finished our sound check. The guys were hanging out all over the place waiting for our time to go on. We had about an hour or something.

In the trailer next to mine I hear that they've got a problem going on and I didn't know quite what it was, but it seemed like Stan Turrentine or one of the guys wasn't there, and why didn't they get Mulligan to take his band on early to cover for him. Well, they came to my trailer and I said, "Listen, I don't know if we can get the guys together so fast because they're all over the place." So they put a call out on the loudspeaker, which makes my band sound like they're late, and I went for it because I've always been cooperative in shows and I hate to see the guys putting a thing on have problems like that. So in my naivete, I was still being cooperative about stuff like that, helping the other guy out.

They call for Gerry Mulligan's band to please come, so the guys all come back. "What's happening?" So I tell them they want us to go on because Turrentine's guys aren't there yet. So okay; we go on stage. It's now sundown and they'd hired some guy to do the lights who's some kind of, in quotes, "artist," who I'm thinking realizes that the important thing here is the lights; the music just exists for him to express his art. It was so beautiful in the sunset that they didn't want to turn on the bandstand lights and spoil it. Well, of course, my guys are trying to read music in the dark, so I finally went to my side of the stage and said, "Will you please turn these goddamn lights on, we can't see a thing out here. Please!" And the upshot of that was this guy pulled such a bitch on me. I go on and this guy is in the wings and he's screaming like a banshee at me for spoiling his show and, ultimately, he sued me. The light guy sued me!

Everybody said, "You've gotta be kidding, man; you're lucky I don't sue your ass for all your unprofessional nonsense." Anyway, when we got off stage, I hear this great hilarity going on in Turrentine's part of the compound, and they're all laughing at the way they put it over on Gerry Mulligan; he didn't want my band to follow him because he's more important than I am anyway. And by God, man, they were just delighted at all the problems we had and that he got his own way and made a fool out of me. I stood and listened to this shit and said that was the end of my being cooperative with any musician; they can all go to hell. You tell me what time to go on I'll be there. You want me to go on early, forget it. To be made a fool of and have the whole performance spoiled because somebody is taking out their hostility on me. I had never met the man, don't know the first thing about him. And he had never met me and doesn't know me, so why am I his enemy? Well, I don't know.

There are fools enough in the world to go around, but there are some things that happened like that, that were so totally unnecessary and a total change from anything I'd ever experienced. Because I really grew up in the business in the days when, if something happened to one band, the other guys helped them; if something happened to somebody else's band, I would help them. If you needed somebody to sub, we'd fill, you need a horn . . . One time I was playing with my quartet and as it happened, half of them showed up late because they had gone to the wrong town. I'm on stage and Duke's guys are playing for me and we're improvising a show. I start to play, and all of a sudden, the sound of notes stopped coming out of the horn. There was just the sound of air coming through, and I felt something warm in my left hand and all the keys had fallen off! Now, this can happen on a saxophone, because the posts are held on by solder, and the solder on one post had let go and it was a key point on the horn and all the keys on that side dropped off—and I'm left standing there holding my horn. Duke looks around and laughs and the next thing I know, I walk off to the side of the stage and Harry Carney's coming up with his horn. He hands me his horn to play and says, "Here, take this."

You know that's more of the thing that I was used to, where guys liked each other and helped each other and there was fun involved. It was kind of a joy, kind of a family feeling. It was the way the vaudevillians made you feel, like it was some old tradition of the theater that you were part of, that felt good, especially for someone like me who felt like an outsider all through my childhood.

33

"ENTENTE FOR BARITONE SAXOPHONE AND ORCHESTRA"

DURING THE PERIOD when I was working concerts with Dave Brubeck, Dave had done a lot of stuff for symphony at that point. He always reminded me, I'll never forget, we were in a restaurant named the Purple Cow in Cincinnati. We were on tour somewhere and afterward we sat up for hours because Dave was feeling frustrated. He wanted to write and he just couldn't bring himself to do it, and he always told me that I did the Dutch Uncle number on him, saying, "Dave, you know what you should do, you should just write, forget about it and write," and I stayed on his case and by God, he did. It started him. He's written a lot of stuff for orchestra and chorus.

I was lucky that the period that I was playing with him, he was doing some of this stuff with the Cincinnati Symphony. So the first experience I had playing with a symphony was playing on these things of Dave's. He wrote a couple of sections that were especially for me to play. I really enjoyed it so I started thinking at that point: where can I get material to play with an orchestra, because that's the hardest thing to really conceive of. It's not just a question of putting a jazz musician with an orchestra. The material that they're going to do together has to mean something to both sides. You can't have the orchestra sitting there providing cushions for soloists, because that doesn't really add up to much interest in the way of music. And it always made more sense, or it was certainly more logical, to adapt the jazz soloist to the orchestra, but then you lose the jazz element altogether. So what to do? And it's been a touch-and-go relationship all along. There have been some very nice things written along the way, but most of the stuff that's been written is really kind of catastrophic in terms of musical value. But that started me trying to come up with some kind of a repertoire to be able to play concerts with orchestras.

I commissioned at that point, Frank Proto, who's a composer who plays with the Cincinnati Symphony, and he wrote, I guess he called it a concerto, but I'm not sure that it's strictly a concerto in form. It was relatively successful and we performed it a couple of times with symphony, but it pointed up the difficulties as much as made use of the possibilities. Probably the main difficulty is if you're going to have improvisation with your orchestra, how do you go about it?

Now this was always a problem, even with jazz writers, and of course this is something that most composers who write for the symphony are not really aware of: that there's a special kind of an approach required to write a successful chord progression for an improviser. Symphony writers fall into the same trap frequently, which is to write a complicated chord progression that doesn't really relate to a song-like melody. It's like a series of chords; there's not necessarily a progression. As a consequence, it throws a tremendous load on the soloist to make some kind of sense, some kind of a form, a structure over this progression that adds up to music. And it happens a lot. It even happened in the piece that Eddie Sauter wrote called "Focus" that Stan Getz recorded. Stan did a hell of a job in improvising on this thing, but Eddie never gave him a place to settle. There was no real feel about it that it starts some place, that this is going on in the middle, and this is an ending, so there was a shape to it.

Now, Stan's the best at making sense out of meaningless progressions of anybody I've ever encountered. But how long can you do it? You've got somebody improvising for five minutes and there's no real shape to the thing. It becomes repetitive and shapeless and this often happens. This has been one of the problems in trying to build a repertoire for myself. I've always meant to get back to Frank on that, and see if we couldn't work on it, because the orchestral parts are great. But some of the parts that are based around improvisation don't really make me feel good, and if I don't feel good, then the concerto for me doesn't have any meaning. It's got to be something that I can get on top of and enjoy playing like the way I do with a jazz band.

We wound up having the same problem with a piece that Harry Freedman wrote for me. They had a thing for my fiftieth birthday at the

Gerry with baritone saxophone.
© FRANCA R. MULLIGAN

Canadian Broadcasting Corporation, and they commissioned Harry to write a piece and called it "Celebration." Well, the piece is a knockout, it really has a lot of good stuff in it, but we've always run into the same problem and we're still wrestling with it. We were supposed to perform it this year, and then I guess something happened to the funding of the concert. It's not surprising since the economy has been so messed up, in Europe as well as here.

But we were looking forward to trying it again, because we were still trying to solve the problem of what to do to make the improvisation really make sense in relation to the whole. I'm the same way in that I need to have points of arrival. There have to be things in the structure of a solo segment that have a sense of form to them, so that it isn't just rambling on and on and playing lots of arpeggios, running chords and all that, because that doesn't mean anything to me. It only means something to me if I can compose something in relation to what is there, and in order to do that, I've got to have a firm base for it. I've tried various things with composers to get them to . . . if you write a progression, you must have something in mind, even a fragment of a melodic direction. Please write those things down to give me a hint of where you're going with it, because a cord progression is too amorphous a base.

It's one thing if you're dealing with a chord progression on a tune that you know. I could play "All the Things You Are" all night, nice chromatic progression like that, but no matter what you're doing, it's always in relation to the melody. It was written in relation to a melody. So it's of a piece. But just to come up with a chord progression that wanders all over hell, that's probably where you're going to wind up, is hell!

I finally wrote a piece for symphony, a solo piece for myself that, both the period of writing and the times that it's been played, have been very rewarding for me. I wrote it when we spent a lot of time in Italy. Some years we've spent more time than others. One year I guess we were there for three or four months at a stretch. And during that period, the head man at La Scala was a man who had been in charge of the theater at Bologna when I did my first tour in Italy in the 1950s. Now he was in charge of La Scala and gave me permission to come to the orchestra rehearsals anytime I wanted to.

In its way, that was probably the biggest single benefit that helped me get this piece written for orchestra, because I could leave the apartment that we'd rented in Milan, and five minutes on the subway or a fifteen-minute walk, and I was at La Scala. Every morning I could go to rehearsals, and I would usually come back and work on the piece in the afternoon. Hearing and having the sound of the orchestra, having the live sound in my ears, kept me going on the thing. In its way it was the hardest thing for me to do, to constantly try to recapture the sound of the instruments so that I could write for them.

So being able to hear them every day, and on top of that, what they were playing this season was Puccini's *Turandot*, the last thing that Puccini wrote. And the orchestra parts on that, the orchestration and the ideas were just so beautiful, such fantastic and intricate writing. And, of course, they start the rehearsals with the orchestra by itself. Lorin Maazel was conducting, so every morning I would go over there and they're working on the orchestra parts, and I go home in the afternoon and I write. So I am quite sure that some of the voicings and devices of Puccini's turned up in my pieces in one guise or another. But it's such a fantastic piece of work. Then, as they went on, they started to add the voices to it. It was a magnificent piece of writing, *Turandot*. That's remained my favorite opera piece.

The story of the first performance of that is kind of heartbreaking and awe-inspiring. Toscanini was conducting, and on the premier performance they played it through, they performed it through until it got to the point where Puccini died before he actually finished it. He wrote almost the whole thing, but it was only the last few minutes that some associate of his, or a student or somebody, finished it from his notes. But Toscanini stopped and put down his baton and turned to the audience and said, "And that's as much as the master wrote," and left the pit. Then after that, the next night and from then on, they did the piece with the ending that had been put on. But that's one of those, even when I hear that story, it makes my hair stand on end.

Zubin Mehta, Gerry, and the New York Philharmonic Orchestra, Avery Fisher Hall, Lincoln Center, New York, December 1989.
© JORJANA KELLAWAY

Now I wind up doing more straight symphonic concerts than I do pops concerts, and it's a totally different kind of repertoire and a different audience. Usually when I do stuff with symphony orchestras, we'll do only the orchestra pieces; the one piece that I wrote is like a suite, called "Entente for Baritone Saxophone and Orchestra," which doesn't use the quartet. The other piece is an arrangement of "K-4 Pacific," which does use the quartet, and then usually the rest of the program is based around other material. Like the first half, for instance, Zubin Mehta did it with the New York Philharmonic where we did the whole week. We were the regular subscription concert series, and he played two Beethoven pieces in the first half. The second half we came on and played "Entente," then he had us play two pieces with the quartet by ourselves and finish up with "K-4 Pacific," which made a really nice, well-rounded concert. "K-4" is a great thing to close with; the band loved to play it, and Zubin would really throw himself into it.

Zubin Mehta and Gerry, backstage at Avery Fisher Hall, 1989.
© JORJANA KELLAWAY

One of the nights when we played it, you know, the last chord is held out and he's got the stick up high and when he gives the cutoff, the stick went flying out his hand and flew halfway back into the orchestra of the theater. We all broke up, it was so great. Oh God, what a great time we had. That was really a high point.

34

"BRIGHT ANGEL FALLS"

LITTLE BIG HORN was recorded in 1983. It has a different kind of rhythm section with synthesizers, but to me it was basically a straight-ahead album. It's just different rhythm treatments, but I think it was perceived as kind of a rock-oriented album, and as a consequence, it kind of got lost in the cracks.

Michael Brecker was one of the ensemble Dave Grusin brought in to play on it. We had dynamite guys in the ensemble, but they came in when we were overdubbing ensemble stuff. God, if we had brought them in earlier, we might have had them play some solos, but that's not what we were thinking about. Dave has such good experience with recording techniques. It's always a pleasure doing things with him. Dave really arranged a lot of those pieces that we wound up doing, because we started out with that album in an altogether different way. It was like taking the quartet into a studio and recording a lot of the repertoire that hadn't been recorded, and we started out doing that and it never really came to life. Dave and I talked it over and said it's not going work because it doesn't feel like we've got an album out of it. Things are all right, but what's the use.

So we revamped our thinking about it, and I had some new things that we were trying. Dave said, "Well, let's try this and we'll get these guys in the rhythm section; they'll be able to put something on that, that would do for that," and so on and so on, and came up with an idea that was, again, the thing of doing a setting for each piece, which that album is. There's not one band on it, although to me it's a very coherent album with a continuity of sound and style. But going from piece to piece, it's different instrumentation, different players, and a different atmo-sphere, and it fits.

But there are a couple of things on there that are real favorites of mine that I always enjoy hearing. The thing that we did with Dave on the synthesizers on "Under a Star" is so beautiful. And watching him put this thing together was fascinating, because what he did with the two synthesizers, but with totally different timbres, was to play things; like he'd do eighths with himself, or he'd play four bars on one and then go into an accompanying mode, and then he would go back with the other synthesizer and have a solo coming out of it. And so the whole thing is just a gorgeous setting, a perfect setting for the piece. It's one of those things; it's a melody I enjoy playing anyway, but with that setting, man, it was like really having a cushion. So there were a lot of things about that.

Also, what happened on it, there was the one piece that we ended up calling "Bright Angel Falls." Franca and I had done something with the quartet in Phoenix, and we drove up with a couple of young friends to see the Grand Canyon. And I saw this place called Bright Angel Falls and I loved that. Because, originally I called this thing "The Sun Is Green" and everybody was so confused, "What does he mean, the sun is green?" So I wound up calling it "Bright Angel Falls." Anyway, it's a kind of blues, with a hint of gospel orientation to it, piece.

Just as we started to play the thing in the studio, Dave looked out the window of the control room, and outside he saw Booker T. Jones. He said, "Come on in, come on in, man; I've got something here for you to play." And he sits Booker T. down at the piano, and Dave goes over to the Fender Rhodes and they proceeded to do this thing. They looked it over and they played a couple of sections and said, "Okay, let's go," and these two guys put me away, man. Booker T. just tore the thing up. Just sat down, and it was kind of a complicated little piece, too, with interludes, and then a progression that's kind of deceptive because it sounds like it's going one place and it goes there, and then it backs up and then it goes around that place. It was really fun, and they just tore it up, the two of them. It really came out great. So I have very, very good memories of *Little Big Horn*.

The project with Scott Hamilton was a project that I wanted to do because I always enjoyed the series where I met somebody, like *Gerry Mulligan Meets Ben Webster*, and Desmond and so on. And I heard Scott Hamilton play, and it was obvious to me that his heroes, like Zoot Sims and Ben Webster, were the guys that I liked so much, so I thought that would be an interesting combination to do one of the *Mulligan Meets* things with him.

I had met Carl Jefferson in Europe at one of the festivals, and I remember spending time waiting for a plane together, probably somewhere in Copenhagen. We got to talking about it and I told him I would like to do this project with Scott, and so we agreed to do it. I wrote a bunch of music for it, just about everything as far as I can remember. It was fun to do; he's a very talented player and the album came out well. I never did anything else with Carl because we kind of got into a little bit of a contretemps about something that kind of precluded an easy relationship of recording. But I was glad to do that one album.

Of course there were other people that recorded for Concord that I would have done things with, but, as I say, this kind of hostility grew up between Carl and me. I think probably one of the things was that Carl has kind of a desire to be a father figure to all of the people that are part of his stable. And I don't really want a father. I left home a long time ago and I had enough of that.

I guess it was that thing again of wanting to do something with an ensemble and I had decided it was time to pursue, a little bit at least, the tentet idea. The tentet was a little bit different format than the *Birth of the Cool* nonet, and I felt probably it was a little bit more flexible for the concert presentation. When I say concert, often I'm thinking of the festivals, which are the main outlet for a bigger band. Because, where are you going to work with it unless you're in a position to put together a whole tour of single-concert engagements? And in this country, it's not really practical, whereas it would be practical in Europe; it's too expensive getting the band there.

So I think what we probably did was talk to George Wein about it, and he said he'd like to have that for the summer coming up. So it was like planning ahead what kind of a program to plan for next year's festivals. And in the process of doing it, I talked to Larry Rosen and Dave Grusin to see if their company was interested. And they were. They liked the idea of having the thing.

Then they thought about it for a while and I guess they talked it over with their people and said what they would really be interested in is to have the pieces that were recorded originally with the *Birth of the Cool*, and would I re-do those? I said I could re-do those and call it *Re-Birth of the Cool*, and that's what we wound up doing. I didn't mind doing it. I would like to have done some things with the tentet with new material because I wrote some new pieces for it, but I also was glad of having the chance of doing an album on an important label, because that was going to help the band on a summer tour. So we went ahead and did it that way with exactly the tunes that were done originally.

Now, getting that music together was a challenge because the music has long since been lost. I had some of the tentet music, but I had none of the *Birth of the Cool* music. Miles was supposed to have it. He always said that he did, but as it turned out he didn't, and some of the pieces had been transcribed already. I had worked on a couple of them when Lee Konitz was doing a thing for the Smithsonian, and he asked me if I would do it. He said he had tried to get the things transcribed but didn't have any luck getting them to sound right and would I do it? I said, "I'll do it, but you have to sit there with me while I do it. I'm not going to sit there by myself."

So he came up here and I spent a couple of days re-doing these things, and he sat and slept a lot, but I said, "If I'm going to go through this, you're going to go through it too." I did a couple of the things that ultimately Gunther Schuller published in his publishing company. So there were a few things. There were a couple of things that Gunther had saved from the date that he was on, which was very lucky—the two things that Gil Evans had written. Gunther said if he'd had any idea that Miles was going to lose that music or be so careless with it, he would have taken all of the music and stashed it away somewhere. I wish he had, but I feel some blame involved too, because I should have known that Miles would be careless with the music. John Lewis and I should have taken care of our own things, because that's the way it was.

I had talked to Miles about doing it. I told him when I saw him a couple of weeks after he had done the Montreux thing, and he was feeling very up about that. He was pleased that he had done it and thought that it came out well. Later on I talked to him on the phone, and he didn't feel quite as enthusiastic about it because he thought the band didn't have any sense of dynamics like Gil had done, and in general he wasn't as pleased with it.

Anyway, when I talked to him, I said I was thinking of putting this thing together for next year and I was probably going to record all of the stuff that we recorded originally. He said, well, let him know because he might do it with me. I said, "Okay." But that's one of those things. By the time I got the date set up, which was just about that time that I went to get in touch with him, he had started having strokes and that was the end of it. He died not long after that. It would have been interesting to try to do something with him again because he and I hadn't done anything for years. Instead, we wound up doing the album with Wallace Roney and Phil Woods.

The fascinating thing to me was the music, the feel, how an arrangement changes with different people playing it. So there were different values that came out of it in the re-doing, and I was pleased because I really put it together and was glad to do the *Birth of the Cool* stuff, because I'd never followed through on any of it. I was always curious how it would feel to use that as concert music, because we originally started out as a rehearsal band; then we worked in a club with it and then recordings, but we never worked in a concert setting. So I was kind of anxious to see how it worked, both the structure of the arrangements and how much I could change the structure of the arrangements to adapt them to more soloists, and the sound of the instrumentation itself.

Well, I felt in the end that the *Birth of the Cool* instrumentation was a little weak for a concert, especially festivals, and that's all we played with it, festivals. We played very few places where we were indoors in an orchestra hall. I think indoors in an orchestra hall it would have worked fine, but having the tentet set up with the second trumpet and extra baritone, it gave enough extra guts to it to feel a little more at home in these big settings. You feel like you can get lost in some of these places, and especially because what we were dealing with was totally an acoustic ensemble, and the whole thing was based on the blends that we could get between the instruments, and then hope that they could do an ensemble amplification, not a microphone on each instrument. In the end they wound up trying to do that—mics on every instrument—so you're at the mercy of the sound engineer mixing it, and you know a lot of times I really don't think that it came off well.

But it was, for me, a very important learning experience and ultimately, the following year, they wanted me to bring the thing down to Brazil, just for two or three concerts. Well, I didn't argue with them; I said, "Two or three concerts—it's a long way to go for two concerts. It must be very expensive for them; it's a long flight." But we did it, and it's sort of like the thing finally gelled. It came together, and we had a couple of really great nights. The band sounded good and it felt good, and I think the summer before that, the experience of having done those concerts, paid off so that it was a rewarding experience finally. And that instrumentation can work. There are things, acoustically, that kind of make basic difficulties. How do you balance the six original horns, which were tuba, baritone sax, trombone, French horn, alto sax, and trumpet? It's bottom heavy. But it's possible for the tuba parts to be played in a way so that the whole thing will blend. Then with the tentet instrumentation, it became much lighter on top having the second trumpet, and it worked very well.

In fact, one of those nights was the night in Sao Paulo. It was one of those things where it was supposed to be recorded on dat tape, but the dat machine broke down so they didn't record it, and we were depending on their dat machine, so we didn't set up ours, because they were taking it off the board. So that happened to me about three times that year, things that I really wanted. You know, usually everything is recorded, but it always happens, man; the things you really want are the things that they missed. And that was like the best night that we had. Two years' experience with that thing.

35

MUSIC, FREEDOM, AND RACE

THERE'S PROBABLY NEVER BEEN a time when more people were saying one thing and meaning another. Our absolute ability to deceive ourselves is one of the wonders of the age. This century has become quite dangerous because we're experimenting with things that, first of all, we don't realize we're experimenting; it's just become our way of life, but it is an experiment. Because we've taken a people and proceeded to change their world around them totally. Everything about our existence is different than it was a century ago.

Well, this doesn't seem to bother people very much. You can't interest kids in it because, a century ago, what does that mean to them? It should mean something because they're the same people. They haven't changed; they think they've changed but they haven't. So what's happened then is you've got electric lights, which means that your ways of living, to the rising and setting of the sun, is different. You've got automobiles, which means that your conception of time and space and your ability to move around, is different. You've got mechanical reproduction of sound, which means that you can have music whenever you want it. It's no longer some kind of a special event to get dressed up and go to hear an orchestra, or even to go to a local saloon and hear a group; whatever, it's different.

We're totally surrounded by ever-present and ever-ready entertainment, to the point that we've taken up all of our mental time with all of these toys. We don't use our minds anymore. We don't have to because people want to be entertained. Look at our sports. You know, the big thing in sports is not to be a participant. The fun of playing a game with friends or whatever, no! It's a spectator ritual that's taken over the rituals that have been lost by the wayside with the disintegration of the rituals of previous centuries, many of which were connected to religion. These changes are so basic to the human condition that I see it as an experiment, because we don't really know what is the outcome of changing the world around us.

I remember, a long time ago, reading a thing. I can't remember what it was or which of the Greek philosophers that it was because I read it in a compilation. I wasn't reading one man's work. But anyway, the writer put forth the idea that he'd like to be in the position of the gods and be sitting up above the clouds and watching people and watching people function in their daily lives. Then he would like to have the power that the gods would have, to change the music of this people and then watch the people change accordingly.

Well, I always thought that was one of the hippest things that I had ever read. This, to me, is precisely what's happened in this century. That the music became more and more . . . let's put it this way: the music became less and less the outcome of the sort of development that had happened in music previously. In previous centuries there was some logic, in human terms, of the development of all music, whether it's folk music or symphonic music. I mean, these things are more obvious than the more organized and more sophisticated kinds of music, such as symphonic music. You can see how men brought to bear their ideals and their intellect to function in relation to this music. So the music progressed in all kinds of directions, in its construction and sonority and so on.

What's happened in our time, instead of it being some kind of an intellectual development, it's one based totally on emotions that happens, more or less, by accident. I mean, the day that some guitar player got a hold of an amplifier and turned it up too loud and it distorted the sound, it started a revolution and a new approach to music. But what we have now is a popular music to a great extent, and by this I mean the popular music that's probably most influential with the young generations, is based on distortion. It's based on electrical accident. It's not based on something that's the content of the music itself.

This being the case, we're dealing with something that's outside the human experience, and you don't know what's going to happen with things like this. What we're able to do with the kind of artificiality of the volume of this kind of other worldly sort of electronic playing that's such a basis of the music, we can bring about sort of incipient states of hysteria, and it's like these things happen without our being either conscious of it or aware of the long-term effect. Maybe in the end it will have no effect at all.

I say that because maybe somebody will say it at this point. I don't believe that. I don't think we get away with the rest of the things that are going on. The breakdown of any sort of taste or standards, with a misreading of the concept of freedom. I don't think we understand very well. I came to have the freedom that what freedom really means is not just the question of doing what you want in the face of the community. Freedom is a responsibility. People seem to think that freedom is theirs by right and I say, man, look around the world because we're in a pocket of a small group of people who really enjoy a kind of freedom that is new to the world. This has only existed in the last couple of centuries and you have to use it or you lose it. People shouldn't really try to delude themselves that we can't.

The elements to curtail individual freedoms have been rampant in the United States all along, and in this century we've seen some fine examples of it. I mean, the kinds of corruption of ideals that went on in the days of the House Un-American Activities Committee in the 1930s. To see some of the films of those hearings and to see what kind of circuses these men were running for their own aggrandizement, because these men were what they were as political symbols, the government felt justified in putting them to death, even though they were pretty sure they hadn't done what they were accused of. It sort of didn't matter because they were just anarchists. Or Joe McCarthy; if you attack first and smear the other person, well, they're so busy trying to clean the shit off themselves that nobody pays any attention to them.

Joe McCarthy destroyed lots and lots of people and he was backed by lots and lots of people.

So we have to be aware that these strains exist very, very strongly in our background and they're still at it today. There are people out there that want to legislate what they think is right for everybody. A good example is the battle over abortion. People should believe what they want. You don't believe in abortion, fine, that's great. But how dare you take the attitude against the other people who feel that it's a necessary tool in the modern world. And we see what happens, man. They don't believe in abortion, which means, don't kill that fetus, and they turn around and kill doctors and nurses. How do you justify that? By what twist of what kind of mind justifies this kind of belief and this kind of behavior? What it means, though, is we have to be very careful because the forces of evil are very, very strong in the makeup of our country and all countries. But our country is the first country that has given people the rights and freedoms to the extent that we have them here, and if you abuse those rights and freedoms, you're going to wind up destroying it. We may be well on our way to doing it.

We may survive yet another backlash into ultraconservatism. I think we probably will. Especially when the reality becomes obvious and the inevitable happens, because this whole balanced budget amendment to the Constitution is the silliest thing. You know, people want to hear that. I mean, it's so totally unrealistic. So, what's going to happen is, if they pass the thing, then it gets right back to the problem that we're in. Where do we take the money from?

Well, I'll tell you where the money's going to come from. It's going to come from education. It's going to come from social services, it's going to come from the arts. It's going to come from any kind of medical care that doesn't show up too readily, like the stuff that's outside the center that nobody looks at. I mean, it's an old story. Ronald Reagan is alive and well and kicking us all in the butt.

This century has been incredible for change in relationships between the races. Some of the problems have naturally gotten worse instead of better. Ignoring it is not going to make it go away, and revising history is going to make a lot of white musicians very angry, which will help to bring more division between us. And who needs it? We don't need division. That's not what jazz is supposed to be about, because one of the other things that jazz was . . . became an idiom that brought people together. It gave a common language between two cultures that opened up all sorts of possibilities of communication. And the final result is that it became a world-class art music that's been a useful idiom for people around the world.

Now, if you start messing around with it too much and you throw elements away, it won't be jazz anymore, and I suppose people like me, well, I won't be around to be bothered, but if I were, I probably would find it boring, because to me the interest is precisely that. It's the coming together that's important. Our similarities are more important than our differences, and unless we can find ways of accepting each other on our own terms, then we're in a lot of trouble.

There's a lot of turmoil in the jazz scene now, which people don't like to talk about. Journalists writing about jazz are trying to pretend it doesn't exist. Come on. You cannot hide the fact that all the grant money goes to the black guys, not to the white guys. You can't hide the fact that when they put together a jazz program at Carnegie Hall, or at Lincoln Center, they get black guys to lead them and to run them and be the whole show. And you can't deny the fact that they don't really do any shows on white guys. It's like the division, in some ways, has never been more pronounced, and pretending that it doesn't exist is not going to make it go away.

I feel kind of stymied because the doors have been closed in my face in this country, and I don't really understand why. I don't like it very much. But mostly I just put it out of my mind and keep on doing what I'm doing.

I think that the revisionist history has got to be held in a little bit of check. Let's not write the white musicians out altogether, because I don't think we would be doing our culture any favor by doing that.

36

THE QUARTET

So THINGS HAVE GONE along pretty smoothly for years, and I've had one group after another, all based on the idea, on the simple idea, of the quartet. The piano, bass, and drums and baritone sax, and I've been lucky to always have good players. When somebody needs to leave for some reason, the guys always send in replacements for themselves, and they want to make sure that they send in good players. Always has been, you know: send in the best players they can find, whether they're well-known younger, older guys, or unheard-of younger players. So in that regard we've been very lucky.

We approach the music in a way to try to give it as much of an ensemble feeling as possible. That may be the most ensemble-minded quartet of a soloist with a rhythm section! But I don't just think of it as myself as a soloist with a rhythm section. I try to find approaches that expand the capabilities a little bit, and to use some of the principles of orchestration to give different colors. Otherwise, I think a single-instrument quartet can be quite boring, and I can be guilty of a lot of things, but one thing I don't want to be guilty of is boring people. So that's always a challenge.

Playing an instrument that's in a lower register already is a challenge because, you know, you go an octave lower and people don't hear as easily, and they tire of the register because it takes more effort to listen to it. So I think people are better able to stand an evening of an alto, or a trumpet with rhythm section. Playing baritone is another kind of challenge to be able to sustain melodic interest.

I thought about it so long ago it's second nature now, but to approach a melody as if it were an octave higher than it actually is, as if I were playing it an octave higher than I am, to give me a freedom with the melody itself and not be trapped in thinking in that register. Because you put some of those things on the piano keyboard and you realize how low they are. So I trick you into not knowing that!

Every instrumentation has its built-in limitations, and one of the things about doing anything in any field is, you have to accept your limitations to start with or you're always going to be frustrated. So what happens is, I've worked on pieces to try to sustain interest in the piece itself, so that the interest is built in.

A piece like "Curtains," it's a long piece. It's a long composition, and it didn't take us very much playing before it felt like a controllable form. It's not to be taken lightly, though, because you've got to understand that progression and don't mess with it. There were a couple of things like that. And we go through periods where we'll play that and it will come out to be an altogether different piece, night after night, even though they're dealing with the same form and the same materials. And it winds up being altogether different.

So in this way, what is in one way a limitation, an element of freedom becomes possible because we're able to do the thing without big consultations between each other. And if we do it at a different tempo, or we do a different groove, or we wind up in a different kind of atmosphere in some section of the chart, it just sustains interest in the piece for us. I've done a few pieces like that, that have been successful. We really enjoyed playing them. They're fun. "Curtains" is one; "Midas Lives" is another. And there's interest built into the progressions themselves. So once we get them under our hands as far as memory is concerned, you can have a lot of freedom with them.

Ideally, I don't know what it's going to feel like when we play it. The things that I know what they're going to sound like usually don't get played for very long. We'll play them and they'll say, "Well, that was fun. Now, let's do something else!" I don't know, maybe that's it. It feels too complete. But to bring a new piece in, I don't really know what's going to happen, and the guys start messing around with it and we play it and we try different things and maybe try different tempos; take it apart and take the blowing progression apart as a way of making it a more interesting progression, or one that hangs together better, or is more logical. And blowing on it to try to find elements that you can use to make ensemble sounds. Where can you shift gears? And how do you end it? It's a process that even though that's what we're searching for, happens in a different way on every piece, because every piece is different.

I think this is a process that evolved over the years. I'm just more aware of it, and in more control of it.

I'm pleased with the way *Dragonfly* came out, as an album, because it's taking elements that are quite different from each other and putting them together into a single whole program, and it works for me. I think that it does that. I'm not disturbed by the differentness of one instrumentation, one group of guys, next to other tracks by different groups. So it has a cohesiveness that I try to achieve in albums. And I think it worked in that.

I've come to an age where I've got a limited number of years left to function, but I'm functioning the best I ever did. I'm a very lucky person. I'm still able to muster up enough of an audience around the world to live in a way that is very nice indeed, travel around the world and have an interesting life for myself and my wife, and we have a grand time.

INDEX